Sociocultural Theory and L2 Instructional Pragmatics

SECOND LANGUAGE ACQUISITION
Series Editor: **Professor David Singleton**, *University of Pannonia, Hungary* and Fellow Emeritus, *Trinity College, Dublin, Ireland*

This series brings together titles dealing with a variety of aspects of language acquisition and processing in situations where a language or languages other than the native language is involved. Second language is thus interpreted in its broadest possible sense. The volumes included in the series all offer in their different ways, on the one hand, exposition and discussion of empirical findings and, on the other, some degree of theoretical reflection. In this latter connection, no particular theoretical stance is privileged in the series; nor is any relevant perspective – sociolinguistic, psycholinguistic, neurolinguistic, etc. – deemed out of place. The intended readership of the series includes final-year undergraduates working on second language acquisition projects, postgraduate students involved in second language acquisition research, and researchers and teachers in general whose interests include a second language acquisition component.

Full details of all the books in this series and of all our other publications can be found on http://www.multilingual-matters.com, or by writing to Multilingual Matters, St Nicholas House, 31–34 High Street, Bristol BS1 2AW, UK.

Sociocultural Theory and L2 Instructional Pragmatics

Rémi A. van Compernolle

MULTILINGUAL MATTERS
Bristol • Buffalo • Toronto

Library of Congress Cataloging in Publication Data
A catalog record for this book is available from the Library of Congress.

British Library Cataloguing in Publication Data
A catalogue entry for this book is available from the British Library.

ISBN-13: 978-1-78309-139-3 (hbk)
ISBN-13: 978-1-78309-326-7 (pbk)

Multilingual Matters
UK: St Nicholas House, 31–34 High Street, Bristol BS1 2AW, UK.
USA: UTP, 2250 Military Road, Tonawanda, NY 14150, USA.
Canada: UTP, 5201 Dufferin Street, North York, Ontario M3H 5T8, Canada.

Copyright © 2014 Rémi A. van Compernolle.

All rights reserved. No part of this work may be reproduced in any form or by any means without permission in writing from the publisher.

The policy of Multilingual Matters/Channel View Publications is to use papers that are natural, renewable and recyclable products, made from wood grown in sustainable forests. In the manufacturing process of our books, and to further support our policy, preference is given to printers that have FSC and PEFC Chain of Custody certification. The FSC and/or PEFC logos will appear on those books where full certification has been granted to the printer concerned.

Typeset by Techset Composition India(P) Ltd., Bangalore and Chennai, India.

Contents

Acknowledgements	vii
Transcription Conventions	ix

1 Introduction — 1
    Introducing Sociocultural Theory and Second Language
        Instructional Pragmatics — 1
    Sociocultural Theory as a Basis for Educational Praxis — 9
    Research Context and Data Sources — 23
    Overview of the Chapters — 27

2 Appropriateness in Language Learning and Language Teaching — 29
    Introduction — 29
    Theoretical Foundations of Appropriateness — 30
    Pragmatics as Mediated Action: A Pedagogical Framework — 42
    Conclusion — 62

3 Understanding Learners as People — 64
    Introduction — 64
    Education and the Development of Personalities — 66
    Internalization as Personalization — 76
    Emotion and Instructional Pragmatics — 85
    Conclusion — 90

4 Developing Awareness of Pragmatic Knowledge Through
   Verbalized Reflections — 93
    Introduction — 93
    Language as a Psychological Tool — 95
    Monologic Verbalized Reflection — 98
    Dialogic Verbalized Reflection — 109
    Conclusion — 117

5	Developing Pragmatic Knowledge Through Appropriateness Judgment Tasks	120
	Introduction	120
	Dynamic Assessment and Pragmatic Knowledge	122
	Dynamically Administered Appropriateness Judgment Tasks as Transformative, Developmental Activity	128
	Pre-enrichment and Post-enrichment Appropriateness Judgment Tasks	144
	Conclusion	150
6	Developing Performance Abilities Through Strategic Interaction Scenarios	153
	Introduction	153
	Dynamic Assessment and Pragmatic Performance	156
	Human Mediation and the Emergence of Controlled Performance	162
	Orientation, Execution and Control	171
	Conclusion	181
7	The Future of Vygotskian Approaches to Instructional Pragmatics	184
	Introduction	184
	Implications for Research	188
	Implications for the Classroom	196
	Implications for Teacher Education	202
	Final Comments	207
	References	209

Acknowledgments

I thank first and foremost the students with whom I have worked over the years, who have helped to shape my view of language, language learning and language teaching as I explored various approaches to integrating sociolinguistic and pragmatic features of discourse into classroom pedagogy. In particular, I extend my gratitude to the eight learners of French who participated in the study upon which this book is based, for without them the framework for instructional pragmatics illustrated here would not exist. I am also indebted to the late Mr Gil Watz, whose endowment for a dissertation fellowship in applied linguistics at the Pennsylvania State University provided financial support for the original study reported on in this book. I would also like to thank my many friends and colleagues for their substantive support and stimulating conversations, which have directly and indirectly shaped the present work in many ways. I am particularly grateful to the following people whose comments, questions and critiques about my work over the years have had a significant impact on the framework for instructional pragmatics presented in this book: Lawrence Williams, Celeste Kinginger, Jim Lantolf, Joan Kelly Hall, Heather McCoy, Steve Thorne, Matthew Poehner, Kwanghyun Park and Kimberly Buescher. I would also like to acknowledge the Department of Modern Languages and the Dietrich College of Humanities and Social Sciences at Carnegie Mellon University who provided material support for the completion of this book. Finally, many thanks are due to my editor, Laura Longworth, and to an anonymous reviewer whose comments, questions and critiques have helped to strengthen the book in many ways.

Transcription Conventions

The following conventions are used throughout this book for transcribing spoken interaction. They are intended to provide detail about the sequencing, timing and delivery of the talk while at the same time making transcripts of interactions accessible to a wide audience.

+	short pause
++	long pause
+++	very long pause
(2.0)	timed pause (2.0 seconds or more)
.	full stop marks falling intonation
,	slightly rising intonation
¿	raised intonation (not necessarily a question)
↑	markedly higher pitch relative to preceding talk
↓	markedly lower pitch relative to preceding talk
(word)	single parentheses indicate uncertain hearing
(xxx)	unable to transcribe
((comment))	double parentheses contain transcriber's comments or descriptions
-	abrupt cutoff with level pitch
:	indicates elongated delivery (each colon represents one extra beat)
underline	underlining indicates stress through pitch or amplitude
=	latched utterances
[...]	indicates that a section of the transcript has been omitted
[	onset of overlapping speech
]	end of overlapping speech
CAPITALS	capital letters indicate markedly loud speech

1 Introduction

Introducing Sociocultural Theory and Second Language Instructional Pragmatics

Aim and scope of the book

The purpose of this book is to construct a framework for second language (L2)[1] instructional pragmatics that is grounded in Vygotskian cultural-historical psychology, most often referred to in applied linguistics and L2 acquisition (SLA) research as sociocultural theory (SCT) of mind (see Lantolf & Thorne, 2006). Vygotskian SCT provides a powerful theoretical account of human development that recognizes the central importance of social relationships and culturally constructed artifacts in transforming biologically endowed psychological capacities into uniquely human forms of mental activity. From the perspective of SCT, the sociocultural domain is not merely a set of factors that trigger innate developmental processes within the mind/brain of the individual. Instead, it is the primary source, and principal driver, of mental development. When extended to formal schooling, including L2 education, such an orientation to human psychology compels us to engage in educational praxis wherein instruction drives development rather than following an assumed progression of innate developmental stages. As Vygotsky (1978: 89) forcefully argued, the only good instruction 'is that which is ahead of development'.

Although this book is about the teaching of L2 pragmatics, it is not intended to present a set of teaching techniques or tips from which one can pick and choose at will. Instead, it aims to illustrate a coherent, systematic pedagogical program based on the principles of SCT. This not only includes recommendations for materials design and teaching practices, but also – and more importantly – a reconceptualization of the object of instructional pragmatics. Teachers will certainly find the book useful, and the data excerpts analyzed throughout are intended to show how an SCT approach to instructional pragmatics works in practice. Teachers are also encouraged to think about ways of adapting the pedagogical framework to suit their own needs and to work within institutional constraints. However, the reader should bear in mind that the pedagogical recommendations assume a particular perspective on the nature of language, pragmatics, mental development, and so on, that is derived from SCT. It is therefore necessary to understand the theoretical framework in order to appreciate the developmental significance of the specific pedagogical practices illustrated in this book. The chapters – whose contents are described at the end of this introduction – are organized with the aim of leading the reader through the components of the theoretical framework, using empirical data to illustrate the aspects of the theory under discussion as they apply to L2 instructional pragmatics.

The data used in this book were collected as part of a study of US university learners of French who participated in a pedagogical enrichment program that was designed to incorporate Vygotskian principles into L2 instructional pragmatics (more details are provided below). Although the data deal exclusively with French, the study serves to illustrate the principles and components of an SCT framework for instructional pragmatics. The framework can certainly be adapted for use in the teaching of any other language.

Defining pragmatics

The focus of pragmatics is on the way people accomplish actions through language. For example, a common area of inquiry examines the realization of speech acts such as invitations, apologies and requests. Inviting someone to a party, apologizing for being late, and requesting to borrow a book are all actions that can be – and are more often than not – accomplished at least in part through written or spoken language. Other actions accomplished through (or at least fundamentally shaped by) language include problem-solving, teaching, reflecting particular world views, creating and maintaining interpersonal relationships, performing social-relational roles and identities, and so on. How these actions are accomplished – that is, the language choices made by speakers – and their effects on other people are in turn subject to various communicative constraints and affordances. In this respect, Crystal (1997) offers a useful definition of pragmatics as a user-centered perspective on language-in-use.

> [Pragmatics is] the study of language from the perspective of users, especially of the choices they make, the constraints they encounter in using

language in social interaction and the effects their use of language has on other participants in the act of communication. (Crystal, 1997: 301)

Crystal's definition is particularly well suited for research into L2 pragmatics because it allows for any instance of language use, learning and development to be studied from the perspective of pragmatics (Kasper & Rose, 2002). It follows that, with regard to L2 instructional pragmatics, any feature of discourse can be taught as pragmatics as long as the focus of pedagogy remains on language users' choices, constraints and effects of language use during communication.

From the perspective of SCT, the ability to accomplish actions through language is mediated by the sociocultural resources available to a person. Mediation refers to Vygotsky's (1978) proposal that higher forms of human cognition are accomplished through the integration of cultural tools, including language, cultural scripts and concepts. These resources – or mediational means – include language forms as well as a person's knowledge of which forms may or may not be appropriate for a given speech event. Also relevant here is Leech's (1983) and Thomas's (1983) now-classic bifurcation of pragmatics into *pragmalinguistics* – the intersection of pragmatics and grammar – and *sociopragmatics* – the intersection of pragmatics and culture. Both pragmalinguistic and sociopragmatic knowledge mediate social action.

Pragmalinguistics entails knowledge of the conventional linguistic means through which social actions can be accomplished (e.g. the various ways of requesting the loan of something such as *Give me that book* versus *Could I borrow that book?* versus *I was wondering, if it isn't too much of a bother, whether you might consider loaning me that book, just for a little while*). In this way, pragmalinguistics encompasses the conventional linguistic tools used to mediate social action. However, speakers do not simply use any and all pragmalinguistic resources randomly or inconsequentially. Instead, sociopragmatic knowledge intervenes to mediate the choices speakers make from among these pragmalinguistic resources in light of present goals for the course of action and potentially changing circumstances. Sociopragmatic knowledge involves an understanding of the conventions of 'proper' or 'appropriate' social behavior, including what to say to whom and when, as well as an understanding of the social consequences of conforming to or breaking those conventions (see Chapter 2). In short, sociopragmatic knowledge mediates the choices speakers make in implementing the available pragmalinguistic resources in the accomplishment of social action. This relationship is depicted in Figure 1.1 as three interlocking ovals. Social actions are goals to be accomplished (e.g. inviting someone to dinner), and these actions are mediated by the means available to speakers (pragmalinguistics), the selection of which is

4 Sociocultural Theory and L2 Instructional Pragmatics

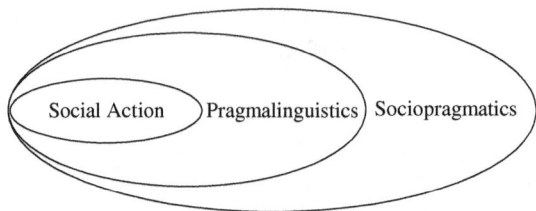

Figure 1.1 Interwoven nature of social action, pragmalinguistics, and sociopragmatics

in turn mediated by speakers' knowledge of sociocultural schemas, concepts and social relations (sociopragmatics).

In sum, mediation lies at the center of a sociocultural conceptualization of pragmatics. Social actions, pragmalinguistics and sociopragmatics are interwoven facets of goal-directed activity. As language users, we employ linguistic resources with an objective in mind, and we use our knowledge of sociocultural schemas to choose the resources that can be used to achieve our goals the way we want to achieve them. While this view certainly includes conventional patterns of meaning and language use, the emphasis on agentive language use leaves open the possibility that the way in which we want to accomplish a given goal may break social conventions. In other words, we can *choose* to conform to or reject conventions of appropriate social behavior because we know what the consequences of doing one thing or another may be given present circumstances. It is this information – clear, systematic sociocultural schemas – that is often missing from L2 pragmatics instruction.

Teaching pragmatics

Research inspired by Kasper's (1997) call for investigations into the teachability and learnability of L2 pragmalinguistics and sociopragmatics has suggested that classroom learners do indeed benefit from some form of instruction. (Thorough reviews are provided in Alcón Soler & Martínez-Flor, 2008; Ishihara, 2010; Kasper, 2001; Kasper & Roever, 2005; Kasper & Rose, 2002; Martínez-Flor & Usó-Juan, 2010; Rose, 2005; Rose & Kasper, 2001; Taguchi, 2011; Takahashi, 2010.) Yet this research has yielded mixed findings regarding the efficacy of implicit versus explicit approaches to teaching. In some cases, implicit conditions – which involve the provision of positive evidence of pragmatic forms and corrective feedback on infelicitous learner language – appear to be as beneficial as explicit instruction in developing pragmalinguistic knowledge. However, the literature suggests that explicit instruction in which metapragmatic information is provided is more beneficial than implicit instruction in developing sociopragmatic knowledge (Takahashi, 2010). Sociopragmatic information, it seems, is more difficult for learners to deduce from positive evidence than is pragmalinguistic form. As such, some explicit intervention is helpful in drawing learners' attention to sociopragmatics.

As noted above, explicit instructional conditions provide metapragmatic information about the various forms being taught, including judgments of politeness and formality. In this way, SCT partially aligns with non-SCT research into instructional pragmatics that privileges explicit instruction because sociopragmatic knowledge is argued to mediate pragmatic action. However, the SCT framework diverges from more traditional approaches in how it conceptualizes the object of explicit instruction. In traditional approaches to instructional pragmatics, metapragmatic information is typically presented as a set of doctrinal, norm-referenced rules of thumb, or what van Compernolle and Williams (2012c: 185) refer to as 'narrowly empirical representations' of conventions (see also van Compernolle, 2010a, 2011b), that provide learners with little information about the meaning potential of the linguistic forms they are acquiring and are, in at least some cases, inaccurate. Instead, the SCT framework compels us to design coherent concept-based instructional materials in order to mediate learner development (see the discussion of systemic-theoretical instruction, below). A similar critique has been leveled against mainstream instructed SLA research, where the grammatical rules presented to students are often unsystematic and fraught with exceptions, ambiguities and inaccuracies (Lantolf, 2007).

One representative example of the unsystematicity of traditional approaches to instructional pragmatics is illustrated in Martínez-Flor and Usó-Juan's (2006) '6Rs' framework. Their recommendations are intended to assist L2 English learners in developing their pragmatic abilities in the speech acts of requesting and suggesting and 'to gradually make learners pay attention to the importance of the contextual and sociopragmatic factors that affect which of the two speech acts has to be made and how' (Martínez-Flor & Usó-Juan, 2006: 44). The approach begins by introducing learners to two important issues in pragmatics: first, the difference – and relationship – between *pragmalinguistics* and *sociopragmatics* (following Rose, 1999); and, second, the three central social variables presented in politeness theory (Brown & Levinson, 1987) – that is, *social distance, power* and *degree of imposition*. Martínez-Flor and Usó-Juan provide explanations and examples of these factors and their effect on politeness in language (see Table 1.1) as a teacher's guide to discussing sociopragmatic factors with their students. Although this orientation to teaching pragmatics is interesting, and on the surface appears to articulate with the SCT framework presented in this

Table 1.1 Sociopragmatic factors

Explanation of factors for teachers	Effect on level of politeness
Social distance 'refers to the degree of familiarity that exists between the speakers (e.g. Travel Agent – Customer, do they know each other?)' (p. 58)	Politeness increases with degree of social distance
Power 'refers to the relative power of a speaker with respect to the hearer (e.g. Hotel Manager – Receptionist, rank within a company)' (p. 58)	Politeness increases with degree of power difference
Imposition 'refers to the type of imposition the speaker is forcing someone to do (e.g. to borrow money versus to borrow a pen)' (p. 58)	Politeness increases with degree of imposition

Source: Adapted from Martínez-Flor & Usó-Juan, 2006

book (i.e. teaching concepts), there are two fundamental problems with the way in which social distance, power and degree of imposition are supposed to be explained to learners.

First, these three social variables are represented as static and preexisting the communicative context. Consequently, language use (i.e. the selection of pragmatic forms) is represented as reactive with no mention of the ways in which the qualities of social relationships (i.e. social distance and power) are *created through* language. Likewise, the explanation of imposition suggests that specific request and suggestion types always impose on the hearer in the same way. For instance, it is implied that borrowing money is always a great imposition while borrowing a pen is not, regardless of the context of the request. This certainly cannot be the case, since asking a classmate if one may borrow his or her only pen during an exam would be a much greater imposition than asking a good friend if one might borrow some change to buy a drink from a vending machine. It should also be noted that the explanations are generally vague. For example, the terms *power* and *imposition* are actually used to define the concepts of *power* and *imposition*. These definitions, therefore, can have very little explanatory value.

Second, the chart misrepresents the relationship between the three social variables and politeness. On the one hand, the concept of politeness as construed by Brown and Levinson (1987) is not explained, and there is no mention of the notion of face or that of a face-threatening act to contextualize the theory. Consequently, teachers and learners may impose their own everyday understandings of politeness (i.e. as in being polite or respectful), which are highly variable from one individual to the next. On the other hand, the politeness effects shown in the right-hand column are not systematic. Although there is certainly a correlation between social distance and politeness, as Brown and Levinson conceived of it (i.e. the convention may be to use more polite forms when there is increased social distance), it is not a steadfast rule. There are many reasons for which a speaker may use a conventionally less polite form in interaction, and it is certainly true that when interactional factors (e.g. conversational repair) are taken into account, conventionally less polite forms are not interpreted as impolite (Kasper, 2004). More importantly, however, the context of Martínez-Flor and Usó-Juan's (2006) explanations (i.e. presenting the pragmalinguistic resources for making requests and suggestions) inaccurately conflates form and meaning by implying that some linguistic forms are inherently more polite than others. Such is certainly not the case. For example, it can be impolite to use a so-called 'polite' form between intimates as it may create unwarranted social distance.

Excerpt 1.1 shows the result of learning unsystematic rules of thumb for displaying politeness, specifically the overgeneralization of a politeness rule. As part of a preenrichment phase of the study reported on in this book, Susan (a pseudonym) was asked to identify which second-person address form (i.e. the familiar *tu* vs. polite *vous*) she would use in a variety of social situations, in this case when meeting a good friend's girlfriend, Sophie, for the first time. The situation was somewhat ambiguous because, although Sophie was described as a peer and the friend of a friend – factors that favor *tu* – she was also a stranger – a factor that, according to the rules of thumb, favors *vous*.

Excerpt 1.1

1	**Tutor:**	What about the second one. +++ Jean's girlfriend Sophie.
2	**Susan:**	I would probably say *vous*. just because I haven't met her before,
3		+ and its goes back to the whole respect thing, I think,
4		+ and even though, + she's my age, and + the girlfriend of my friend,
5		+ I still just + because I'm meeting her for the first time, +
6		I feel like I would just default to *vous*,
7	**Tutor:**	okay.
8	**Susan:**	to be respectful,

In selecting her response, Susan applied her rules of thumb for politeness/respect. Specifically, because she had never met Sophie before, Susan opted to choose *vous* (line 2), conventionally described as the polite form of address in French-language textbooks (van Compernolle, 2010a, 2011b). Although Susan seemed to acknowledge the potential importance of age and the relationship between Sophie and Jean (line 4), she reverted to her default respectful choice (lines 5–8), *vous*, because she did not actually know what do in this situation. Susan failed to recognize that because of their similar age and Sophie's potential friend status as the girlfriend of a friend, her choice of the conventionally respectful *vous* would most likely be seen as strange, or even rude, because it would create an unnecessary social distance between peers with potential friend status (Belz & Kinginger, 2002; Kinginger, 2008). Since Susan had developed only rule-of-thumb-based knowledge of sociopragmatics prior to her participation in the study, she did not have a coherent framework of meanings that she could use to negotiate the ambiguities of the situation presented in the task. As will be demonstrated in this book, the SCT framework for instructional pragmatics develops in learners a systematic, meaning-based orienting basis for making pragmalinguistic choices.

A brief sketch of the SCT framework for L2 instructional pragmatics

The central tenet of the SCT framework for L2 instructional pragmatics illustrated in this book is that instructed L2 development – including pragmatics – is fundamentally a conceptual process (Negueruela, 2008). Culturally constructed concepts – whether spontaneously acquired in the everyday world or intentionally developed through formal schooling – mediate cognition (Karpov, 2003; Kozulin, 1995; Vygotsky, 1986). Concepts are not merely the content of thought but in fact frame thought such that we think through them. Because concepts are culture specific, a large part of L2 development entails 'acquiring new conceptual knowledge and/or modifying already existing knowledge as a way of re-mediating one's interaction with the world' (Lantolf & Thorne, 2006: 5). Here, Agar's (1994: 60) neologism 'languaculture' is important. In Agar's view, the notion of languaculture reflects the union of language and culture, traditionally treated as independent of one another, as a dialectic that 're-establishes the unity between people and their fundamental symbolic artifact' (Lantolf & Thorne, 2006: 5).

From this perspective, instructed L2 pragmatic development may therefore be conceptualized as the appropriation of languacultural concepts and patterns of meaning. In other words, pragmatics is not simply about language in its cultural context – where culture is external to language and impacts upon it from the outside – but, instead, implies the union of the two, where language-in-use is simultaneously an expression of culture and a resource for the reification and transformation of culture. Although some concepts may be similar across cultures, how they are enacted in and through social interaction and communicative activity can be highly variable. For instance, although both American and French cultures have similar conceptions of power–distance relationships, only French has a second-person (i.e. *tu* or *vous*) distinction to encode such aspects of social relationships in the personal pronoun system.[2] Thus, learning to say *you* in French is about much more than mastering a few rules-of-thumb and the morphosyntax of second-person verb phrases; it also entails learning to operate within a new conceptual framework, namely that *tu/vous* choice in French both reflects and creates the qualities of social relationships and points to aspects of one's own social identity (see Morford, 1997; for L2 French, Kinginger, 2008; van Compernolle, 2010a).

Another important tenet of the framework is that the value of conceptual knowledge is directly linked to its relationship with practical activity – that is, *use* (Vygotsky, 1997, 2004). It is never enough to acquire new conceptual knowledge detached from its context of use, and pedagogies that value explicit knowledge of the object of study (e.g. language) must include learning activities that link this knowledge to action. The objective is to apply and transform knowledge through practical activity. Within the framework, knowledge and use, theory and practice form a dialectic in which each dynamically exerts an influence on the other. Vygotsky was clear that this dialectic, *praxis*, was fundamental to any theory of education and cognitive development.

These first two claims find support in Paradis's neurolinguistic theory of bilingualism and L2 acquisition (Paradis, 2004, 2009). Paradis presents evidence that a great deal of adult SLA is subserved by the declarative memory system and, as such, is fundamentally a declarative or conscious process. This model accounts not only for metalinguistic knowledge developed through explicit forms of teaching but, as Paradis argues, such processes as noticing, deduction, and so on, that are not always treated as part of consciousness in the SLA literature. The result, he contends, is that adult L2 learners rely extensively on whatever form(s) of conscious knowledge they have when using the L2. Through use of the L2, access to this knowledge can be sufficiently 'speeded up' (i.e. accelerated) to be perceived as automatic. Paradis's theory complements Vygotskian pedagogies that assign great significance to the quality of conscious (conceptual) knowledge in adult L2 development. In short, if adult L2 learners rely extensively on declarative knowledge, the quality of that knowledge becomes a central pedagogical concern (Lantolf, 2007).

Sociocultural Theory as a Basis for Educational Praxis

The purpose of this section is to introduce the reader to the core theoretical assumptions of SCT – as proposed by Vygotsky – that form the basis for the SCT framework for L2 instructional pragmatics illustrated in this book. These ideas are revisited and elaborated in the following chapters, so the following paragraphs serve simply as a concise overview of the central theoretical tenets of SCT. For a comprehensive account of the theory, and its extension to L2 development, the reader is referred to Lantolf and Thorne (2006).

Mediated mind

The central tenet of Vygotskian SCT is that the human mind is mediated by culturally constructed artifacts. In contrast to dualistic, reductionist accounts of human mental functioning, which assume that mental processes either originate in one's environment (upward reductionism, behaviorism) or are biologically specified within the mind/brain of the individual (downward reductionism, innatism) (see Valsiner & van der Veer, 2000), Vygotsky posited a dialectical (i.e. organic, unitary) relationship between the biologically endowed and the culturally constructed. Human consciousness, for Vygotsky, emerged from the unity of biologically specified mental abilities and the internalization of culturally constructed mediational means. The integration of these mediational means in cognitive activity effectively reorganizes and reshapes biologically endowed cognitive processes into higher forms of specifically human psychological functions. In short, 'biology provides the necessary functions and culture empowers humans to intentionally regulate these functions "from the outside" (Vygotsky, 1997: 55)' (Lantolf, 2006: 70). The human mind, therefore, is not coterminous with the brain but incorporates culturally based mediational means (Wertsch, 1998).

Vygotsky's understanding of the mind as mediated led him to propose that humans interact with the world through indirect or auxiliary (mediational) means. Thus, whereas the leading psychological theories of Vygotsky's time posited a direct stimulus-response relationship between subject and object, Vygotsky insisted that cultural artifacts allowed humans to create their own indirect, auxiliary relationship with the world. Through mediational means, 'the direct impulse to react is inhibited, and an auxiliary stimulus [i.e. a mediating artifact] that facilitates the completion of the operation by indirect means is incorporated' (Vygotsky, 1978: 40). He continued:

> this type of organization is basic to all higher psychological processes. . . . [The auxiliary stimulus] transfers the psychological operation to higher and qualitatively new forms and permits humans, by the aid of extrinsic stimuli, *to control their behavior from the outside* [italics in original]. The use of signs leads humans to a specific structure of behavior that breaks

away from biological development and creates new forms of a culturally-based psychological process. (Vygotsky, 1978: 40)

Vygotsky (1978) represented this indirect (mediated) relationship between subject and object as a triangle (Figure 1.2) in which the subject acts on the object via tools and signs. It should be noted, however, that Vygotsky never argued that direct stimulus-response processes did not exist in humans. Rather, he insisted that such processes belonged to a class of lower (i.e. not culturally based) psychological functions that humans shared with other animals, especially primates. Higher forms of culturally based psychological processes, however, incorporate cultural tools (i.e. mediational means), which allow humans to control their lower (i.e. natural or biologically specified) psychological processes. As Cole (1996) points out, 'natural' (i.e. unmediated) functions are located along the base of Vygotsky's triangle in that there is a direct stimulus-response process, whereas cultural (i.e. mediated) forms of cognitive activity 'are those where the relation between subject and environment (subject and object, response and stimulus, and so on) are linked through the vertex of the triangle (artifacts)' (Cole, 1996: 119). Higher or culturally based forms of mental activity include such things as voluntary attention, intentional memory, and logical thought and problem solving, which of course rely on biologically specified functions in the brain but which are formed through the integration of mediating artifacts. For instance, intentional memory depends on one's working and long-term memory capacities (i.e. biology) but also on artifacts (i.e. culture) allowing for the intentional control over these functions – that is, remembering what one wants to remember when one wants to remember it, and how one wants to remember it. An illustrative example from my own experience as a blues and rock guitarist – and one that is undoubtedly shared by others – is the use of tablature, or tabs. Tabs depict the strings of the guitar and the progression of fingering positions to be played on each string (e.g. open, first, second, third fret, and so on). Tabs are important not only for reminding the guitarist

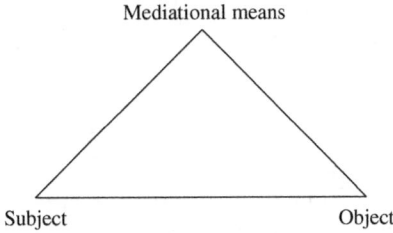

Figure 1.2 Mediation triangle

which notes are to be played in what order but, more importantly, the most relevant fingering positions to play the sequence of notes as well as how the notes should be realized (e.g. slides, bends, hammer-ons, pull-offs), as indicated by various symbols integrated into the tab chart. Tabs are commonly used without actual sheet music, so the guitarist must already be familiar with the song (e.g. rhythm, melody, time signature, tempo). In this way, tabs are a useful, culturally based means for remembering the song and how the song is to be played.

It is important to note that, within Vygotsky's theory, artifacts are understood to be much more than physical objects isolated from human activity. Instead, artifacts can only be understood as a constitutive aspect of the activity in which they are incorporated (Cole, 1996). Understanding an artifact thus entails an understanding of how its use fulfills some aspect of human goal-directed activity and in turn comes to constitute that activity. In this regard, Wertsch (1998) offers the useful concept of the *human-agent-acting-through-mediational-means* to describe the unity of human activity and artifacts.[3] In other words, artifacts are not simply instrumental or supplementary material objects that humans can use to accomplish some action (e.g. the concepts of *cultural toolkit* or *person-plus* proposed by Wells, 1999 and Perkins, 1993, respectively). Human goal-directed activity and integrated artifacts cannot be truly understood independently of each other because 'artifacts assume their character from the activities they mediate' (Lantolf & Thorne, 2006: 67). To illustrate this point, we can return to the example of guitar tabs described above. Guitar tabs may mediate the learning of a song or a particular riff, they may mediate playing during individual practice or rehearsal with a band as a reminder of when to play what and how, or they may mediate one's performance on stage. Although the physical object remains the same, its status as artifact is different in each context: it may be a learning tool or an intentional memory device.

Although Vygotsky's (1978) own research focused primarily on the mediating potential of tools and signs (e.g. physical objects and symbolic artifacts, such as language) introduced during the course of activity (Wertsch, 2007), other scholars have expanded the notion of mediational means to include less explicit forms of mediation. Wartofsky (1973; as cited in Cole, 1996), for example, distinguished a three-level hierarchy that includes primary artifacts (e.g. tools and signs), secondary artifacts (e.g. modes of action using primary artifacts) and tertiary artifacts (e.g. imagined worlds that influence how we perceive the material world). For his part, Cole (1996) highlights the importance of cultural models, schemas and scripts (which he categorizes as secondary artifacts following Wartofsky's [1973] model) in structuring thinking processes and how we integrate primary artifacts into the activities we participate in. Wertsch (2007) distinguishes among explicit forms of mediation, which are intentionally introduced during the course of activity (e.g. physical objects, adult assistance), and less transparent, or implicit, mediating artifacts, such as internalized concepts. For the purposes of the present book, I simply wish to identify three broad categories of interrelated, or interwoven (Cole, 1996), mediational means or artifacts: *tools and signs*, *concepts* and *activities*.

Tools and signs include material objects (e.g. hammers, pen and paper, calculators, computers) as well as semiotic systems, foremost among which is language (Vygotsky, 1978, 1986). As noted above, tools and signs are only understood to be artifacts in the Vygotskian sense within the context of the activities they mediate. For example, language is understood to be a mediating artifact only within the context of language-mediated activities, not as the set of decontextualized and isolated sounds and structures privileged in formalist approaches to linguistics (Cole, 1996; Lantolf & Thorne, 2006; Leontiev, 1981; Thorne & Lantolf, 2007). This perspective compels us to understand language as activity, or *languaging* (Becker, 1988) – that is, as a semiotic process in which meaning is created in and through concrete communicative activity.

Concepts mediate human activity because they constitute systems of meanings that frame human mental activity (Vygotsky, 1986). As discussed in greater detail below, Vygotsky distinguished between *everyday concepts*, which spontaneously arise through extensive empirical experience, and *scientific concepts*, which are abstract yet systematic understandings of objects of study (Davydov, 2004; Galperin, 1989, 1992; see below). Because conceptual knowledge, whether everyday or scientific, comprises networks or associations of meanings as well as relations among objects and other concepts, they fundamentally frame how humans know and act upon the world. As such, concepts mediate mental activity and, by extension, how humans use tools and signs in concrete material activity.

Activities themselves also mediate human behavior and cognition. Routinized patterns of interaction, cultural models, scripts and schemas provide frameworks through which and within which humans operate (Cole, 1996; Engeström, 1987). Activities comprise rules (conventions), divisions of labor, and available mediating artifacts (i.e. tools and signs, concepts) that are appropriate for the accomplishment of the activity in progress. In this regard, Cole (1996: 126) notes that cultural scripts '[specify] the people who appropriately participate in an event, the social roles they play, the object [i.e. artifacts] they use, and the sequence of actions and causal relations that applies'. Knowledge of the roles, appropriate mediating artifacts and sequences constituting activities is constructed from one's experiences participating in phenomenologically similar events. In turn, this knowledge mediates one's orientation to participation in future events.

Internalization and zone of proximal development

Another core concept within SCT is that of internalization. Vygotsky argued that mediational means are internalized through participation in culturally organized activity. The process of internalization, therefore, links the social and the internal-psychological in a dialectical unity – it is the process by which mediational means (i.e. culture) are incorporated into one's cognitive system. It is important to note that Vygotsky conceived of the social as psychological or, put another way, as the intermental plane. This is apparent in his description of the genetic law of development (Vygotsky, 1978), which holds that higher psychological functions are at first mediated by others before growing inwards (Frawley, 1997) to exist on the individual, or intramental, plane. The idea that internalization is a form of inward growth is crucial: internalization is not simply the acquisition of cultural tools; rather, it is a transformative process of appropriating cultural tools and making them one's own (Lantolf & Thorne, 2006). At the same time, it should also be recognized that internalization is bidirectional. As Zinchenko (2002) points out, internalization entails simultaneous *growing in* and *growing out* because it is a process that reorganizes the person–environment relationship and thus must have an external, or outward, dimension. (For extended discussion of the bidirectional nature of internalization, the reader is referred to Lantolf & Thorne, 2006: 151–178.)

One of the central themes running throughout this book is that internalization is a process of personalization of mediational means. Although it will be more fully discussed later (see especially Chapter 3), the concept of personalization is important enough to warrant some preliminary comments here. As noted above, internalization involves making something one's own, which entails the transformation of mediational means. In this way, the concept of internalization distinguishes the SCT perspective from acquisition models of development (Kozulin, 2003) because the growing in and growing out processes fundamentally change the qualities of mediational means. In other words, learners do not simply acquire prepackaged knowledge or skills, but instead integrate these in ways that are personally meaningful in relation to concrete material activity. The evidential basis for determining development, therefore, centers on the degree to which the mediational means are personalized. As will be illustrated throughout this book, different learners, though provided with the same pedagogical materials, internalized the mediational means in different ways, forming their own personal relationships with meanings (sociopragmatics) and forms (pragmalinguistics).

To be sure, internalization/personalization does not occur in a vacuum. Rather, as Vygotsky made clear in his formulation of the genetic law of development, higher (i.e. mediated) psychological functions appear first on the intermental plane. As Kozulin (2003: 17) writes, for Vygotsky, development (i.e. internalization) 'depends on the presence of mediating agents in the [learner's] interaction with the environment'. Vygotsky's concept of the zone of proximal development (ZPD), often described as the difference between what one can do alone and what becomes possible with support, represents the pathway through which mediational means are internalized. In this regard, Holzman (2009) offers an insightful discussion of the ZPD concept in which she identifies three interpretations of it: (1) a measurable property of an individual; (2) an approach to interacting with learners to support them in tasks; and (3) a collective and transformative activity characterized as a cooperative undertaking between individuals (see Poehner & van Compernolle, 2011). Holzman notes that the third interpretation is closest to Vygotsky's original proposal.

Understanding the ZPD as collective activity through which mediational means may be internalized offers a powerful way to conceptualize the organization of learning environments. This reading of Vygotsky does not limit discussions of the ZPD to measurable learning potentials or diagnostics of abilities, nor does it rely solely on the concept of assistance, which Vygotsky took for granted in his writings about the ZPD (Chaiklin, 2003). Instead, focus is on cooperatively engaging learners in personalizing the mediational means available to them. In this way, mediating agents, such as teachers, in fact encourage differences to emerge across individual learners (see Chapter 3). In short, ZPD activity entails creating the conditions for qualitative changes in consciousness to occur (Lantolf & Thorne, 2006) as learners simultaneously grow in (internal mental activity) and grow out (external mental and material activity).

Educational praxis and the artificial development of mind

Praxis – the unification of theory and practice – is one of the central commitments of sociocultural educational psychology. Vygotsky argued that, while practice was formerly the mere application of theory, which 'had practically no effect on the fate of the theory' (Vygotsky, 2004: 304), it was to be its highest test for his new psychology (Lantolf, 2008). In short, Vygotsky believed that it was inadequate for educational psychology to limit its scope to the description of naturally occurring developmental processes; instead, he argued, psychology's true objective was to be 'a science of the laws of variation of human behavior and of the means of mastering these laws' (Vygotsky, 1997: 10).

Vygotsky was careful to emphasize that his perspective on developmental education was not equivalent to experimental pedagogies that were primarily concerned with 'the solution of purely pedagogical and instructional problems by means of experiment' (Vygotsky, 1997: 10). Instead, his commitment to praxis meant that educational psychology was 'concerned with *psychological* investigations applied in the field of education' (Vygotsky, 1997: 110). For Vygotsky, formal education had the objective of promoting the 'artificial mastery of natural processes of development' (Vygotsky, 1997: 88) – that is, intentionally promoting development through pedagogical intervention. In contrast to Piaget and other contemporary educational psychologists, who believed that instruction should follow natural developmental stages, Vygotsky argued that learning in a schooled context had the potential to cause particular kinds of cognitive development that were unlikely to occur in non-schooled (everyday) contexts.

> Vygotsky considered education to be a specific form of cultural activity that had important and unique developmental consequences. ... [E]ducation is not just an undertaking whereby knowledge is obtained, but it is indeed an intentionally organized (i.e. artificial) activity that restructures mental behavior. (Lantolf, 2008: 16)

According to Vygotsky, one of the key differences between natural or everyday development and artificial (intentional) development exists at the level of conceptual knowledge, in particular the distinction between everyday and scientific (or theoretical) concepts (Vygotsky, 1986).

Everyday concepts constitute empirical knowledge (Karpov, 2003) and are based on 'an immediate observable property of an object' (Kozulin, 1995: 123). There are two types of everyday concepts: spontaneous and nonspontaneous. *Spontaneous* everyday concepts are generally inaccessible to consciousness without special education. For example, children acquire the grammar of their first language nonconsciously, and their appropriate use of the language does not depend on any conscious understanding of it. However, this knowledge can become open consciousness through schooling (e.g. learning grammar rules and parts of speech). *Nonspontaneous* everyday concepts are developed through conscious learning processes, whether in the everyday world or in formal educational contexts. As such, they are open to conscious inspection (i.e. awareness). For instance, the nonspontaneous everyday concept of a circle is formed through the conscious abstraction of objects with the same or similar geometric shape with which one has had more or less extensive experience, 'such as wheels, pancakes, bracelets, [and] coins' (Lantolf, 2008: 21). This kind of knowledge is akin to rules of thumb in language teaching: it provides some practical guidelines, but it is not coherent, nor is it part of a larger system.

Scientific concepts, by contrast, 'represent the generalizations of the experience of humankind that is [sic] fixed in science' (Karpov, 2003: 66). They encompass the essential features of a given set of objects, which may not be immediately observable. To revisit the example of the concept of a circle, the scientific concept is 'a figure that appears as the result of a [360-degree] movement of a line with one free and one fixed end' (Kozulin, 1995: 124; as cited by Lantolf, 2008: 21). The scientific concept describes all possible circles. As Kozulin (1995: 124) notes, this definition of a circle 'requires no previous knowledge of round objects to understand'. Scientific conceptual knowledge of language therefore entails an understanding of the essential features of language. As argued in this book, this kind of knowledge is semiotic rather than structural. Of course, structure/form is important, but a holistic, systematic understanding of meaning potential must be the core of instructed L2 development. In other words, while traditional approaches to instructed SLA in general, and L2 instructional pragmatics in particular, have privileged form, the SCT framework begins with meanings, specifically underlying conceptual meanings relevant to linguistic practices.

Vygotsky (1986) acknowledged that everyday and scientific concepts have their own strengths and weaknesses. Everyday concepts are rich in empirical evidence and closely tied to everyday lived experience. However, because they are empirical (i.e. exemplar-based), everyday concepts often lack generalizability, and they may not be transferable to circumstances that a person has not encountered before. Scientific concepts, however, have the advantage of being abstract and systematic, thus making their use applicable to the full range of possible circumstances. They are also explicit and therefore available for conscious control. Yet scientific concepts are not necessarily linked to empirical experience. Therefore, it may take a long time for a learner to be able to accelerate his or her control over the concept in practice. Keeping in mind Vygotsky's commitment to praxis (i.e. the unification of theory and practice), he argued that 'for scientific knowledge to be of value it must be connected to practical activity' (Lantolf, 2008: 21). In other words, acquiring scientific knowledge without developing the ability for use results in empty verbalism, or 'knowledge detached from reality' (Vygotsky, 1987: 217). Consequently, pedagogies based on Vygotskian principles must find a way to link abstract theoretical knowledge with concrete practice. In the case of instructed L2 development this means, on the one hand, promoting systematic metalinguistic knowledge and, on the other, creating the conditions for the application, and possible transformation, of such knowledge in performance (e.g. speech or writing). And in contrast to traditional instructed SLA approaches to mapping forms onto meanings, the SCT framework aims to map meanings onto forms (see below). In other words, conceptual meanings come first, and can then be extended to relevant linguistic forms. In this way, instructed L2 development – conceived of as a conceptual process (see above) – is characterized as the 'ascent from the abstract to the concrete' (Ilyenkov, 1982: 135; see also Davydov, 2004, described below).

As noted above, instructed SLA has traditionally focused on the acquisition of forms as means for creating and interpreting meaningful utterances. Accordingly, it is the forms that are privileged in the first instance, and as those forms are acquired they may be mapped onto message-relevant meanings. For example, in many beginning-level French textbooks, past tenses are taught in a stepwise fashion, starting with the preterit (*passé composé*). Units focusing on past tenses in textbooks usually describe the appropriate formation of the *passé composé* (i.e. selecting the appropriate auxiliary verb, *être* 'to be' or *avoir* 'to have', and adding the past particle of the main verb). Practice exercises then reinforce the structural dimension of past tense use. Only later, when the imperfective is introduced (which also starts with a focus on forming the imperfective, i.e. verb endings), are learners then presented with information that is relevant to the meaning of past aspect (i.e. the choice between the perfective and imperfective aspect) – for instance, foregrounding or backgrounding information in a past narrative to move the plot forward or to contextualize actions. Thus, what is privileged first is mastery of the formal features of past tenses and only once these are assumed to be under learners' control are the meanings made available to them. SCT reverses this through concept-based instruction, by focusing first on the meaning and significance of verbal aspect and then mapping those meanings onto the relevant past tense forms, as illustrated in the work of Negueruela (2003).

Meaning, therefore, is not simply about 'getting the message across' (i.e. denotational meaning of utterances) but about the perspectival and representational nuances that are possible in the language one is learning (i.e. psychological meaning). Both types of meaning are certainly important, and they interact in important ways. However, when conceptual meanings are foregrounded, learners are given access to a more systematic and thoughtful orienting basis (i.e. motives) for choosing between forms. It is also important to note that the kind of concepts that are privileged in SCT-grounded pedagogies are those that are relevant for communicative action and meaning making. Thus, while knowledge of verb paradigms may be conceptual in nature, the content of the concept is limited to formal, structural properties of the language and do not necessarily function semiotically. By contrast, appropriation of the grammatical concept of aspect or the sociopragmatic concept of social distance, for example, can foster in learners a systematic and semiotically oriented basis for interpreting and creating meaning in communication that is not limited to a closed set of forms. Aspect is, after all, relevant not only for past tense (there are also perfective and imperfective present and future aspects, realized in different ways in different languages) or even verb forms (lexical aspect may be realized also via verb choice and adverbs), just as the concept of social distance is relevant to many pragmatic features of language, not just address forms or speech act realizations.

Systemic-theoretical instruction

Following Vygotsky's position on the value of conceptual knowledge in formal educational practice, Galperin (1989, 1992) and Davydov (2004) developed concept-based approaches to instruction. Although differences do exist between the Galperinian and Davydovian models – known respectively as systemic-theoretical instruction (STI) and movement-from-the-abstract-to-the-concrete (MAC) – both approaches treat scientific concepts as the minimal unit of instruction. As Ferreira (2005: 55) notes, despite differences in these approaches, both Galperin and Davydov promoted conceptual instruction that 'is explicit, linked to the leading activities [of learners], ... focused on conscious awareness of what and why one is doing what one is doing, ... and aims at developing autonomy and creativity in students'. The main difference between Galperin's and Davydov's respective approaches is in developing orienting models of scientific concepts for instruction.

For Galperin, the model is inflexible, a procedure used to accomplish error-free action (Haenen, 1996: 190). For example, Negueruela (2003) developed flow charts for teaching the concept of aspect in L2 Spanish. These flow charts led learners through the process of selecting appropriate tenses for the meanings they wanted to create. As such, although Negueruela's study enabled learners to make creative, agentive choices regarding verbal aspect, the flow charts served as a step-by-step guide for selecting appropriate tenses without error. For Davydov, however, the model is flexible enough to guide learners through quasi-investigation of a concept. The model encompasses the essence of the discipline and serves as a tool for the development of theoretical thinking. Ferreira (2005), for instance, used Davydov's (2004) notion of a germ-cell model for teaching the concept of genre in an ESL writing course. A germ-cell model is essentially the core kernel of the concept to be appropriated that encapsulates its essence and can be elaborated and modified as learners are guided through a quasi-investigation of the concept. In the case of Ferreira's study, the model was open to evaluation and revision as learners developed an understanding of the mutual influence of language and context represented in 'the *abstract communicative principle* (ACP)— LANGUAGE ↔ CONTEXT' (Ferreira, 2005: 19). Thus, rather than providing a step-by-step flow chart or diagram to produce error-free action, the germ-cell model gave learners an orientation to exploring the concept of genre. (For an extended comparison of STI and MAC, see Ferreira, 2005.)

It should be noted that, although Galperin, and later Davydov, focused on teaching experiments (STI, MAC), this research fundamentally addressed the problem of the development of mind within Vygotsky's overall project.[4] What Galperin in particular demonstrated through his STI experiments was that mental activity was not a mysterious internal process occurring solely within the brain of the individual. Instead, mental activity arose in and through practical, material activity, which was goal directed (i.e. purposeful) and always linked to the problems of real-life material activity. As Stetsenko and Arievitch (2010) write:

> the mind gradually arises in development ... out of material activity because it serves the need to thoroughly examine emerging, new situations and to anticipate the consequences of actions within these situations prior to their physical execution. (Arievitch, 2010: 244)

And in a later passage:

> acting on the internal plane retains all the characteristics of human real-life activity – it is an active process of solving problems that exist out in the world and of searching for 'what is to be done next' given present conditions and future goals. (Arievitch, 2010: 244–245)

Thus, whether carried out on the internal or external plane, actions are goal directed: 'mental actions are carried out in the medium of meanings' (Stetsenko & Arievitch, 2010: 245), whereas material actions are executed in physical activity. It is noteworthy that neither Galperin nor Davydov considered mental activity to occur only internally (privately), but also included externalized forms of thinking. Take, for instance, the example of an architect who draws blueprints and revises them before actually constructing a building (Lantolf & Thorne, 2006). In essence, the building was constructed on the symbolic plane (i.e. in the blueprints) prior to its execution during construction. Thus, the architect's thinking was materialized in the blueprints.

Concept-based pedagogy is therefore grounded in three basic principles (Lantolf & Thorne, 2006). First, as mentioned above, concepts serve as the basic unit of instruction. Concepts are systematic representations of objects of study that guide learners' actions during concrete material activity. The two remaining principles aim to support the internalization of relevant concepts: materialization of the concepts (e.g. in the form of pedagogical diagrams) and verbalization (e.g. explaining the concept as such and explaining one's performance in relation to the concepts). As Lantolf and Thorne (2006: 304) note: 'These three principles are derived from [Galperin's] general theory of human mental functioning according to which mental activity is controlled by three processes: orientation, execution, and control.' The orientation process (i.e. the planning function) 'determines what and how something is to be done' (Lantolf & Thorne, 2006: 304). The execution process represents the actual activity, while the control process is responsible for evaluating whether, and to what extent, the orientation (i.e. plan) was successfully executed. Thus, the goal of concept-based pedagogy is to provide students with an orienting basis for action such that both mental and material activities are guided by coherent, systematic explanations of how to plan and execute actions, while at the same time enabling students to control and evaluate those actions in relation to their understanding of the activity's goals. This approach has the potential to develop students' agency, defined as the socioculturally mediated capacity to act and to assign meaning to one's actions, including its contextually sensitive significance, given the constraints and affordances arising from one's relationship with the environment.

Concept-based L2 instruction

To date, a number of studies have shown that internalized linguistic concepts serve a powerful mediational role in L2 development and use. Such studies have investigated the teaching of tense, aspect and modality in Spanish (Negueruela, 2003, 2008; Negueruela & Lantolf, 2006), Spanish locative prepositions (Serrano-López & Poehner, 2008), genre in an ESL academic writing course (Ferreira, 2005), the concept of voice in French (Knouzi et al., 2010; Lapkin et al., 2008; Swain et al., 2009) and Spanish literature and metaphor (Yáñez Prieto, 2008). In what follows, I provide a description of the research carried out by Negueruela and Swain and colleagues, cited above, as these projects have been the primary models for the design of the study reported on in this book.

Negueruela (2003) implemented a concept-based approach to instruction in an intermediate-level US university Spanish composition and grammar class. Students were presented with pedagogical models (diagrams) of the concepts of mood, aspect and tense, assigned six at-home audio recorded verbalization tasks in which they explained to themselves the relevant concepts, and engaged in several spontaneous spoken-interactive tasks outside of class over the course of a 16-week academic term. Negueruela documented in great detail how learners' verbalizations (audio recorded by learners at home) developed from rule-of-thumb-based explanations of the use of perfective and imperfective tenses to conceptually grounded, meaning-based understandings of the role of tense in assigning a particular aspectual perspective on a given event. This shift was suggestive of these learners' thinking about language no longer as a set of rules to follow but as a system of meanings from which they could choose to fit their specific communicative purposes. Negueruela also documented marked improvement in these learners' spoken performance, namely their agentive (i.e. voluntary, controlled) use of tense to assign specific meanings (aspect) to the events described. Although the learners continued to struggle in performance, as evidenced by faltering control over linguistic forms from time to time, Negueruela explained that this should not be surprising since conceptual knowledge typically develops ahead of performance abilities (Valsiner, 2001). Elsewhere, Negueruela (2008) has described the internalization of categories of meanings (concepts) as leading to a zone of potential development (ZPOD). For Negueruela (2008), the ZPOD entails the internalization of categories of meanings (i.e. concepts), which sets the stage for the (potential) development of communicative performance abilities.

Swain and colleagues (Knouzi et al., 2010; Lapkin et al., 2008; Swain et al., 2009) developed a one-time concept-based instructional intervention to teach the concept of voice in an intermediate-level Canadian university L2 French course, with a much more experimental design compared to Negueruela (2003) (i.e. with a formal pretest, posttest and delayed posttest). Their primary focus was on the role of verbalization, or *languaging*, in the internalization of linguistic concepts. Their study consisted of developing written concept explanations cards and pedagogical diagrams depicting the concepts for the learners to study independently in class. During an in-class intervention, students were prompted to speak to themselves (i.e. verbalize their thinking) in the presence of a researcher as much as possible. Their results indicated that all learners improved their understanding of the concept of voice, as measured by definition data (i.e. explaining the concept of voice) and a worksheet in which they identified voice in a text and explained how it functioned. However, interindividual differences were found; most notably the amount and quality of languaging varied across the learners. Their analysis, reported on in detail in Swain *et al.* (2009), suggested that high languagers (who performed better than the other groups on a posttest and delayed posttest) produced significantly higher rates of *self-assessment* and *inferencing* languaging units. Swain *et al.* (2009) identified three forms of inferencing:

> (a) *Integration*: the participant uses information presented in previous cards ...; (b) *Elaboration*: the participant does not only show evidence of retaining the information presented previously but also appropriates the information either by incorporating it into prior knowledge ... or by incorporating several pieces of information of the explanatory text ...; (c) *Hypothesis formation*: the participant forms a hypothesis based on what he or she has already learned or understood. (p. 11)

Self-assessment refers to languaging units in which the learner monitors or evaluates his/her understanding of the concept. Based on their findings, Swain *et al.* (2009: 22) argued that 'it is not just that high languagers language more, but that they use language in qualitatively different ways, ways that mediate those processes important to the understanding of cognitively complex ideas'.

What both of these research programs illustrate is that the internalization of conceptual knowledge is a key component of L2 development. As described earlier, concept-based pedagogy emphasizes three aspects of mental actions: orientation, execution and control. Internalized concepts provide an orientation to action, and they also serve to control, monitor and evaluate action. Thus, conceptual knowledge is foregrounded as the central component of developing the ability to control one's actions voluntarily in order to achieve one's goals and to respond to present and potentially changing circumstances.

Research Context and Data Sources

The SCT framework for L2 instructional pragmatics proposed in this book draws from a study of a concept-based approach to developing advanced L2 pragmatic abilities among US university learners of French (van Compernolle, 2012). This book elaborates upon the theoretical and methodological underpinnings of the study and illustrates the practical extension of the SCT framework to the domain of L2 instructional pragmatics.

Design of the study

The study was designed to explore the extension of Vygotskian pedagogical principles, specifically STI, to L2 instructional pragmatics. To this end, a six-week pedagogical enrichment program was developed to allow students to meet one-on-one with a tutor outside of their normal class. The following materials and tasks were included in the study (details of the materials design and task administration will be fleshed out in the relevant chapters):

- A 36-page concept-based course book, which included written concept explanations as well as pedagogical diagrams depicting the concepts (see Chapter 2), served as the center of the enrichment program. Using the course book, the learners engaged in monologic and dialogic verbalized reflections in which they considered the qualities of the concepts (see Chapter 4).
- Appropriateness judgment questionnaires (AJQs) in which learners were to select appropriate pragmatic forms in a variety of social-interactive situations and to explain their choices (see Chapter 5).
- Spoken-interactive scenarios, modeled after Di Pietro's (1987) strategic interaction methodology, in which the learners planned the scenario, performed it, and discussed their performance with the tutor (see Chapter 6).

In addition, semi-guided language awareness interviews (LAIs) were included in order to assess the qualities of the learners' metapragmatic knowledge. Table 1.2 provides an outline of the study's design.

Table 1.2 Outline of the research design

Session	Procedures
1	• Pre-enrichment LAI • AJQ 1 • Scenarios 1 and 2
2	• Introduction of concept-based materials • Verbalized reflection • AJQ 2
3	• Scenarios 3 and 4
4	• Verbalized reflection (diagrams only) • AJQ 3
5	• Scenarios 5 and 6
6	• Post-enrichment LAI • Repeat AJQ 1 • Scenarios 7 and 8

Session 1 of the program represents an attempt at assessing learners' actual level of development (i.e. what they know and are able to do independently at the start of the program), including a LAI, an AJQ, and two strategic interaction scenarios aiming to elicit informal and formal speech (see above). This first session also served as a diagnostic assessment in that the researcher noted specific areas of difficulties for each individual to be followed up on in subsequent sessions.

Sessions 2–5 represent the enrichment program proper. During this period, the participants were introduced to the concepts via the concept explanations and diagrams (session 2), asked to verbally reflect on the concepts (sessions 2 and 4), and cooperatively worked with the researcher/tutor on various AJQs (sessions 2 and 4) and strategic interaction scenarios (sessions 3 and 5) to develop their conceptual knowledge and performance abilities. The enrichment program aimed not only to provide multiple opportunities to engage in similar tasks but also to withdraw mediation progressively. Thus, while verbalized reflections during session 2 took place while the participants had access to the full verbal concept explanations, they had access only to the pedagogical diagrams during session 3. Similarly, during interactive tasks (i.e. AJQs, scenarios), the researcher/tutor sought to provide the least explicit assistance required to position the participants to contribute maximally to the task.

Session 6 was designed to mirror session 1 as a means of comparing preenrichment and postenrichment metapragmatic knowledge and performance abilities. As such, the participants engaged in another LAI centered on the same guiding questions as in session 1, the same AJQ used in session 1 as a means of directly comparing preenrichment and postenrichment performance, and scenarios that were very similar to those used in session 1.

Participants

The participants in this study were all undergraduate learners of French enrolled in an intermediate-level (second year) oral communication and reading comprehension course during Fall 2010 at a large public research university located in the northeast United States. The rationale for recruiting from among this population was twofold. First, although students enrolled in Second year courses are generally communicatively capable in French, their experience with the language is generally limited to what is taught in formal educational contexts. As such, their awareness of, and ability to use, the range of sociolinguistic and pragmatic variants available to French speakers is limited. Second, students enrolled in intermediate-level coursework have already completed the university's foreign language requirement and are therefore pursuing their studies in French for their own purposes, such as a personal interest in the language, a desire to study abroad in the future and/or a professional/career-related goal.

Volunteers were offered compensation for their time in the amount of $60 for the study, which was prorated at $10 per session. Initially, 15 students expressed interest in the study. However, only ten students were eventually able to arrange meeting times with the researcher. Of these, two students withdrew from the study before it began without citing a reason for doing so. The remaining eight participants all completed the study.

Table 1.3 displays basic information about these eight participants, including the pseudonym selected by, or assigned to, each participant, gender, and previous studies in French at the middle school, high school and university levels. Five were females and three were males. All eight participants had previously taken French in middle and/or high school, including high school French at the Advanced Placement level 4 and/or 5.[5] Six participants had taken one or two French courses (French 3, the final semester of the basic language sequence,[6] and/or an intermediate grammar course) at the university prior to enrolling in the oral communication and reading comprehension course. The remaining two, Leon and Pierre, had not taken any university-level French courses. In addition, although all eight participants had had a number of years of previous French studies, none reported having had more than very little exposure to the language outside of a formal classroom setting. None of the participants was a French major or minor at the time of the

Table 1.3 Participant information

Pseudonym	Gender	Previous studies in French: Years in middle school	Previous studies in French: Years in high school	Previous studies in French: University courses
Nikki	Female	2	4	French 3
				French Grammar
Susan	Female	1	4	French 3
				French Grammar
Leon	Male	2	4	—
Pierre	Male	1	4	—
Mary	Female	—	4	French Grammar
Stephanie	Female	1	4	French 3
				French Grammar
Laurie	Female	1	4	French 3
Conrad	Male	2	4	French 3

study, although some were considering pursuing a minor, or at least advanced-level coursework, and/or participating in a study abroad program.

Overview of the Chapters

This introduction has outlined the key components of the SCT framework for L2 instructional pragmatics to be elaborated in the six remaining chapters of the book. As I mentioned at the outset, this book is not simply a teacher's guide with hints or tips for teaching pragmatics. Instead, its purpose is to present a coherent pedagogical framework based on Vygotskian cultural-historical psychology. To this end, each of the remaining chapters deconstructs a particular theoretical issue in L2 instructional pragmatics from the perspective of SCT, drawing empirical support from the study described above. Although each chapter can be read as a stand-alone piece, it is helpful to read them in the order in which they are presented in order to fully appreciate the theoretical and practical arguments constructed throughout this volume.

Chapters 2 and 3 delve further into the theoretical and empirical underpinnings of the SCT framework for L2 instructional pragmatics. In Chapter 2, the history of the concept of appropriateness in language learning and language teaching is traced and critiqued in order to arrive at a conceptualization of appropriateness that is commensurable with SCT. Two central concepts are proposed: (1) that sociopragmatic meaning exists as a dynamic and malleable indexical field (Eckert, 2008; Silverstein, 2003; van Compernolle, 2011a); and (2) that pragmatics must be seen as mediated action. Chapter 3 addresses SCT's approach to understanding learners as people-acting-through-mediational-means. The chapter includes discussions of personality development, self, identity, agency and emotions.

Chapters 4–6, then, specifically address the components of the proposed pedagogical framework. Each of the chapters documents the findings of the study in relation to the theoretical claims of the framework. Chapter 4 considers the relationship between thinking and speaking and the role of verbalization in concept formation. Chapter 5 focuses on the development of concept-based pragmatic knowledge as an orienting basis for action during problem-solving tasks, with specific emphasis on the role of cooperative dialogue in driving development. Chapter 6 then links the development of conceptual knowledge to the development of spoken performance abilities. In particular, Chapter 6 explores how dynamically administered strategic interaction scenarios served to develop learners' controlled performance abilities.

Chapter 7 concludes the book. The discussion includes a summary of the SCT framework and its central claims regarding instructed L2 pragmatic development. However, the principal aim of the chapter is to construct a praxis-oriented future for Vygotskian approaches to L2 instructional pragmatics. To this end, the findings of the study reported in the book are then discussed in terms of their implications for research, classroom teaching and teacher education programs.

Notes

(1) Second language (L2) will be used throughout this book to refer to any language learned beyond one's first, whether second, third, foreign, and so on.
(2) Of course, English speakers can encode types of relationships through alternative means, such as titles and honorifics, use of last names versus first names, and so forth. However, the pronoun *you* does not itself encode information about social relationships as do the French pronouns *tu* and *vous*. In other words, the French language predisposes speakers to attend to social relationship qualities in the grammar of second-person verb phrases, whereas this information is only optionally encoded periphrastically in English.
(3) Lantolf and Thorne (2006) argue with Wertsch's (1998) use of *agent* in this term. In their view, 'there are no uniquely human actions that are not mediated. ... human agency appears once we integrate cultural artifacts and concepts into our mental and material activity' (Lantolf & Thorne, 2006: 63). For this reason, Lantolf and Thorne enclose *agent* in parentheses.
(4) It should be noted that Galperin conducted STI experiments not in controlled laboratory settings, but in classrooms. In line with Vygotsky's (1997) position on developmental education, Galperin sought to perform psychological investigations in educational contexts by intervening in the development of real learners. In this way, he was interested not only in teaching methods, but more importantly in tracing the development of mental activity as it arose in and through pedagogical activity.
(5) Advanced Placement (AP) courses are designed to provide high school students with an opportunity to earn one or more semesters of college-level credit through examination. The exception here is Stephanie, who had four years of high school French but had not taken AP-level French.
(6) None of the participants was required to take French 3 at the university. However, those who chose to take this course did so because they felt they needed a refresher course for whatever reason (e.g. some stated having had bad high school teachers or having done poorly on an AP exam).

2 Appropriateness in Language Learning and Language Teaching

Introduction

This chapter addresses the concept of appropriateness as it has been conceptualized in the language learning and teaching literature in general and in the L2 pragmatics literature in particular. Appropriateness refers to a social judgment of the acceptability of some instance of language in context. Crystal (1997: 421), for example, defines appropriate language as 'any use of language considered to be compatible with a given social situation'. But how do we define what is compatible with a particular context and what is not? Consider the data in Excerpt 2.1, where Leon had been asked to decide which second-person pronoun (i.e. the more familiar *tu* or the more formal *vous*) he would use with a favorite teacher and to explain his choice.

Excerpt 2.1

```
1  Leon:  ((silently reads situation)) so again. this is (xxx) he's one
2         of my favorite teachers, + even though he may be forty
3         years old, um + if I've had him for like a while, I feel like
4         I'm familiar with him, there's a very good chance I'd actually
5         use the tu form, + even though often + um teachers use the vous,
```

Conventionally, students are expected to use *vous* with teachers, a rule of thumb that is always presented in learner textbooks. However, Leon selected *tu*. This is an unconventional choice, and in many situations, it could be seen as inappropriate and carry with it negative social consequences. However, Leon's choice of *tu* could be construed as appropriate. He certainly understood the potential relevance of the age difference and the social convention to use *vous* with teachers (lines 2–3, 5). Yet, from his perspective, 'favorite teacher' was a category of persons with which one had a familiar relationship (line 4). Therefore, 'favorite teacher' was a category of persons with whom Leon felt comfortable using the more familiar *tu*. The question is whether there is a single appropriate response or use of language that is compatible with a situation or if multiple responses can be considered compatible with it when language users' orientations to situations are taken into account (Dewaele, 2008). In other words, we have to ask whether, and to what extent, pragmatic *conventions* are equivalent to *appropriateness* in language use. This question has obvious, and significant, implications for how pedagogical materials aimed at developing learners' pragmatic abilities are designed and implemented in educational contexts.

The remainder of this chapter has two objectives. First, it aims to problematize the theoretical foundations of the notion of appropriateness in order to propose a conceptualization of it that is commensurable with sociocultural theory (SCT). Second, and in line with the SCT perspective on appropriateness, it develops a rationale for choosing pedagogical concepts relevant to L2 instructional pragmatics, based on the framework of mediated action.

Theoretical Foundations of Appropriateness

For the first half of the 20th century, the field of linguistics – and, by extension, the domain of language learning and language teaching – focused almost exclusively on studying language as an abstract system that was separable from the people who used it and the social contexts in which it was used. De Saussure (1913/1959) proposed a distinction between *langue* (the abstract system) and *parole* (the actual use of language). He argued that, if linguistics were to become a true science on par with physics, biology, chemistry, and so forth, its object of study must be limited to the objective truths about the abstract system (*langue*) and, thus, must exclude what he saw as the often flawed and variable performance of language (*parole*). Chomsky (1965) made a similar argument as he was developing a generative theory of syntax – *linguistic competence* (the innate, deep semantic knowledge of the linguistic system that allows native speakers to formulate and process well-formed sentences) was pitted against *linguistic performance*, with the former being heralded as the objective and, therefore, the proper object of study in linguistics.

In the 1960s, however, there emerged a number of alternative, functional-pragmatic perspectives on language. These included Austin's (1962) doctrine of locutionary, illocutionary and perlocutionary acts, and Searle's (1969) reinterpretation of Austin's proposals as speech act theory. This perspective holds that language not only had a referential or semantic meaning but in fact accomplishes social actions through its use. Halliday's (1973, 1978) systemic-functional linguistics, which adopted a sociological-semiotic perspective (as opposed to an innatist psychological-semantic perspective based on a 'built-in' hierarchal syntax), also put contextualized language use at its center. The then-emerging field of sociolinguistics (e.g. Gumperz & Hymes, 1972; Hymes, 1964, 1972; Labov, 1972) provided insight into the nature of actually performed language with an emphasis on appropriateness and its relationship with a variety of sociocultural factors.

Within the field of language teaching and language learning, insights from these functional and sociolinguistic perspectives were quickly adopted. In particular, Hymes's (1964, 1972) work on the ethnography of communication, and his concept of *communicative competence*, received much attention as a potential framework to broaden the scope of the field beyond well-formed, or formally accurate, sentences to include communication and social appropriateness (Canale, 1983; Canale & Swain, 1980). As will be fleshed out below, Hymes's ideas were appropriated and reinterpreted as the bases for communicative approaches to language teaching and testing.

Parameters of communicative competence

As noted above, the notion that social appropriateness constitutes an important aspect of language learning (first or additional) derives from the work of Dell Hymes (1964, 1972). Hymes was unhappy with the way that formalist approaches to linguistics had abstracted language from its sociocultural context of use and, in many cases, even went so far as to disqualify analyses of language-in-use from the field of linguistics proper. Although Hymes recognized that the ability to understand and produce grammatical utterances was important, he argued that *linguistic competence* (Chomsky, 1965) was never enough. Instead, he insisted that, as children acquire language, they also acquire the sociocultural knowledge required to use language appropriately. As Hymes (1964: 110) wrote:

> it is not enough for the child to be able to produce any grammatical utterance. It would have to remain speechless if it could not decide which grammatical utterance here and now, if it could not connect utterances to their contexts of use.

Hymes referred to this ability to use language appropriately as *communicative competence*. To investigate language acquisition and use from the perspective of communicative competence, Hymes developed a set of empirical research questions to be carried out in ethnographic studies that centered on four 'parameters' or criteria: whether, and to what extent, a particular use of language is formally possible, feasible, appropriate and actually performed.

Hymes's first criterion engages with more traditional or formalist schools of linguistics that focus on the grammaticality of possible sentences or utterances, particularly Chomsky's (1965) work on transformational grammar. By *formally possible*, Hymes meant whether, and to what extent, the linguistic system allows a given combination of sounds or words to be judged as grammatically acceptable. In this sense, Hymes's term is similar to Chomsky's notion of *linguistic competence*. However, Hymes's possibility parameter differs in two important ways. First, he included not only linguistic grammaticality but also other culturally significant forms of nonlinguistic behavior, which, like language, have their own sets of grammatical rules (e.g. when, where and with whom to shake hands). Second, Hymes was not interested in an abstract, idealized speaker-hearer as Chomsky was, but instead he was firmly committed to understanding what people can actually do in and with language. In this sense, Hymes's possibility parameter is 'dependent both upon (tacit) knowledge and (ability for) use' (Hymes 1972: 282). Importantly, for Hymes, what is *possible* to do in and with language is not co-equivalent with what is deemed to be correct usage in normative reference grammars. Instead, the possible encompasses what may be done and understood between people who share a common and conventionalized, yet malleable, semiotic system. This is a crucial distinction between Hymes's conception of the possibility criterion and traditional views of grammaticality because it recognizes that language users are able to creatively manipulate their semiotic artifacts.

The three remaining criteria are related to the actual performance or production of language. *Feasibility* refers to the psycholinguistic dimension of a speaker's capacity to process formally possible utterances either in production or comprehension, including 'memory limitation, perceptual device(s), [and the] effects of properties such as nesting, embedding, branching and the like' (Hymes, 1972: 285). The feasibility criterion holds that not all formally possible utterances can be feasibly processed. Canale and Swain (1980: 4) illustrate this point with the following sentence: 'The cheese the rat the cat the dog saw chased ate was green.' The sentence is *formally possible* (i.e. grammatical) because it follows the rules of English for embedding relative clauses. However, it cannot *feasibly* be automatically processed. Indeed, it takes quite a bit of conscious processing to understand the relationship between the main clause (i.e. *the cheese was green*) and the embedded relative clauses (i.e.

the rat ate the cheese, the cat chased the rat and *the dog saw the cat*). Of course, Hymes (1972: 281) underscored the fact that feasibility was a relative notion that was dependent upon the 'means of implementation available'. For example, Canale and Swain's illustrative sentence can be more feasibly processed in written form, where a material artifact (i.e. text) is produced, than in spoken interaction, where language is ephemeral. In fact, it is doubtful that many people would be able to spontaneously produce or automatically process such a sentence in spoken interaction.

Appropriateness entails the sociocultural and pragmatic effectiveness of a given utterance that is formally possible and feasible 'in relation to a context in which it is used and evaluated' (Hymes, 1972: 281). Just as not all formally possible utterances are feasible, not all feasible utterances are appropriate in all contexts. Instead, the appropriateness of a given utterance depends on its relationship to specific sociocultural activities. Hymes therefore argued that the *speech event* ought to serve as the minimal unit of analysis rather than the utterance or sentence in isolation. For this, he developed a mnemonic device to describe the elements of a given speech event known as the SPEAKING model (Hymes, 1972), shown in Table 2.1. By using the SPEAKING model, Hymes sought to understand what forms of linguistic (and nonlinguistic)

Table 2.1 Hymes's SPEAKING model

Element		Description
S	Setting and scene	The *setting* is the time, place and physical environment of a speech event; the *scene* describes the psychological or cultural definition of the setting, including formality, sense of seriousness or playfulness, and so on.
P	Participants	Who is involved in a given speech event, including the speaker(s) and audience.
E	Ends	The purpose or goal of a speech event and its outcomes.
A	Act sequence	The form and order of actions that comprise the speech event.
K	Key	The cues that point to the overall tone and/or manner of the speech event.
I	Instrumentalities	Linguistic forms and speech styles used in the speech event.
N	Norms	The social rules governing what forms of action and interaction are recognized as acceptable/appropriate during the speech event.
G	Genre	The type of speech event taking place.

behavior constituted specific speech events or social activities. In this way, Hymes's notion of appropriateness is not about predefined or static judgments of what constitutes proper and improper social behavior but instead addresses the way in which language simultaneously reflects and shapes activity types (Levinson, 1992). Put another way, speech events are in large part determined by the qualities of the elements described in the SPEAKING model, which in turn come to be associated with what is recognized as appropriate language in the context of a particular type of speech event. It is important to note that Hymes's conception of appropriateness does not exclude the possibility that unconventional language use can be entirely appropriate. Rather, unconventional uses of language can be socially significant and meaningful, for instance when speakers diverge from conventional patterns and meanings to initiate or respond to a shift in activity types, sarcasm, humor, and so forth (van Compernolle, 2011a).

The fourth criterion – whether, and to what extent, something is *actually performed* – goes to the heart of Hymes's theory of communicative competence as a theory of *language use*. As Hymes (1972: 286) noted, 'something may be possible, feasible, appropriate and not occur'. In other words, there may exist many imaginable possible, feasible and appropriate utterances, but it does not mean that all of them will actually be performed at some point in time. Instead, there are probabilistic conventions of language use that determine which subset of formally possible, feasible and appropriate utterances will be used during a given speech event. At the time Hymes was developing a theory of communicative competence, this particular claim was largely speculative (Cook, 1999: 65); findings from quantitative sociolinguistics in the 1960s and 1970s (e.g. Labov, 1972) and, later, in corpus linguistics (e.g. Biber, 2006) have provided evidence of the probabilistic nature of language-in-use. It is important to note, however, that Hymes did not intend to disqualify low-frequency or non-occurring utterances from his research program in favor of only those utterances that could be frequently observed. Instead, for Hymes, this was a research question to be explored through empirical investigations.

The four parameters of language advocated by Hymes represent a solid theoretical foundation for explorations of communicative competence. However, it should be kept in mind that Hymes's intent was not to develop a strict or formalist doctrine for language analysis but instead to promote an approach that sought to investigate the relationship among the four components of communicative competence and, by extension, 'the circumstances in which the demands of one may outweigh the demands of another' (Cook, 1999: 65). There are certainly times when the use of some instance of language that is not formally possible is perfectly acceptable, just as there are times when it is perfectly appropriate to use a form of language that has never before occurred. Authors, poets and comedians, for instance, frequently use language in unconventional ways for stylistic effect. Such is also naturally within the capacity of everyday language users whose communicative competence enables them to intentionally and meaningfully manipulate their semiotic artifacts to meet their communicative needs.

Communicative competence in L2 teaching and testing

The rise of communicative competence within the field of L2 teaching and testing emerged in the 1960s and 1970s as language educators and research became increasingly frustrated with traditional pedagogical approaches, namely grammar-translation and audiolingualism. Hymes's socially oriented perspective on *language-in-use* proved to be a welcome alternative for those interested in foregrounding communicative ability in language pedagogy. One early example is provided in Savignon's (1972) study of the coping strategies employed by learners of French to achieve successful communicative interaction. Savignon argued that the ability to express, interpret and negotiate meaning in context was ultimately more important than one's formal knowledge of grammatical rules in isolation, because knowledge of a grammatical rule does not necessarily imply the ability to use that rule for communication.

In an important reinterpretation of the concept of communicative competence, Canale and Swain (1980) outlined the theoretical bases for communicative approaches to L2 teaching and testing. Engaging with and expanding upon Hymes's (1972) work, Canale and Swain proposed a three-part model of communicative competence, which included *grammatical competence, sociolinguistic competence* (comprised of two subcomponents, *sociocultural competence* and *discourse competence*), and *strategic competence*. Importantly, Canale and Swain eliminated Hymes's notion of *feasibility* 'since perceptual strategies, memory constraints, and the like would seem to impose themselves in a natural and universal manner' (Canale & Swain, 1980: 16). In short, they argued that knowledge of feasibility was irrelevant for L2 teaching and testing *in practice* because language users typically neither produce nor encounter instances of language that are not feasible.

Grammatical competence refers to knowledge of and ability to use the linguistic system, including lexis, phonology, morphosyntax and semantics. In other words, grammatical competence is the knowledge of what is *formally possible* in Hymes's terms. The role of a speaker's grammatical competence, according to Canale and Swain (1980: 30), is 'determin[ing] and express[ing] accurately the literal meaning of utterances'. It is noteworthy that Canale and Swain (1980: 29) did not endorse any particular linguistic theory to describe grammatical competence, nor did they maintain that 'a theory of grammar is directly relevant to [L2] pedagogy'.

Sociolinguistic competence addresses the *social meaning* of utterances, and in this way articulates with Hymes's notion of *appropriateness*. As noted above, sociolinguistic competence is comprised of two subcomponents. *Sociocultural competence* refers to the appropriateness of utterances 'within a given sociocultural context depending on contextual factors such as topic, role of participants, setting, and norms for interaction' (Canale & Swain, 1980: 30). In addition, sociocultural competence entails knowledge of and ability to use particular grammatical forms to convey an appropriate register or style of language (e.g. sociostylistic and pragmatic variation). *Discourse competence* refers to knowledge of and ability to create cohesion and coherence in language. Canale and Swain's definition of sociolinguistic competence thus resonates with the components of Hymes's SPEAKING model (see above).

Strategic competence encompasses communication strategies used 'to compensate for breakdowns in communication due to performance variables or to insufficient competence' (Canale & Swain, 1980: 30). In this way, strategic competence articulates with the survival or coping strategies identified by Savignon (1972), which included a speaker's ability to cope with momentary lapses in memory, inattention, miscomprehension, and so forth, as well as gaps in one's lexical and grammatical knowledge during communicative interaction. In their model, Canale and Swain highlighted two categories of communication strategies: those related to grammatical competence (e.g. strategies used to compensate for insufficient control over grammatical forms) and those that relate to sociolinguistic competence (e.g. strategies used to compensate for insufficient sociocultural knowledge).

The components of communicative competence identified by Canale and Swain (1980) have served as the basis for discussions of communicative approaches to L2 teaching and testing. Canale (1983) slightly modified the original model by separating discourse competence from sociolinguistic competence as a distinct fourth component of communicative competence. Savignon (1983, 1997) contributed to discussions of classroom practices for communicative language teaching, and Bachman (1990) formally developed a communicative approach to language testing based in large part on the models presented in Canale (1983) and Canale and Swain (1980). Although these models (among many other discussions; see Widdowson, 1989, 2003) contributed to further defining the individual components of communicative competence, they did not substantially contribute to operationalizing a functional model of the interrelations among them. It was not until an influential paper by Celce-Murcia et al. (1995) that the individual components were respecified, elaborated and reorganized into a relational model.

Celce-Murcia et al.'s (1995) model of communicative competence refines and elaborates the four components presented in Canale and Swain (1980) and Canale (1983): (1) grammatical competence, redubbed *linguistic competence*; (2) discourse competence; (3) sociolinguistic competence, which they rename *sociocultural competence*; and (4) strategic competence. Importantly, they also add a fifth component, *actional competence*, to reflect the notion that communicative competence is a theory of language use. They define actional competence as 'competence in conveying and understanding communicative intent, that is, matching actional intent with linguistic form based on the knowledge of an inventory of verbal schemata that carry illocutionary force (speech acts and speech act sets)' (Celce-Murcia et al., 1995: 17). Although pragmatic ability is present in the Canale and Swain model under sociolinguistic competence, Celce-Murcia et al. distinguish it as actional competence in order to separate *actional intent* from *sociocultural factors*.

Although Celce-Murcia et al.'s discussion and elaboration of the constituent components of communicative competence is enlightening, the real contribution of their paper is the organization of them into a functional-relational model. As noted above, previous discussions of communicative competence focused primarily on defining the components involved, but there was no real attempt to operationalize how they related to one another.

At the center of their model is discourse competence, which reflects the importance that the authors ascribe to issues of discourse cohesion and coherence, deixis, genre (formal schemata) and conversational structure. Discourse competence itself then both shapes and is shaped by sociocultural competence, linguistic competence and actional competence. As Celce-Murcia et al. (1995: 9) explain:

> our construct places the discourse component in a position where the lexico-grammatical building blocks [i.e. linguistic competence], the actional organizing skills of communicative intent, and the sociocultural context come together and shape the discourse, which, in turn, also shapes each of the other three components.

Strategic competence, then, links all components together as 'an ever-present, potentially usable inventory of skills' (Celce-Murcia et al., 1995: 9), enabling speakers to negotiate communicative actions and cope with problems as they arise. Celce-Murcia (2007) has further refined this functional-relational model of communicative competence to include *interactional competence*, which integrates actional competence from the Celce-Murcia et al. (1995) model and conversational competence using insights from conversation analysis (Sacks et al., 1974), as well as *formulaic competence* to emphasize the importance of routines, collocations, idioms and lexical frames in discourse.

As discussed above, models of communicative competence have focused primarily on what is formally possible in language (grammatical or linguistic competence) and what is appropriate in context (sociolinguistic or sociocultural competence, discourse competence). The criterion of what is actually performed (probability) underlies each of the various components. In addition, as we have seen in the discussion of Celce-Murcia et al.'s (1995) model, the ability to use language (actional competence) has also emerged as a distinct and crucial component of communicative competence (see also Widdowson, 1989). However, as elaborated in the following section, Hymes's original ideas – which were developed in the form of empirical research questions – have been reindexed to fit the (perceived) needs of language educators and, in many cases, the original concept of communicative competence, as potentiality and ability has been replaced by a rather strict doctrinal approach to pedagogy (Leung, 2005; Widdowson, 2007). This is particularly relevant for discussions of *appropriateness*, both in the sense in which Hymes used the term to refer to sociocultural conventions (e.g. the SPEAKING model) and in relation to what is deemed appropriate for teaching and learning in a classroom context.

Critical perspectives on appropriateness

Cook (1999) notes that models of communicative competence, while welcome alternatives to traditional grammar-centered approaches to language competence, led to a tendency to over-emphasize appropriateness at the expense of what is formally possible, feasible and actually performed. Likewise, the rise of corpus linguistics has led to an overemphasis on what is actually done (i.e. authentic uses of language attested in corpora), 'which can be at the expense of developing knowledge of what is possible and appropriate' (Cook, 1999: 65). What Cook points to is a reconceptualization of Hymes's ideas – originally conceived as empirical questions – for the purposes of language pedagogy that centers on the identification of a clearly defined set of linguistic practices that count as the language, viewed as an abstract system, which can be standardized and codified for use in normative reference grammars and learner textbooks (see also Widdowson, 1989).

Leung (2005) argues that, when applied to English language teaching, the original meanings of Hymes's ideas vis-à-vis a set of ethnographic research questions were reindexed for language teaching professionals concerned with what to include in teaching materials and curricula. As he writes, 'Hymes's research-oriented ideas have gone through an epistemic transformation: from empirically oriented questions to an idealized pedagogic doctrine' (Leung, 2005: 124). The source of such a transformation, according to Leung, is that language teachers and materials developers are not directly concerned with situated, ethnographic research into the processes by which communicative activity is achieved. Instead, 'they are more directly concerned with what information or content should be included in the curriculum and how such content should be worked on in the classroom' (Leung, 2005: 125). Leung continues:

> The need to specify what is to be taught and learned inevitably turns research questions, which allow the possibility of both instability in existing knowledge and emergence of new knowledge, into pedagogic guidelines and principles which have to assume a degree of stability, transparency and certainty in existing knowledge. (Leung, 2005: 125)

In short, curricula and materials designed around communicative approaches to language teaching came to be based on an idealized native speaker. There is some irony in this transformation inasmuch as Hymes's original ideas were themselves part of a critique of Chomsky's (1965) idealized speaker-hearer living in a homogenous speech community and highly abstract notion of linguistic competence. The result is that the notion of appropriateness in language is no longer judged on the basis of observation and ethnographic research, but 'according to some normative assumptions of language practice set in an imagined social exchange' (Leung, 2005: 131).

In response to the influence of corpus linguistics in language teaching, Widdowson (2007) argues that Hymes's (1964, 1972) four interrelated principles of whether, and to what extent, some instance of language is formally possible, feasible, appropriate and actually performed have been abandoned in favor of a view of language that privileges only the attested utterances of native speakers. In essence, the creativity and meaning potential of the possible has been left by the wayside, having been deemed incorrect or inappropriate for learning if not attested as having actually been performed. The result, writes Widdowson, is that '[s]uch conflation disregards the obvious fact that the reality of actually performed language depends on its appropriate relationship with context, and that *a use of language can be entirely appropriate without being attested as having been actually performed* [italics added]' (Widdowson, 2007: 219). Elsewhere, Widdowson (2003) has suggested replacing the notion of communicative competence, associable in many ways with the Chomskian notion of linguistic competence (cf. Chomsky, 1965), with the concept of communicative capacity. Communicative capacity does not entail 'replications of native speaker realities' (Widdowson, 2007: 218) but instead refocuses attention on the meaning-making possibilities offered by the language, even if such possible utterances do not reflect probabilistic native speaker conventions. In short, communicative capacity entails a critical awareness (van Lier, 1988) of the relationship between Hymes's four kinds of judgments and the ability to act upon them to create meaning.

Dewaele (2008) offers an insightful discussion of appropriateness from an emic, or user-relevant, perspective based on opened-ended questionnaire data elicited from bi- and multilinguals. In line with the arguments presented by Leung (2005) and Widdowson (2007), Dewaele insists that a purely etic framework of what counts as appropriate and inappropriate language use can never fully capture the dynamic nature of how appropriateness is negotiated and evaluated in situated communicative activity. In other words, Dewaele recommends complementing more static assessments of appropriateness, which may be motivated by doctrinal pedagogical or curricular factors, with L2 users' own perspectives on and explanations of what they consider to be appropriate. In this sense, although conventions of use may be observable from the outside, appropriateness actually entails locally constructed and dynamic evaluations of and orientations to what is being said and how it is being said from moment to moment within a given communicative interaction.

A sociocultural response

It should by now be clear that the notion of appropriateness, while central to every discussion of communicative competence, is one of most ambiguous terms used in the L2 learning and teaching literature. In fact, the notion of appropriateness has become polyvalent within discussions of communicative approaches to language teaching. On the one hand, and in relation to Hymes's original use of the term (see above), there is the question of what counts as appropriate language use in particular sociocultural contexts – that is, how contextualized language use can be judged as appropriate or inappropriate. On the other hand, there is concern regarding what is appropriate for teaching and learning, or put another way, what the inclusion and exclusion criteria may be for developing curricula, syllabi, language teachings materials, tasks, and so forth.

As will be further elaborated in this chapter, the perspective I take on judgments of social appropriateness – as Hymes used the term – centers on two fundamental parameters:

(1) The degree to which a particular instance of language use – whether conventional or unconventional – is interpretable by one's interlocutor(s) or audience given the discourse situation in which language is being used.

(2) The degree to which a particular instance of language use – whether conventional or unconventional – is effective in reflecting and (re)shaping activity types, social relationships and/or social identities.

The phrasing *the degree to which* in both criteria is meant to suggest a continuum, and in this way foregrounds the fact that the appropriateness of language-in-use is rarely – if ever – a binary appropriate/inappropriate, right/wrong dichotomy. Instead, there may be many varying degrees of appropriateness judgments ranging from completely inappropriate, to not quite appropriate, to sort of appropriate, to pretty much appropriate, to completely appropriate, and everywhere in between. In addition, I opt to use the terms *conventional* and *unconventional* as replacements for Hymes's grammatical/formally possible criteria in order to respecify the notion of possibility to reflect the contingency of language-in-use (van Lier, 2004), meaning that what is possible in language depends on both the design (speaker intention) and interpretation (interlocutor) of an utterance. Conventionalization (i.e. the regularization of patterns of language use) provides speakers with resources for designs of meaning, but speakers need not always reify conventionalized patterns of language and meaning (van Compernolle, 2011a).

These two criteria also depend on the specific activity type in which language is used, which necessarily implies an interlocutor or audience, whether physically present (as in the case of face-to-face spoken interaction) or physically and/or temporally displaced (as in the case of writing). In this sense, appropriateness is interactional – a particular instance of language cannot be judged without reference to what is going on, what other participants are doing, how language is being interpreted, and so forth. The point here is that appropriateness cannot be reduced to rules of use in a doctrinal way (e.g. rules of thumb, prescriptivism, formulas for use). This is why concepts (meanings) are important for language pedagogy. By promoting the internalization of categories of meanings, and how these meanings in turn map onto linguistic forms, there is the potential to avoid prescriptivism and unsystematic pragmatic knowledge (e.g. rules of thumb) in favor of sociopragmatic creativity and intentionality that is performed on the basis of meaning. This implies that some consideration of unconventional uses of language is also needed, whether this entails grammatically/structurally unconventional language use (i.e. divergences from linguistic conventions) or simply unconventional in the sense that a particular grammatical form, word, topic, and so on is not typically used in some context (i.e. divergences from social-context-specific conventions).

Pragmatics as Mediated Action: A Pedagogical Framework

Overview

As noted in Chapter 1, *mediated action* is the central tenet of the SCT framework for instructional pragmatics. It is important to keep in mind that a mediated action perspective on pragmatics does not necessarily favor adherence to social conventions. Instead, the concept of mediation implies conscious control over one's choices, including the ability to break with pragmalinguistic and/or sociopragmatic conventions in order to achieve a desired effect in light of present circumstances, constraints, and potential conflicts and/or points of tension. Figure 2.1 expands upon the mediated action perspective described in Chapter 1.

The three interlocking ovals represent, from left to right, *outcomes* (i.e. the action accomplished through language use), *pragmalinguistics* (i.e. the language used to accomplish an action) and *sociopragmatics* (i.e. the social meanings indexed through the use of language). The social action oval is located within the pragmalinguistic oval, which is meant to suggest that pragmalinguistics mediates social action. In turn, the pragmalinguistics oval is within (i.e. is mediated by) the sociopragmatic oval. This arrangement of the three domains for pragmatics is intended to emphasize the primacy of the sociopragmatic domain in the mediated action framework. The two solid arrows linking sociopragmatics to pragmalinguistics, and pragmalinguistics to social action, indicate this relationship. This is not to say that social actions cannot be accomplished without knowledge of the sociopragmatic domain; they can

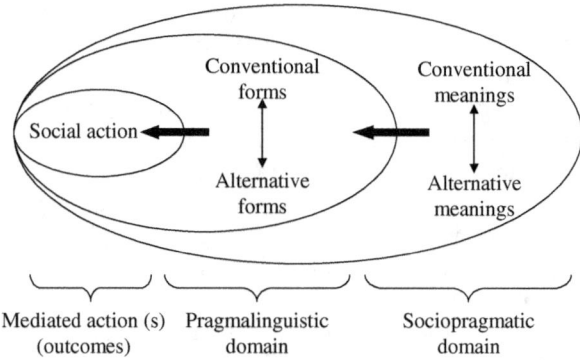

Figure 2.1 Pragmatics as mediated action

be, and frequently are, in child language acquisition (Tomasello, 2003) as well as in adult L2 socialization where learners use pragmalinguistic resources and create social meanings without fully understanding those meanings and the potential consequences of their actions (Kinginger, 2008). The mediated action framework is a guide for L2 instructional pragmatics, which, according to the SCT perspective illustrated in this book, ought to place the greatest emphasis on the internalization of categories of meanings – that is, the sociopragmatic domain.

As noted earlier in the discussion of appropriateness, the mediated action framework recognizes the potential importance not only of conventional language and patterns of meanings but also, and crucially, unconventional pragmalinguistic and sociopragmatic alternatives. Conventions and their alternatives are often in conflict. In Figure 2.1 this conflict, or tension, is represented by the dashed arrows connecting conventional and alternative meanings, and conventions and alternative forms, within the sociopragmatic and pragmalinguistic domains, respectively. Adhering to, or breaking with, conventions can be motivated by a variety of factors. The way speakers want to position themselves in relation to another person or persons (e.g. creating distance or intimacy) and the kinds of special effects possible when speakers flout conventions (e.g. impoliteness, humor) can make different meanings, and by extension particular forms, relevant in situated discourse (van Compernolle, 2011a). Advanced L2 pragmatic abilities therefore depend on the degree to which learners develop a systematic conceptual framework that mediates such choices in language. Excerpt 2.2 provides one example of how learners, as a result of systematic concept-based instruction, can deal with, and resolve, these tensions.

Excerpt 2.2

1	**Steph:**	((finishes explaining that she wants to use *vous* to create distance))
2		I don- cuz at the <u>same</u> time I would want to <u>show</u> my perso<u>na</u>lity↗=
3		=cuz like it's a + it's a program + it's like a <u>wai</u>tress and a
4		or a front desk↗ so you're gonna need to be like + welcoming↗
5	**Tutor:**	okay.
6	**Steph:**	so I wouldn- I wouldn't wanna necessarily use <u>nous</u> and *ne pas*.=
7		= cuz that would be like + too stiff. and like for me. if I were + (xxx)
8		in this <u>role</u>. I wouldn't wanna be like + I would wanna show that
9		I'm more laid back, I'm not like + <u>uppity</u> or whatever. so prob-
10		so <u>I</u> would probably use <u>on</u> and *pas*.
11	**Tutor:**	okay. + so *vous* for the + relationship. [distance.]

12	**Steph:**	[mhm]

12 **Steph:** [mhm]
13   and then *on* and *pas* to show like + my personality. I guess.
14 **Tutor:** okay.

For this scenario, Stephanie was preparing to adopt the role of a student being interviewed for a work-study program in France. The director of the program was going to call her to speak about working either at the front desk of a hotel or as a server in a restaurant. Conventionally, a job interview situation would call for the use of conventionally more formal linguistic forms (see below) – in this case, the second-person pronoun *vous* 'you', the first-person plural pronoun *nous* 'we', and the so-called complete negative *ne [verb] pas* structure. In planning her performance, Stephanie opted to use the more formal *vous* to maintain an appropriate social distance, while at the same time deciding to use the less formal first-person plural pronoun *on* 'we' and to omit the preverbal negative particle *ne*. Although the use of *on* and the omission of *ne* are certainly unconventional choices, Stephanie's decision is informed by her sociopragmatic knowledge. In fact, as she pointed out, for the positions she was interviewing for (i.e. front desk clerk or a restaurant server), the less formal *on* and *ne*-omission represented the appropriate way to position herself as welcoming (line 4) and to show her personality (line 13). It is also important to note that Stephanie was certainly aware of the pragmalinguistic alternatives (i.e. *nous* and *ne*'s presence), but that she judged the social meaning of using those forms as inappropriate for the situation (lines 6–9). It is clear that not all interviewers would orient to the use of more informal language as appropriate, and there could be negative social consequences for not adhering to social conventions, but this is beside the point. At issue here is that Stephanie had developed a systematic orienting basis for making meaningful choices about how she wanted to position herself vis-à-vis her interlocutor through the use of pragmalinguistic forms. Thus, Stephanie's choices were appropriate from the vantage point of mediated action.

This is, of course, a very different kind of appropriateness from that which is typically the subject of L2 pragmatic competence, and it should be recognized that Stephanie's unconventional choice may not be oriented to as appropriate by an interlocutor in a nonpedagogical setting. Nonetheless, the appropriation of concept-based pragmatic knowledge has the potential to serve Stephanie as a tool for dealing with unintended negative consequences that may arise from her pragmatic choices in the future. The point is that her thinking in this instance was mediated by a meaning-based orientation to the communicative problem. Her choice of pragmalinguistic forms was appropriate for creating her intended meaning.

Orders of indexicality as the leading pedagogical concept

The SCT framework for L2 instructional pragmatics centers on promoting the internalization of sociopragmatic categories of meanings that can then be mapped onto relevant pragmalinguistic forms. The aim, following Negueruela (2008), is to assist learners in creating a zone of potential development (ZPOD) – that is, a concept-based orienting basis (i.e. metalinguistic knowledge) that sets the stage for the development of learners' communicative abilities. What this requires is a leading concept that is abstract and systematic, but that serves to guide learners through a quasi-investigation (Davydov, 2004) of the object of study – in the case of the present study, French pragmatics. The concept of quasi-investigation is important: it recognizes that the locus of knowledge is with the instructor (i.e. in the form of social mediation and pedagogical materials), but at the same time emphasizes the active role that learners must take in internalizing mediational means (i.e. concepts and pragmalinguistic forms). In essence, learners are neither passive recipients of prepackaged knowledge nor are they expected to be totally independent agents tasked with acquiring the requisite knowledge (Kozulin, 2003). Instead, in cooperation with a mediating agent (e.g. a teacher), they are led through an investigation of a leading concept, a process that involves a set of subconcepts and linkages to illustrative pragmalinguistic forms. In short, the focus of the approach is on concepts rather than forms. Forms are certainly important, but in the SCT framework for L2 instructional pragmatics, they serve to illustrate how the concepts are instantiated in concrete communicative activity.

The selection of a leading concept for the SCT framework for L2 instructional pragmatics is motivated by two factors. First, the concept must have a central focus on meaning rather than pragmatic forms or types of pragmatic actions. In other words, the concept cannot only be useful in explaining concrete pragmatic conventions, but must be abstract enough to encompass all possible instances of language used for pragmatic purposes. Second, the concept must be amenable to didactization – that is, to be simplified for pedagogical use, including being presentable in the form of a didactic model, without compromising its coherence and systematicity.

With these two criteria in mind, Silverstein's (2003) concept of *orders of indexicality* is particularly attractive, not only for its focus on the meaning potential of any instance of language but also for its commensurability with Vygotskian cultural-historical psychology (see van Compernolle, 2011a). Silverstein describes the orders of indexicality in terms of the dialectics of sociolinguistic phenomena. The dialectic, according to Silverstein, is the relationship between indexicals (e.g. language forms) and various degrees of social meaningfulness. An n-th order (first-order) indexical is a feature of language that can be associated with a particular group (e.g. region or socioeconomic status) or semantic function (e.g. number-marking), indexicalities that can be discovered through traditional observational methods in linguistics. However, an $n + 1$-th order (second-order) indexical has been assigned 'an ethno-metapragmatically driven native interpretation' (Silverstein, 2003: 212) and thus carries meaning in terms of one or more local ideologies, while an $(n + 1) + 1$-th order (third-order) indexical is a feature that has come to be perceived as meaningful within another supra-local ideological schema. Second and third-order indexical meanings are not necessarily accessible to researchers through observational methods alone, and while third-order indexical meanings are often open to conscious inspection (e.g. they are talked about in relation to ideology), second-order social meanings are by and large unconscious to native speakers of a language (i.e. these are the gut reactions to particular speech patterns that non-linguists are not typically able to articulate). To uncover these social meanings requires the adoption of more emic, ethnographic approaches to understanding a particular languaculture (Agar, 1994) that account not only for linguistic performance but the ways in which members of a community experience, and make sense of, their sociolinguistic worlds (Eckert, 2008; Johnstone & Kiesling, 2008; van Compernolle, 2011a).

Johnstone and Kiesling's (2008) study of the monophthongization of /aw/ in Pittsburgh English (e.g. such that the word *house* is pronounced [ha:s]) provides a good example of how the indexical order operates. First-order indexicalities include geographic provenance (e.g. monophthongization of /aw/ is a distinctive feature of the Western Pennsylvania dialect) and socioeconomic status (e.g. higher frequencies of the monophthong are present in the speech of working-class Pittsburghers relative to middle class and professionals). Second-order indexicalities include speakers' dispositions to, and local beliefs about, being a Pittsburgh insider (e.g. who is a real Pittsburgher). Third-order indexicalities extend beyond the local context such that monophthongization of /aw/ has become enregistered as a distinctive feature of Pittsburgher identity – for instance, tourist tee-shirts with creative spellings of words to reflect stereotypical Pittsburgh pronunciation (e.g. *downtown* spelled *dahntahn*). Monophthongization of /aw/ can thus index multiple levels of meaning, particularly those relevant to the construction of localness and insider status (see also Johnstone, 2011).

The orders of indexicality provide speakers with the basic ingredients for making meaning, or to borrow the New London Group's (1996) terminology, designs of meaning. Variational practice entails the active process of staking claim to any number of meanings and ideologies indexed by existing language patterns. In turn, the active design of meaning participates in the propagation of these new potential indexicalities, hence the dialectic between conventionalized meanings available for use and the creative redesigning of meanings (Silverstein, 2003). Thus, speakers do not simply draw from a sociolinguistic toolkit but ultimately have the potential to transform the patterns and meanings in and through discourse. The notion of designs of meaning articulates with Vygotsky's (1986) (see also Wertsch, 1985) distinction between *meaning* – the relatively stable meaning of a word – and *sense* – the psychological meaning assigned to a word in concrete communicative activity (van Compernolle, 2011a). Although knowledge of the meaning, or *sense*, potential of linguistic variants may be in large part implicit for native speakers of a language, from the point of view of the SCT framework for L2 instructional pragmatics, the goal of pedagogy is to make the potential indexical meanings of language explicit and open to conscious inspection on the part of learners. In this regard, Silverstein (2003) provides a conceptual framework for elucidating the sociopragmatic domain, knowledge of which can then be mapped onto the pragmalinguistic forms that mediate social action.

Figure 2.2 displays the pedagogical diagram depicting the orders of indexicality that was used in the SCT framework for instructional pragmatics illustrated in this book. The diagram is designed to depict for learners the dialectics of conventions, stereotypes and local construction of meanings. Two-way arrows are meant to suggest that each component exerts influences on the others in an ongoing and potentially unending process of meaning making. The box at the top right of the diagram represents first-order indexicality, described here as observable conventions of language use. The box at the bottom right represents third-order indexicality, described to students as stereotypes about language use. The larger box on the left represents second-order indexicality, described as the way in which people use conventional patterns of and stereotypes about language to construct meanings. The larger size of this box is meant to focus learners' attention on the active design of meaning (New London Group, 1996; van Compernolle, 2011a), which is also the principal emphasis of the SCT framework for L2 instructional pragmatics – that is, promoting learners' capacity to design their own meanings in relation to the possible interpretations of their use of particular pragmalinguistic forms.

It should be noted that, in practice, the concept of orders of indexicality is not as visible or overtly oriented to as the subconcepts of self-presentation, social distance and power (see below). This is because the subconcepts help

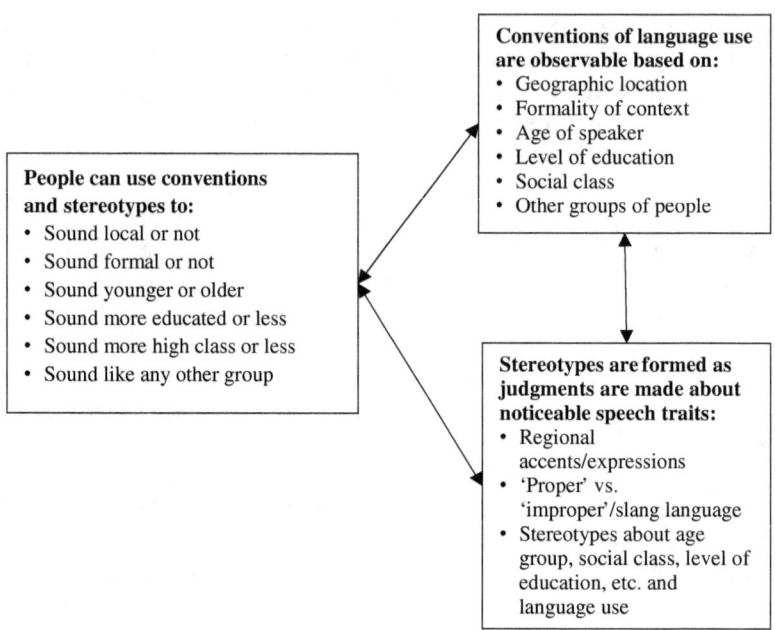

Figure 2.2 Pedagogical diagram depicting the indexical order

to concretize the leading concept, specifically how second-order indexical meanings are realized in concrete communicative activity. Nonetheless, the idea of style, of indexicality, is always present because the subconcepts represent a way for learners to engage with the highly abstract concept of the indexical order and how conventions and stereotypes are resources to be used in the construction of locally relevant sociopragmatic meanings.

Pragmalinguistic forms

Within the SCT framework for L2 instructional pragmatics, it is not sufficient to present an abstract concept like orders of indexicality and then leave learners to their own devices to figure out how the concept applies to real life (e.g. in language use). Rather, learners must be guided through a quasi-investigation (Davydov, 2004) of how the leading pedagogical concept is relevant to them, which entails demonstrating to learners how the orders of indexicality play out in concrete communicative activity. To do so requires the selection of illustrative pragmalinguistic forms on the one hand, and relevant subconcepts that explicate the potential indexical meaning(s) of the illustrative pragmalinguistic forms on the other (see below). In short, the leading concept provides a macro-level framework for the investigation of particular meaning–form relationships available to learners in the language they are studying. It is important to recall that the SCT framework illustrated in this book centers on the teaching of *meanings*. Forms are selected to illustrate how meanings are created in communicative activity. In other words, designing an SCT-informed pedagogy is not about choosing which forms, structures, speech acts, etc. are thought to be important for learners to acquire but, rather, which forms, structures, speech acts, etc. serve to illustrate how the meanings that are thought to be important for learners to acquire are created through language-in-use.

Speakers of French have access to a wide range of pragmalinguistic resources (e.g. polysemy in the pronominal system, morphosyntactic variation) that index a variety of social-stylistic meanings (see Ager, 1990; Beeching *et al.*, 2009; Coveney, 1996). Such resources reflect, and are constitutive of, the sociopragmatic domain, including social-interactive contexts and activity types, interlocutor statuses, the qualities of interpersonal relationships, social identities, and so on. One of the demonstrated difficulties facing L2 speakers of French – particularly those who have learned French predominately, if not exclusively, in a formal educational context – is the discrepancy between the relatively limited range of options presented in pedagogical materials and the language that is actually used in non-educational settings (e.g. native speaker communities). Textbooks often avoid, or at least minimize, explanations of the full range of pragmalinguistic resources available to learners, particularly those resources that are perceived to be informal, nonstandard, or colloquial (Etienne & Sax, 2009).

As an initial attempt at developing the SCT framework for L2 instructional pragmatics, the study reported in this book centered on demonstrating how the orders of indexicality play out in the use of three features of discourse: the second-person pronouns *tu* and *vous*; the first-person plural pronouns *on* and *nous*; and the presence versus absence of the negative morpheme *ne* in verbal negation. The motivation for selecting these features of discourse as illustrative forms was twofold. First, all three are highly salient and frequent in a wide range of communicative contexts, meaning that learners will encounter and need to use them on a regular basis (cf. many phonological and lexical variations that may be less salient and/or less frequently realized in discourse). Second, ample research in native speaker and L2 contexts has been conducted that provides a solid empirical basis for mapping out the potential indexical meanings of the various forms.

Second-person pronouns

Personal pronoun systems are important features of many languages for constructing and maintaining social relationships and identities. This is because pronouns indicating persons 'include reference to specific social relations, knowledge of which is required for the relevant words to be used correctly' (Mühlhäusler & Harré, 1990: 5). The French second-person pronouns *tu* and *vous* are particularly salient examples of the interrelationship between reference to persons and reference to specific social relations. *Tu* is generally considered to be the default singular second-person pronoun: it designates one interlocutor. *Vous*, however, carries the dual roles of both the plural form of *tu* (i.e. *tu* + a 3rd person, or *tu* + *tu*) and the formal, or polite, singular second-person pronoun used in opposition to *tu* (i.e. *vous* = polite or formal *tu*).[1] However, French *tu* and *vous*, like many sociolinguistic features of language, are double indexicals (Silverstein, 2003). As Morford (1997: 5) explains:

> [French *tu* and *vous*] 'index,' or point to, the relative formality of settings and occasions, as well as degrees of deference and/or intimacy between the speaker and addressee; and second, the capacity to signal certain aspects of an individual speaker's identity within the wider social order.

The interpretation of particular aspects of *tu/vous* use have also entered into supra-local ideologies, or what may be referred to as third-order indexicalities, which renders these pronouns capable of indexing a broad array of group memberships, politics and ideologies.

Van Compernolle (2011a) maps out a number of potential indexical meanings of *tu* and *vous* using Silverstein's (2003) framework of orders of indexicality (Table 2.2). First-order indexical meanings are related to the sociolinguistic patterns of use that correlate with macrosociological categories (e.g. region, age, socio-economic status, political leanings). In turn, these conventions, or the 'differentiated correlations among [macrosociological] factors' (van Compernolle, 2011a: 91), may serve as the basis for constructing second-order indexical meanings during the course of concrete communicative activity. To this can be added the metaevaluation of second-order meanings entering supra-local ideologies, or third-order indexicality. Although Table 2.2 depicts these potential indexical meanings in a somewhat static way, van Compernolle (2011a: 91) emphasizes that:

> indexical meanings and associations with particular identities are, of course, not fixed but highly malleable [because they] are activated in the concrete form of the utterance. And utterances are never isolated. Instead, they follow preceding utterances and project futures ones as well.

Table 2.2 Indexical meanings of *tu/vous* choice in French

Orders of indexicality	Potential meanings and/or associations
First-order indexicality	Sociolinguistic conventions can be correlated with various social groups. For example: • generalized T use is widespread in Quebec, whereas T/V distinctions remain conventional in France; • friends and family use T whereas strangers tend to use V; • younger speakers use T more frequently than do older speakers; • conservatives use V more frequently than do left-leaning individuals. These conventions are observable by any linguist and represent only correlations with predetermined social factors.
Second-order indexicality	Sociolinguistic conventions are available as an indexical resource for speakers. Social meaning is attributed to T/V choice based on the correlations noticed by individual speakers. Here, T/V choice becomes a double indexical (Morford, 1997), which can serve to index both the nature of the relationship between two interlocutors and one's social identity. Thus, V can be used to point to first-order indexicalities, such as distance between strangers, non-youthful (non-student) identities, conservatism, etc., while T can be used to point to familiarity, youthfulness, left-leaning politics, etc. To be sure, not all speakers will associate T/V use with the same set of potential second-order indexicalities.
Third-order indexicality	Third-order indexicality entails explicit metadiscourse (or ethnometapragmatics in Silverstein's [2003] terms) about the T/V system, in particular noticing and valuating the second-order indexical meanings according to other ideological schemata. For instance, older, more conservative individuals may view the rise of T among younger, more liberal individuals as a sign of the loss of politeness or respect, and perhaps left-leaning individuals as a whole as rude or lacking respect for others. Young liberals, on the other hand, may see older conservatives as impolite too, because they refuse to use T to mark solidarity with others. Basically, the metadiscourse surrounding second-order indexicality points to associations with other political and ideological schemata (e.g. conventions for politeness/impoliteness, desire for solidarity/distance, desire for egalitarianism/hierarchical social order).

Source: Adapted from van Compernolle (2011a: 91).

Orders of indexicality are levels, or continua, that point to observability and generalization. First-order indexicals are the most readily observable and 'generalizable' inasmuch as basic observational techniques can be used by linguists to uncover them. In this sense, one can correlate demographic info such as age, education level, etc. or claimed relationship statuses (e.g. friends, family, strangers) with *tu/vous* distributions. Second-order indexicals get at the local meaning in language use. Here, it is about a particular design of meaning and interpretation of that meaning in a concrete situation. This is why more ethnographic methods and metalinguistic methods are needed to access this information. It is also why demographic categories as well as relationship categories recur here, but in a more specified way. In other words, it is not the category 'friend' that is important, but how particular persons in specific interactions 'do being friends'. This entails particularization rather than generalization. In turn, third-order indexicals point to broader macrosociological ideologies that transcend observed first-order indexicals and practiced second-order indexical meanings.

Although learner textbooks offer advice for using *tu* and *vous*, explanations typically center on first-order indexicalities, such as relative age, interlocutor status, and so forth presented as rules of thumb (van Compernolle, 2010a; van Compernolle *et al.*, 2011; see also Chapter 1). Such simplistic explanations may lead learners to assume (incorrectly) that *tu/vous* choice is a straightforward affair. Indeed, as Dewaele and Planchenault (2006) found in a study of learner perceptions, learners often judge the *tu/vous* system as easily navigable (based on simplistic rules of thumb) during the early years of study. However, as learners gain experience with, and access to, a wider range of social-interactive settings with French speakers (and, thus, second-order and third-order indexicalities), they begin to notice the more subtle complexities of the system and perceive it as increasingly difficult. Although some learners who have prolonged access to French-speaking communities and meaningful social relationships with French speakers (e.g. during study abroad) do indeed begin to uncover the indexical meaning potentials of these pronouns, their knowledge is often not very systematic but rather comprised of deductive rules derived from their concrete social-interactive experiences (see Kinginger, 2008).

L2 French learners often demonstrate variable or mixed patterns of *tu/vous* use that do not align with native speaker sociolinguistic conventions. Canadian immersion students who begin French instruction at a young age often overuse *tu* because of the preference for *tu* in learner–learner and learner–teacher interactions (Harley *et al.*, 1990; Lyster, 1994; Swain & Lapkin, 1990). However, immersion students who begin later (about 12 years of age) often overuse *vous*-singular (Swain & Lapkin, 1990), given the tendency for such learners to study relatively more formal varieties of

French. (For a detailed overview of research involving Canadian immersion students, see Lyster & Rebuffot, 2002.) Similarly, McCourt (2009) and van Compernolle *et al.* (2011) have documented the quantitative patterns of *tu/vous* variation in a corpus of learner–learner synchronous computer-mediated interactions among US university students of French. Their results demonstrate that not only do learners demonstrate high levels of inappropriate or mixed use of *tu* and *vous*, but that this variation is related to the specific lexicogrammatical structures involved. Their argument is that, in addition to difficulties disambiguating the indexical potential of *tu* and *vous*, learners may also learn specific (semi)autonomous sequences by rote without their being 'associated with the units that comprise them' (Bybee, 2008: 219). It follows that lexicogrammatical motivations may sometimes override learners' metapragmatic awareness as well as their grammatical competence (i.e. the ability to manipulate the morphosyntax of second-person verb phrases) during relatively spontaneous language production.

Research on telecollaboration and study abroad has documented the important role played by participation in social interaction with expert language users in the development of appropriate *tu/vous* use. Belz and Kinginger (2002) investigated the cross-linguistic (i.e. French and German) development of address form use in telecollaborative language learning environments, focusing on two case studies (one learner from each language). In both instances, the telecollaborative partnerships resulted in an increased use of appropriate forms of address following the explicit questioning (on the part of French and German participants) of inappropriate pronoun use by the American learners. Thus, participation in social interactions where there exist social consequences for inappropriate *tu/vous* use is essential for the process of socialization. Similarly, learners of French who participate in study abroad programs often have opportunities to gain access to communities of practice (Lave & Wenger, 1991) in which their understanding of and control over *tu* and *vous* can develop (Kinginger, 2008).

The pronouns on and nous

Another variable feature of the French pronominal system involves first-person plural reference. Whereas most reference grammars and pedagogical texts usually present the subject pronoun *nous* with a first-person plural verb form as the standard variant – as in <u>*nous allons*</u> *au cinéma* 'we're going to the movies' – the subject pronoun *on* with a third-person singular verb form – as in <u>*on va*</u> *au cinéma* 'we're going to the movies' – has all but replaced *nous* in most varieties of everyday, informal, conversational French (Blondeau, 2003; Coveney, 2000; Fonseca-Greber & Waugh, 2003; van Compernolle, 2008b).[2] In fact, Coveney (2000) notes that *nous* use is so infrequent in contemporary

French that it may be considered as a vestigial variant (Trudgill, 1999) whose use is reserved for highly marked contexts. In addition, the *nous* variant can be used to emphasize the exclusion of the hearer from the reference (cf. exclusive *we* in English), or to refer 'to a group seen from the outside' (Coveney, 2000: 467). Van Compernolle's (2008b) analysis of *on/nous* variation in corpus of synchronous computer-mediated French discourse confirmed this finding. At the same time, the author illustrated how the *nous* form has persisted as a resource for the construction of humor or to signal a microshift in style or activity type (see also van Compernolle, 2011a). Thus, while there are clear first-order indexicalities associated with these pronouns (e.g. in terms of formality, speaker age, socio-economic status), the conventions, or associative links, can be capitalized on by speakers in the very local, situated construction of personal meanings.

L2 French learners typically use the more formal *nous* variant at high frequencies, even in contexts where the more informal *on* would be appropriate (van Compernolle & Williams, 2009b). Positive correlations have, however, been found between contact with native speakers of French in non-educational settings and increased *on* use (Dewaele, 2002; Mougeon *et al.*, 2010; Sax, 2003). This is also supported by study abroad research documenting learners' performance before and after a sojourn in a French-speaking country (Regan *et al.*, 2009). To my knowledge, only van Compernolle and Williams have engaged in pedagogical research. They report that language analysis tasks within a whole-classroom ZPD can be effective in raising learners' awareness of variation between *on* and *nous* (van Compernolle & Williams, 2012a). In another study (van Compernolle & Williams, 2012b), the authors showed how developing metasociolinguistic awareness can also lead learners to agentive use of stylistic variants such as *on*, though their performance lags behind their understanding of the meanings of the pronouns.

Presence and absence of ne

The presence versus absence of the proclitic negative particle *ne* in verbal negation is one of the best known stylistic variables in French (Coveney, 1996). Reference grammars and standard pedagogical texts depict verbal negation as involving *ne* (or *n'* in prevocalic position) and one of several postverbal negative complements (e.g. *pas* 'not', *rien* 'nothing', *jamais* 'never') in an embracing structure, as in *il ne vient pas* 'he is not coming'. However, *ne*'s absence, as in *il vient pas* 'he isn't coming', is ubiquitous in nearly all varieties of informal or everyday French. Van Compernolle (2010b) provides a comprehensive overview of sociolinguistic analyses of French negation, highlighting the general trends documented in the literature as they relate to social, stylistic and linguistic factors (Table 2.3).

Table 2.3 Social, stylistic and linguistic factors

Factor	Comments
Region/variety	Lowest frequencies in Canada (less than 1%) and Switzerland (2.5%). Rates in France range from ~1–20% in recent years.
Speaker's age	Older speakers tend to use *ne* more frequently than do younger speakers.
Socio-economic status	Some correlation between SES and *ne* retention, in that middle- and upper-middle SES speakers use *ne* more frequently than speakers in lower SES. Effect less influential among younger speakers than among older ones.
Subject type	*Ne* retention more frequent with nominal subjects and in nonovert subject environments (i.e. infinitive and imperatives) than with pronominal subjects.
Frequency of expression	Frequently occurring expressions, e.g. *c'est pas, (il) faut pas, je sais pas*, may be becoming lexicalized without *ne*. Argument for grammaticalization of clitics and verbs.
Style	More careful speech styles favor *ne* retention, while more relaxed settings favor *ne* deletion. *Ne* can be used productively for stylistic effect, e.g. emphasis, moralizing, etc.

Source: Adapted from van Compernolle (2010b: 451).

L2 French learners tend to use the *ne*-present structure at high rates (van Compernolle & Williams, 2009a). Similar to research on other stylistic variables, contact with native speakers outside of an educational setting positively correlates with increased *ne* omission (Dewaele, 2004; Mougeon et al., 2010; Sax, 2003), especially following a study abroad program (Regan et al., 2009). As with the *on/nous* variable, the only research conducted that incorporates instruction is that of van Compernolle and Williams. They report that explicit instruction is more effective in raising learners' awareness of the meaning of variation when compared to simple exposure alone (van Compernolle & Williams, 2011a), because explicit instruction, through instructional conversations, can provide developmentally rich patterns of interaction in the ZPD (van Compernolle & Williams, 2012a). Subsequent research reported by these authors confirms that more extensive pedagogical intervention to raise learners' metasociolinguistic awareness can also lead to increasing control over these forms during spontaneous language production (van Compernolle & Williams, 2012b, 2012c).

Important differences and the relationship between the illustrative forms

The three illustrative variable features of discourse selected for the study reported on in this book differ in several important ways. As an anonymous reviewer of this book observed, *tu/vous* variation is socially indexical in the sense that it points to relationship categories that are, at least conventionally, rather stable across the lifetime of the relationship, and they only come to mark demographic categories, or social identities, in relation to the distribution of *tu/vous* relationships across a range of encounters. By contrast, stylistic variables (e.g. *on/nous* and *ne*) may be variable within a relationship, and it is their relative frequencies within a communicative event that index social and stylistic factors. In addition, while choices about the use of stylistic variants are to a large extent open to individual preferences, *tu/vous* use entails choices that are more interpersonal and relational in nature – the selection of one or the other of these pronouns is the legitimate concern of the addressee as well as of the current speaker. Relatedly, *tu/vous* use is, to a large extent and in many contexts, highly conventionalized in a way that stylistic variables are not. In other words, and to paraphrase the reviewer's insightful comments, *tu/vous* use is constrained by 'agreed practice' that is in essence external to an individual's choice, and to break with agreed practice may risk construing one's communicative intent as something other than 'legitimate personal meaning'. In light of this substantive and thought-provoking critique, I would like to clarify what I conceive of as the relationship between *tu/vous* choice and the stylistic variables (*on/nous* and *ne*) used in this study to illustrate indexicality. These issues also certainly deserve to be further critiqued and revised in the professional literature.

Second-order indexicalities (see above) are necessarily self-presentational as well as intersubjectively relational because they are dialectically related to first-order (social conventions, probabilistic patterns) and third-order (supra-local ideologies) indexicalities. They are self-presentational because linguistic practices point to and are interpreted as claims of belonging to various social groups, whether etically defined (e.g. gender, age, social class) or more locally constructed (e.g. communities of practice). In turn, they are intersubjectively relational because linguistic practices also point to and are interpreted as a sort of social-relational positioning (e.g. Bucholtz & Hall, 2005) vis-à-vis one's interlocutor. In other words, because linguistic practices can mark and can be interpreted as cues as to a speaker's real or perceived membership status in culturally recognizable groups, they simultaneously – and dialectically (Silverstein, 2003) – impact upon real or perceived claims of relationship status between interlocutors (e.g. in-group versus out-group status, perceived similar or different social categories, perceived similar or different ideologies). This applies equally to *tu/vous* choices and stylistic variants, albeit in different ways, as noted above, as well as to first meetings and/or transient relationships and established and ongoing relationships across contexts.

Pragmalinguistic choices participate in the initiation and reification of the perception of social identity and relationship qualities. *Tu/vous* choice does this in a very explicit way because the use of one pronoun or the other typically remains categorical within a relationship once a *tu/vous* relationship has been established (i.e. speakers do not normally alternate between the two pronouns, with the exception of a shift that marks a change in relationship status, for instance shifting from *vous* to *tu* as an index of the development of a closer or more intimate relationship), so a first use of *tu* or *vous* can index identity and relationship information (i.e. it is not question of relative frequencies of *tu/vous* use within a relationship, as with stylistic variables). Established practices are also very salient and, in a wide range of social-interactive contexts, they are highly conventionalized. Nonetheless, choices are meaningful, even if the choice is conventional: a conventional choice, say *vous* in a service encounter, reifies the range of social meaning potentials available in the indexical field, whereas an unconventional choice challenges, and has the potential to transform, established practice (Eckert, 2008; Silverstein, 2003; van Compernolle, 2011a). Stylistic variables are meaningful to the extent that their relative frequencies point to social and identity-relevant categories, and they interact with address forms in establishing social relationship qualities as a functional sociolinguistic system. For instance, the intersubjective adoption of a relatively 'informal' style (e.g. *on*, absence of *ne*) in a reciprocal *vous* relationship mitigates or downgrades the degree of social distance in the relationship. In essence, it is like saying, 'Yes, there is some degree of distance, but we seem to claim membership in at least some of the same or similar social groups (first-order indexicalities) and share some of the same ideologies vis-à-vis language use (third-order indexicalities)'. By contrast, when stylistic choices are not reciprocal, there is an implicit, if not overt, claim of being different.

Subconcepts

As noted above, the leading concept of orders of indexicality provides a macro-level framework for understanding the social meaning potential of pragmalinguistic practices. However, subconcepts are necessary for explaining the particular meaning potentials available to speakers in relation to specific pragmalinguistic practices. In the present study, three sociopragmatic subconcepts were selected as important for learners to appropriate: self-presentation, social distance and power/relative status.

Self-presentation

The first subconcept, self-presentation, was presented as the first step in choosing to use either *tu* or *vous*-singular, *on* or *nous*, or negation with or without *ne*. The concept was depicted (Figure 2.3) as the difference between presenting oneself as *tee-shirt-and-jeans* versus *suit-and-tie*, prompting learners to consider the consequences for presenting oneself in one or the other way in various social-interactive contexts. For instance, the initial written concept explanation read as follows:

> The first step in choosing to use either *tu* or *vous*-singular, *on* or *nous*, or negation with or without *ne* is to decide how you want to present yourself, keeping in mind the conventional uses of these forms. *Tu, on* and negation without *ne* are all conventionally informal ways of using French. They are associated with informal speech, laidback/cool attitudes, friendliness, youthfulness and liberalism in everyday contexts. By contrast, *vous, nous* and negation with *ne* are all conventionally more formal ways of using French. They are associated with formal contexts, academic speech, upper class speech, conservatism and formal writing. Remember that you can use these conventions to create the meanings you want to create. A helpful way of thinking about how to create

Figure 2.3 Pedagogical diagram depicting self-presentation

meaning is to ask yourself: Am I tee-shirt-and-jeans (*tu, on,* negation w/o *ne*) or am I suit-and-tie (*vous, nous,* negation w/*ne*) right now? Then think about the consequences of presenting yourself as tee-shirt-and-jeans or suit-and-tie in different contexts.

The diagram was meant to encompass the potential indexical claims (Eckert, 2008; van Compernolle, 2011a) invoked in the use of one variant or another in a simple yet systematic fashion, based on culturally relevant images the learners most likely already recognized. The *tee-shirt-and-jeans* image was meant to suggest such potential meanings as youthfulness, informality, coolness, and so on, while the *suit-and-tie* image drew on associations with conservatism, professionalism, formality, and so forth. It should be noted that the following concept cards, as well as discussions between the tutor and the learners, also made it clear that mixing elements of *tee-shirt-and-jeans* and *suit-and-tie* (e.g. using *vous,* but also *on,* and ∅...*pas*) was not only possible but an important semiotic resource. Individuals may have different interpretations of these images and their relationship with language because we all experience the sociolinguistic world differently (Johnstone & Kiesling, 2008). Individuals therefore necessarily differentially attribute indexical meanings to semiotic (linguistic and imagistic) artifacts. As such, variability across individuals in the interpretation of this diagram – as well as all other diagrams used here – should not be seen as a weakness of the design of the study but, to the contrary, as a strength of it in that the materials allow for individuals to internalize these concepts as their own (see Chapter 3). Internalization, as Vygotsky conceived of it, was not about the acquisition of prepackaged knowledge but the process of appropriating culturally constructed artifacts and transforming them as one's own (see Lantolf & Thorne, 2006: chapter 6).

Social distance
Social distance was presented as the degree of familiarity and/or intimacy between two or more individuals, which may be previously established or not (e.g. existing relationships versus strangers). Thus, *tu/vous* choice was explained to maintain, establish or possibly change the degree of social distance in a given relationship and was depicted as *closeness* versus *distance*. The written explanation read as follows:

> Marking closeness or distance can be achieved, in part, through your choice between *tu* and *vous*. You can point to closeness by using *tu* and distance by using *vous*. Your choice of pronoun, therefore, has real consequences for your relationships.

The pedagogical diagram depicted the concept as two persons standing close together (*tu*) as opposed to two persons standing with space between them (*vous*) (Figure 2.4).

Relative status

Relative status, or power, was explained in terms of *tu/vous* symmetry. While closeness or distance may be indexed via symmetrical *tu-tu* or *vous-vous* use, constructs of power (i.e. power over another person) may be brought into focus by establishing an asymmetrical *tu-vous* relationship. Ager (1990) gives the example of police officers using *tu* with suspects and expecting *vous* in return as the sociolinguistic extension of authority and legal power structures. As depicted in Figure 2.5, the difference between symmetrical and asymmetrical *tu/vous* relationships is in the degree of emphasis placed on, or construction of, hierarchical differences between

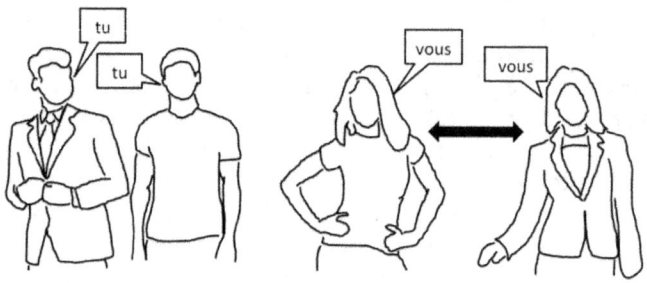

Closeness or distance?

Figure 2.4 Pedagogical diagram depicting social distance

Relative status?

Figure 2.5 Pedagogical diagram depicting relative status/power

interlocutors: two persons at about the same level (symmetrical *tu-tu* or *vous-vous*) versus one person placed above another (asymmetrical *tu-vous*). It should be noted that the seemingly equal status depicted for symmetrical relationships does not mean that institutional or other power/status differences do not exist. However, by establishing or maintaining a symmetrical *tu/vous* relationship, these differences are somewhat downplayed. As the written explanation read:

> Marking relative status can be achieved, in part, by your choice of *tu* or *vous*, as well as the symmetry of *tu/vous* use – that is, both people using *tu* or *vous* versus one using *tu* and the other using *vous*. Symmetry (*tu-tu* or *vous-vous*) can point to solidarity or even equality by downplaying any power hierarchy that might exist. Asymmetry (one person using *tu* and the other *vous*) can emphasize or draw attention to a very visible hierarchy in the relationship – the person called *vous* is being put in a position of power while the person called *tu* is being put in position of lower or no power. For clarification, there is a very strong preference nowadays for symmetrical relationships (*tu-tu* or *vous-vous*). Asymmetrical relationships can be seen as rude or impolite, because of the history related to social class hierarchies a long time ago (for example, nobles called servants *tu*, while servants had to call nobles *vous*).

Summary

To summarize, the course text focused on four principal sociopragmatic concepts: (1) orders of indexicality; (2) self-presentation; (3) social distance; and (4) relative status. An essential part of the concept explanations was the focus on the active design of meanings. Active designing does not of course mean doing whatever one wants; speakers must engage with the conventions of language and meanings available to them and shared by others in their community, but they can manipulate these patterns and meanings to meet their communicative needs (Lantolf & Thorne, 2006). As van Compernolle (2011a) writes:

> Variational practice is fundamentally about tapping into existing language patterns and conventions that are imbued with a broad array of indexical meanings and ideologies in the active process of staking claim to any number of those meanings and ideologies. In short, it entails the option of choosing one common way of saying something from among all available possibilities in the active design of meaning. (van Compernolle, 2011a: 92)

The concepts developed for the study, therefore, aimed to provide learners with an orienting basis for the use of linguistic variants grounded in meanings (indexicalities), any number of which they can stake claim to during concrete communicative activity.

Conclusion

In this chapter, I have outlined the SCT framework's orientation to the notion of appropriateness in language learning and language teaching, the central concern of the field of L2 instructional pragmatics. In contrast to traditional perspectives on appropriateness, the SCT framework for L2 instructional pragmatics does not conflate social conventions of language use with prescriptive rules for proper social behavior. Instead, emphasis is placed on the active design of meaning and speakers' ability to negotiate the indexical field in light of the present and changing circumstances of, and goals for, their communicative interactions.

The concept of pragmatics as mediated action forms the core of the framework. Social actions are mediated by pragmalinguistic choices, and these choices are mediated by one's sociopragmatic knowledge. The sample pedagogical materials presented above were designed in order to develop in learners a systematic, meaning-based orienting basis for understanding the sociopragmatic domain and for selecting pragmalinguistic forms. Thus, the concepts were intended to be internalized as psychological mediators. As emphasized above, however, internalization is not co-equivalent with mainstream perspectives on acquisition, nor does it entail rote memorization. Rather, internalization is about appropriating a psychological mediator as one's own. As such, variability in learners' knowledge is to be expected. In fact, one of the strengths of the SCT framework is that it acknowledges, and embraces, the uniqueness of individuals (see Chapter 3), allowing learners to personalize their psychological mediators to fit their desired selves, goals and dispositions toward L2 use. In other words, what is privileged in the SCT framework for instructional pragmatics is the thoughtful, deliberate use of L2 pragmalinguistic forms that is mediated by a systematic, though personally significant, understanding of the meaning potential of one's choices.

Notes

(1) Readers interested in detailed overviews of French *tu/vous* are referred to the works of Coveney (2010), Gardner-Chloros (2007), Morford (1997), Peeters (2006), van Compernolle (2008c) and Williams and van Compernolle (2007, 2009).

(2) It should be noted that *nous* remains obligatory as a direct object (e.g. *tu devrais venir nous voir* 'you should come see us'), as an indirect object (e.g. *elle nous a dit la nouvelle* 'she told us the news'), as a strong pronoun, such as a doubled subject (e.g. *nous on va voir un film* 'us we're going to see a movie') or an object of a preposition (e.g. *chez nous* 'our place', *c'est à nous ça* 'that's ours [that]'), and as a possessive pronoun (e.g. *on va rester avec notre famille* 'we're going to stay with our family'), even when *on* is used as a subject. The exception is in reflexive structures, where subject and object clitics agree (e.g. *nous nous appelons demain* versus *on s'appelle demain* 'we'll call each other tomorrow').

3 Understanding Learners as People

Introduction

At its core, sociocultural theory (SCT) is a theory of what it means to be a person. In its extension to second language (L2) development, SCT understands L2 learning as much more than the acquisition of particular linguistic forms and L2 learners as much more than processors of input and producers of output. Instead, the SCT perspective entails seeing L2 learners as *people* with diverse histories, emotions and desires, dispositions to and beliefs about language and learning, and complex, dynamic motives for language learning that together shape the qualities of their experiences and outcomes. Therefore, as Lantolf and Pavlenko (2001: 156) point out, 'we should not expect any two individuals to learn and develop in precisely the same way even if the material circumstances, or conditions, of their learning appear similar'. Rather, we must expect individuals to be unique and, as Lantolf and Pavlenko (2001: 157) note in discussing A.A. Leontiev's (1981) perspective on L2 education, we must develop 'a pedagogy that not only recognizes but builds upon [that] uniqueness'.

One of the consequences of such an approach, as extended to L2 instructional pragmatics, is that multiple ways of behaving must be recognized as potentially appropriate, even if they may break with social conventions (see Chapter 2).[1] For example, the data in Excerpts 3.1 (Stephanie) and 3.2 (Conrad) show two different orientations to appropriate, desirable behavior when interacting with a university department's administrative assistant, a 50-something woman who was described on an appropriateness judgment questionnaire as being relatively formal with students.

Excerpt 3.1

```
1   Tutor:  and the fourth one?
2   Steph:  ((reads situation silently)) um, just with the background information
3           that she's relatively formal with students,
4           I would prob- I would definitely use vous.
5           um because + uh she's older so she might expect that,
6   Tutor:  mhm
7   Steph:  from students as well? same with nous and ne pas,
8           I would stick with those.
9   Tutor:  okay.
10  Steph:  um just to make sure that + I don't like + in some way insult her.
11          by using the like more casual laidback conversation.
12  Tutor:  okay.
```

Excerpt 3.2

```
1   Con:    ((reads situation silently)) I would- yeah I would use
2           the same thing as the + um as the past one.
3           so I would use vous and on and pas,
4   Tutor:  okay
5   Con:    vous again for that same + level of respect + ful distance.
6           that we talked about. for my teacher.
7   Tutor:  okay.
8   Con:    and um. + yeah. on and pas. for um +
9   Tutor:  cuz you just wanna be you, ((laughs))
10  Con:    yeah. I'm me. ((laughs))
```

Stephanie's explanation of her choice to use the more formal variants – the more conventional choice – was indicative of her desire to converge with the speech level of her interlocutor (i.e. more suit-and-tie), specifically when the interlocutor may be perceived as being in a higher social position relative to her (e.g. based on age). Conrad, however, had indicated throughout the enrichment program that he wanted to be able to express his everyday relaxed, casual persona in French in a wide range of contexts. His choices for this situation created what he referred to as *respectful distance* through the use of *vous* 'you'-FORMAL but simultaneously represented an assertion of his relaxed, casual identity (i.e. the use of *on* 'we' and the omission of *ne* in negation), a less conventional choice. In both cases, however, Stephanie and Conrad made appropriate choices that were mediated by the concepts they were appropriating.[2]

This chapter addresses how the SCT framework for L2 instructional pragmatics embraces the uniqueness of individuals and encourages learners to develop their own personally significant relationships with sociopragmatic concepts and pragmalinguistic forms. It should be kept in mind that uniqueness is culturally mediated. In other words, following Vygotsky's (1978) account of the genetic law of development, culture – or 'history in the present' (Cole, 1996: 110) – precedes the individual and provides the conditions under which the unique individual may develop through the internalization of culturally constructed artifacts. Thus, the SCT framework both recognizes learner history – culturally mediated uniqueness – and dynamically builds on it to promote conscious control over language by providing materials and tasks that enable learners to internalize new mediational means (i.e. concepts) that have personal significance and relevance to learners' desired ways of being in the L2. The result is that L2 learners can create the meanings they want to create rather than being bound to a set of narrowly empirical norm-referenced pragmatic rules of appropriateness (van Compernolle & Williams, 2012c). As discussed in the preceding chapter, this entails conceiving of pragmatics as mediated action – in particular, acknowledging that the qualities of one's sociopragmatic knowledge mediate pragmalinguistic choices in the accomplishment of social actions. It should also be borne in mind that recognizing and building upon uniqueness is not an 'anything goes' approach to teaching. It is, however, one that provides learners with systematic options for meaning-making rather than doctrinal rules for proper social behavior.

Education and the Development of Personalities

To lay the groundwork for the SCT framework's approach to embracing and building upon the uniqueness of individuals, we must consider Vygotsky's stance toward the development of personalities, which he viewed as inextricably linked to the overall development of mind, including intellect. For Vygotsky, personalities are sociogenetically rooted: they arise in and through our interactions with the world where we internalize culturally based mediational means: 'Cultural devices of behavior do not appear simply as external habit; they comprise an inalienable part of the personality itself, rooted in its new relations and creating their completely new system' (Vygotsky, 1997: 92).

The role of education

Vygotsky and his adherents held that educational activity – including formal schooling as well as upbringing outside of school – played an important role in the formation and continued development of personalities (Chaiklin, 2001, 2002; Davydov, 1995). In discussing the Vygotskian-inspired reform of the Russian education system initiated in the late 1980s, Davydov outlines the position as follows:

> [T]he following general ideas of Vygotsky are basic, ideas that have been set forth and made more precise by his students and followers. The *first idea* is that education, which includes both human teaching/learning and upbringing, is intended first of all to *develop* their personalities. The *second idea* is that the human personality is linked to its creative potentials; therefore, the development of the personality in the education system demands first of all the creation of conditions for discovering and making manifest the *creative* potentials of students. The *third idea* is that teaching/learning and upbringing assume personal *activity* by students as they master a variety of inner values; the student becomes a true subject in the process of teaching and upbringing. The *fourth idea* is that the teacher and the up-bringer *direct and guide* the individual activity of the students, but they do not force or dictate their own will to them. Authentic teaching/learning and upbringing come through collaboration by adults with children and adolescents. The *fifth idea* is that the most valuable methods for students' teaching/learning and upbringing correspond to their developmental and individual particularities, and therefore these methods cannot be uniform. (Davydov, 1995: 13; italics in original)

Davydov's comments are intriguing for a number of reasons.

First, the primary goal of education, according to Davydov's interpretation of Vygotsky, is to develop the personality, and this is linked to developing learners' creative potential. As we have seen in discussing Galperin's (1989, 1992) and Davydov's (2004) work on concept-based instruction, creative potential is dependent on the quality and systematicity of the cultural tools made available to learners (Stetsenko & Arievitch, 2010; see also Chapter 1). Thus, through internalization, personalities may be developed, enriched and/or transformed. This position starkly contrasts with more mainstream approaches to education that seek to develop only the intellect (e.g. skills, content knowledge). In fact, within a Vygotskian dialectic perspective, intellect and personality are not separate – they are unified in the development of mind, each exerting an influence on the other. Second, individuals become true subjects through teaching/learning activity. This is because individual consciousness, and therefore personality and agency, develops through the internalization of cultural tools (Lantolf & Thorne, 2006; Wertsch, 1998). Personalities are not innate or biologically endowed.

They are culturally mediated and, as such, they are open to continued growth and/or modification through education. Third, educators ought to direct and guide learning activity without imposing on learners, which means that learners are given the freedom to engage with the cultural tools in a personal way. Individual particularities, as Davydov calls them, are to be recognized and built upon (Lantolf & Pavlenko, 2001). As a result, individualization of teaching/learning activity is desired over uniformity. This relates to the concept of personalization, discussed later in this chapter.

Personalities, therefore, have a cultural basis – that is, a basis in the education of the person through upbringing and formal schooling. This is not to deny the importance of biology, however. There are certainly neurobiological factors that predispose individuals to different behavioral characteristics (DeYoung, 2010).[3] Yet personality, as Vygotsky understood the concept, was a higher, mediated psychological construct. In fact, Chaiklin points out that Vygotsky used the term personality in two ways, both of which emphasize the cultural, or sociogenetic, foundation of its development:

> [A first use refers] to those human qualities of behaviour that result from cultural development as distinct from biological maturation. A second use is a more precise identification of the specific cultural development, which in Vygotsky's analysis was thinking with concepts, and a self-consciousness of this ability. (Chaiklin, 2001: 239–240).

Both understandings of the concept of personality in Vygotsky's writings are important.

The first use that Chaiklin describes raises the development of personalities to the same level as intellectual development. In fact, it is virtually impossible to separate intellectual and personality development as both impact upon each other in a dialectical unity. This is because 'personality development ... focuses on the development of motives in relation to societal practices' (Chaiklin, 2002: 168). For instance, individuals may have different motives for learning mathematics, chemistry or additional languages (e.g. to pass a course or fulfill a university requirement, to become an engineer or chemist, to teach or to travel the world as a multilingual), and of course these motives can change depending on social material circumstances (Lantolf & Genung, 2002). Education plays a key role in developing motives for societal practices, and hence in developing personalities – why (i.e. motives) people behave the way they do. The second use of the concept of personality in Vygotsky's writings is particularly relevant to the SCT framework for instructional pragmatics described in this book. As Chaiklin (2001) comments in the above quotation, Vygotsky's more nuanced thinking about personality development entails, on the one hand, the appropriation of concepts as psychological mediators and, on the other, conscious awareness of this development. The appearance of conceptual thinking in adolescence signals a qualitative change in psychological abilities – namely, how one understands social reality and social relations (Vygotsky, 1986). Social consciousness develops and is turned inward to regulate internal mental and external material activity, which involves self-awareness of, and the ability to modify, the motives for one's actions. This is a qualitatively new, and more mature, form of personality in comparison to pre-conceptual thinking.[4]

The role of education – particularly formal schooling – is to promote concept-mediated thinking such that learners gain greater volitional control over their actions which is grounded in a coherent, systematic orienting basis for action (Davydov, 2004; Galperin, 1989, 1992; Vygotsky, 1997). This is not just about content mastery or intellectual development. Rather, as Davydov (1995) points out in the quotation given above, this entails empowering learners to be creative as a means of developing their personalities within a formal educational context. And creativity depends on conscious, motivated control over one's actions. The internalization of new and/or modified mediational means – particularly scientific concepts – creates this kind of opportunity. This is a crucial dimension of the SCT framework for L2 instructional pragmatics: the focus is on internalizing sociopragmatic concepts as integral dimensions of one's personality in order to remediate one's L2-mediated interactions with the world. This includes, crucially, awareness of the meaning of, and motives for, one's pragmatic actions. As we will see in the following section, these ideas are central for understanding Self, identity and agency in relation to instructed L2 pragmatic development.

The mediational nature of Self, identity and agency

This section expands upon the discussion of personalities and their relevance to instructional pragmatics. As we saw in the preceding discussion, Vygotsky and his colleagues and later interpreters considered the development of personalities to be an integrated dimension of the development of mind. Formal education has the potential to play a critical role in personality development through the development of concept-mediated thinking. Here, three constructs that are relevant to understanding personalities – Self, identity and agency – are addressed in relation to the concept of mediation within the context of L2 instructional pragmatics.

In discussing the findings of two case studies of intermediate-level US learners of French and their understanding and use of sociostylistic and pragmatic language variants, van Compernolle and Williams (2012b: 246)[5] conclude that:

> the ability to use social and stylistic variation, and to assign meaning and relevance to it, is as much about learning formal aspects of language (e.g. which features of discourse can vary and what such variation means) as it is about learners (re)negotiating and performing their identities in relation to the place of the L2 in their lives, past, present, and future.

The study featured two young women, Casey and Melanie (both pseudonyms), who were enrolled in an accelerated second-year French course in which instruction on the meaning and use of sociolinguistic and pragmatic variation had been integrated into the curriculum (e.g. formal and informal registers). Casey was reserved and studious, and she oriented to the learning of French as an individual academic pursuit. Melanie, the daughter of an Army officer, was already multilingual (English, Spanish, Japanese) and had been raised in Mexico, Germany, Australia and the United Kingdom before moving to the United States as a teenager. Because of her history of language learning as social practice, she oriented to the learning of French as a key to gaining access to additional social networks beyond an academic setting. Van Compernolle and Williams report that Casey and Melanie developed two different dispositions toward variable features of language. On the one hand, Casey demonstrated a preference for maintaining a more formal, academic stance, although she understood, and was capable of using, a more informal style. On the other hand, Melanie actively sought to use a more informal style systematically, which she perceived as central to her goal of creating and maintaining intimate social relationships in the future. As the quotation above suggests, van Compernolle and Williams ascribe the differences between the two women in terms of orientations to variation to the relationship between their histories, present circumstances and desired futures: Casey and Melanie appropriated what they were being taught in ways that were mediated by their histories and relevant to their future goals.

The framework used in the van Compernolle and Williams study, which will be expanded here, was adapted from Wiley's (1994: 18–39) synthesis of Pierce's and Mead's semiotics of the Self. The perspective aligns with the Vygotskian understanding of humans as historical, mediated beings, and of the sociogenetic roots of individual personalities (Chaiklin, 2001; Davydov, 1995; see above) – in fact, the concept of Self here is essentially equivalent to Vygotsky's use of the concept of personality. The Self is an enduring, historical, yet future-oriented, quality of the individual. However, this is not a biologically endowed, monolithic entity. Rather, because the human mind is mediated, the Self is constituted in and through one's interactions with the world: it is the totality of internalized culturally constructed artifacts (e.g. tools, signs, concepts, belief systems). And because humans, as long as they are living, continue to interact with the world, the Self continuously adapts to new circumstances. People may internalize new mediational means and/or modify existing ones across the lifespan, thereby changing the structure of the Self (Pavlenko & Lantolf, 2000).[6]

The link between the Self and the world is found in the multiple identities, or roles, performed by individuals in particular contexts in which they are carrying out goal-directed material activity: 'Identities are the result of (re)negotiating, (re)constructing, and (re)conceptualizing a person's (a self's) relationship to the world' (van Compernolle & Williams, 2012b: 237; see also Block, 2007; Kinginger, 2004, 2008; Lantolf & Pavlenko, 2001; Pavlenko & Lantolf, 2000). In essence, identities mediate between the Self/consciousness and the external world. Figure 3.1 represents this relationship. The Self and the world indirectly impact upon each other at the base of the triangle, as depicted by the dashed two-way arrow. At the apex of the triangle, the Self – or aspects thereof that are relevant to present social-material circumstances – links to identities, which interact with the world. The two-way arrows between the Self and identities, and between identities and the world, are meant to suggest the bidirectional nature of the relationship. Identities emerge in our interactions with the world on the basis of one's Self, and these interactions have the potential to turn inward to impact upon the Self. To recall the discussion of internalization from Chapter 1, this entails both outward (Self-to-world) and inward (world-to-Self) growth. Identities mediate, and are mediated by, the Self and the world.

Norton's (1995, 2000) concept of identity as the site of struggle is useful for further understanding the mediational nature of identities. Norton (1995: 15) conceptualizes (social) identities in terms of subjectivities that are 'multiple and contradictory' and which emerge in our interactions with the sociocultural world:

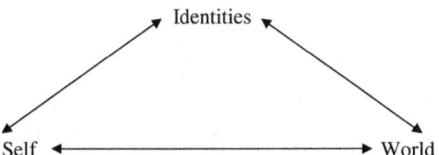

Figure 3.1 Mediational nature of identities

> Subjectivity is produced in a variety of social sites, all of which are structured by relations of power in which the person takes up different subject positions – teacher, mother, manager, critic – some positions of which may be in conflict with others. (Norton, 1995: 15)

A Vygotskian interpretation of Norton's argument conceives of the various subject positions taken up by individuals as the roles, or identities, enacted in the pursuit of goal-directed material activity. These subject positions are at once mediated by the Self and the world. The site of struggle, as Norton suggests, is the locus of human action: what one does given the mediational means available in particular social-material circumstances. Identities are forged in the interaction between the internal Self and the external world. They are, by definition, ephemeral, but because of their bidirectional mediational nature, identities can – for better or for worse – have a lasting and transformative impact upon both the Self and the world.

One of the consequences of viewing identities as mediating between the Self and the world is that we must recognize the unity of human-agents-acting-through-mediational-means (Wertsch, 1998). The Self, as noted above, is not a biologically endowed, or innate, entity, but rather arises through the internalization of culturally constructed artifacts. This is not to say that people are passive subjects. On the contrary, it is the integration of mediational means into our mental and material activity that allows humans to control their behavior from the outside (Vygotsky, 1978). As such, our responses to social-material circumstances allow for agentive choice-making, but our choices are variably afforded and constrained by the mediational means that we have internalized. Agency is the socioculturally mediated ability to act (Ahearn, 2001). There is no agency without cultural mediation: 'human agency appears once we integrate cultural artifacts and concepts into our mental and material activity' (Lantolf & Thorne, 2006: 63). In addition, agency 'entails the ability to assign relevance and significance to things and events' (Lantolf & Thorne, 2006: 143; see also van Lier, 2008). It therefore follows that human agency – and by extension the identities, or subject positions, one enacts in response to social-material circumstances – depends on the qualities of the cultural artifacts and concepts internalized as psychological mediators.

Relevance to instructional pragmatics

The mediational nature of Self, identity and agency is a fundamental tenet of the SCT framework for L2 instructional pragmatics. Put succinctly, the objective of the framework is to create the conditions for the transformation of the Self. As the preceding discussion has made clear, the Self, or consciousness, is historical: it is forged in our interactions with the world where we internalize culturally constructed mediational means. This process is mediated by the various identities, or subject positions, we adopt in the pursuit of concrete material activity, thus creating an indirect, mediated, relationship between the Self and the world. Transforming the Self involves internalizing new, and/or modifying existing, mediational means (e.g. artifacts, concepts) (Lantolf & Thorne, 2006). At issue here is empowering learners to develop alternative forms of agency – new and/or modified options (identities, subject positions) for interacting with the world and for assigning relevance and significance to particular pragmatic practices.

As shown in the van Compernolle and Williams (2012b) study, learners appropriate new tools (e.g. language forms, concepts) to suit their future goals (motives), a process that is inextricably linked to learners' histories (Self). The new forms of agency that may emerge are therefore different for individual learners because 'what is relevant and significant is very much influenced by [their] historical trajectories' (Lantolf & Thorne, 2006: 143). For Casey, pedagogy led her to assign new meaning and relevance to the more formal, academic register she already used: by learning about less formal, everyday language, she began to understand the significance of the more formal register in relation to her Self and future goals for learning French. In Melanie's case, pedagogy opened a new door to the kind of everyday language she privileged in the pursuit of creating close interpersonal relationships: she not only learned new everyday forms and their meanings, but also assigned new relevance and significance to the more formal standard forms she had already learned in previous classes. Consequently, Casey and Melanie were both empowered to adopt modified, albeit very different, subject positions that were mediated by the new tools and concepts they had appropriated. This is how the SCT framework for L2 instructional pragmatics recognizes and builds upon the uniqueness of individuals: by providing coherent, systematic sociopragmatic concepts, it becomes possible to remediate learners' L2-mediated interactions with the world. To recall Davydov's (1995) comments discussed above, this is about pedagogy corresponding to individual particularities with the aim of developing the personality.

To illustrate this point further, we can turn to the language awareness interviews (LAIs) conducted during the pre-enrichment and post-enrichment phases of the present study (see Chapter 1). The LAIs were designed to assess learners' declarative knowledge of the illustrative pragmatic forms selected for instruction, including any rules or concepts that guided their selection of one form or another. Excerpt 3.3 shows part of Leon's pre-enrichment LAI, in which he described his understanding of the second-person pronouns *tu* and *vous*.

Excerpt 3.3

1	**Tutor:**	can you tell me a little bit about what you understand
2		about *tu* and *vous*.
3	**Leon:**	okay. well um *vous*- uh *tu* and *vous*. obviously both mean you.
4		uh *vous* is + either the <u>plur</u>al form, or uh can just be formal,
5	**Tutor:**	yeah
6	**Leon:**	um *vous* you would use with people you hadn't necessarily
7		<u>met</u> yet, or with uh just like + also <u>tea</u>chers and ++
8		people you want to show re<u>spect</u> to.
9	**Tutor:**	uhhuh
10	**Leon:**	or are in a place of au<u>thor</u>ity. as opposed to <u>*tu*</u>.
11		it's just more informal. with your friends. <u>frien</u>d<u>l</u>y.

Leon certainly understood a number of important features of the *tu/vous* system: both pronouns are for second-person address, and *vous* has the dual roles of the plural 'you' and the formal 'you', which contrasts with the more familiar, informal *tu*. He also pointed to several categories of persons with whom to use *vous* (strangers, teachers, persons to whom one owes respect) and *tu* (friends). This is standard textbook-style, unsystematic rule-of-thumb knowledge (van Compernolle, 2010a, 2011b, 2012). Although nothing Leon said was inherently wrong, his knowledge at this point limited the subject positions he could adopt – essentially, Leon was *subject to* external factors, and he did not demonstrate any understanding that he could actively impact upon those factors in this instance. Although Leon had certainly learned the second-person forms and some of the conventions of use, which are in at least some contexts functionally sufficient, he had not appropriated the forms or their meaning potentials as his own (e.g. recognizing that he had the power to transform identity and relationship qualities).

Six weeks later, Leon's post-enrichment LAI (Excerpt 3.4) revealed a dramatic change in his understanding of the *tu/vous* system – namely, that he was not only subject to, but could impact upon, external factors.

Excerpt 3.4

1	**Tutor:**	can you just tell me: + what do you understand
2		about *tu* and *vous*. + first of all.
3	**Leon:**	ok<u>ay</u>, + um:: + well there's:: + just like with
4		all th<u>ree</u> + there's the first consideration, +
5		of um whether I want to present myself
6		informally, or formally,
7	**Tutor:**	okay,

```
 8  Leon:   um: + but tu and vous ((clears throat))
 9           also has: + the two added um + sort of flares,
10           of um of like showing uh some kind of distance,
11           or what kind of degree of distance, +
12           vous obviously is farther away + than tu uh:
13           and then there's also um + a sort of like +
14           hierarchical, + type thing, + where um ++
15           well like reciprocation now I guess.
16           where like if I:: if someone refers to me as tu,
17           it's appropriate for me to respond as tu because uh
18           you know. if they- if they call me vous, and then
19           I respond as tu, + um then there's sort of +
20           like I make a hierarchy.
21  Tutor:  okay.
```

Leon's postenrichment knowledge was mediated by the concepts he had appropriated during the pedagogical program. He articulated a systematic, meaning-based framework for using *tu* and *vous*: one must consider self-presentation, social distance, power and reciprocity. This provides evidence of the development of a new sign-meaning relationship that mediated Leon's thinking, and it is one that opened up new possibilities for enacting new, or modified, subject positions. Leon recognized that he not only had to follow pragmatic rules in reaction to communicative contexts, but that he had the power to shape contexts and the qualities of social relationships. This is a new form of potential agency that is mediated by sociopragmatic concepts.

Summary

From the preceding discussion, I hope to have established the following points regarding personality development and the mediational nature of Self, identity and agency, and the relevance of these concepts to L2 instructional pragmatics:

(1) The personality is an integrated dimension of the human mind that results from cultural development – it is mediated. Specifically, the personality arises in the development of concept-mediated thinking.
(2) Education – including upbringing and formal schooling – develops the personality. This is foundation of the development of one's sense of Self.
(3) The Self is historical but future oriented. It develops through the internalization of mediational means.

(4) Identities, or subject positions, mediate between the Self and the world. This is the locus of *mediated* human action.
(5) By virtue of the mediational nature of identities, the Self impacts upon the world, and the world impacts upon the Self. This bidirectionality allows for inward and outward growth (i.e. internalization).
(6) Agency is socioculturally mediated and entails not only voluntary control over behavior, but also the ability to assign meaning and relevance to actions and experiences. Agency depends on the mediational means available for enacting various subject positions.
(7) Pedagogy has the potential to remediate learners' interactions with the world, which can lead to a restructuring of the Self (i.e. internalization of new and/or modified artifacts and concepts).
(8) Consequently, new forms of agency that allow learners to enact new and/or modified subject positions through the L2 are made possible. This is how the SCT framework builds upon the uniqueness of individuals.

The remainder of this chapter expands upon these ideas in two ways. In the next section, the idea that internalization is a process of personalizing mediational means is elaborated. Then I turn to a discussion of the inseparability of emotions and cognition in relation to instructional pragmatics.

Internalization as Personalization

This section offers further specification of the notion that internalization is a process of personalization (see Chapter 1). This is a crucial concept for understanding learners as people and for viewing instructional pragmatics as an attempt to build on the uniqueness of individuals. Internalization is not simply a process of acquiring new, prepackaged form-function mappings. Rather, it is about appropriating new categories of meaning and mapping those categories of meaning onto L2 forms, which leads to remediated abilities to create meaning in L2-mediated activity. Thus, Dunn and Lantolf (1998: 427) note that 'from the sociocultural perspective, *second* language learners have a *second* chance to create new tools and new ways of meaning. ... In an important sense, L2 learning is about gaining the freedom to create'. The internalization/personalization of mediational means (e.g. forms, concepts) is in essence about developing new potentials for agency – new potentials for enacting personally significant and meaningful subject positions to mediate between the Self and the world through the L2.

Transformation of concepts

As Zinchenko (2002) makes clear, internalization is a bidirectional process that involves inward and outward growth (see Chapter 1). The concept of growth is particularly important for understanding how internalization entails personalization. Inward growth is not co-equivalent with more traditional models of acquisition (Kozulin, 2003; Sfard, 1998) where what is acquired is simply integrated into the mind/brain 'as is'. Rather, humans appropriate mediational means as their own, acting through them in material activity (Wertsch, 1998). This is 'a transformative and reciprocal process whereby the person transforms what is internalized and through externalization potentially impacts the self and the community' (Lantolf & Thorne, 2006: 158). Thus, mediational means may be transformed in outward growth as well.

As described in Chapter 2, the pedagogical materials (i.e. written concept explanations, diagrams) designed for the study reported in this book aimed to abstract meaning potentials of relevant pragmalinguistic forms (e.g. self-presentation, social distance) from conventionalized appropriate contexts of use. The key idea here was to avoid a doctrinal, prescriptive approach to presenting pragmatics to learners that would lead to rote learning and non-thoughtful action. Thus, rather than providing learners with rules to follow, they were presented with categories of meaning (i.e. concepts) and pushed to consider the consequences of indexing different categories of meaning in specific contexts to support critical, thoughtful personalization of the concepts. For example, the self-presentation diagram (i.e. tee-shirt-and-jeans versus suit-and-tie) pointed to categories of meaning such as youthfulness, informality and coolness, in opposition to conservatism, professionalism and formality. During verbalized reflections (see Chapter 4), learners were prompted to externalize their understanding of the concept, including what the consequences of presenting oneself as tee-shirt-and-jeans or as suit-and-tie might be in different social contexts; during appropriateness judgment tasks (see Chapter 5) and strategic interaction scenario performances (see Chapter 6), they were pushed to apply the concepts to concrete social-interactive contexts. Importantly, there was no aim on the part of the tutor to lead learners to believe that tee-shirt-and-jeans was appropriate for certain contexts and suit-and-tie for others. Instead, the point was to engage them in personalizing the concepts for their own purposes – to make them their own. (Recall Davydov's 1995 comments, discussed above, regarding the development of personalities as a process involving creativity and guidance without imposing a teacher's will on the student.) This is not, however, an 'anything goes' argument: the concepts provided the parameters within which learners could make meaningful choices regarding pragmatic actions.[7] Growth is therefore reflected in the appropriation of categories of meaning as personally significant and relevant psychological mediators (see Negueruela, 2008).

Using data collected for the study reported on in this book, van Compernolle and Kinginger (2013) illustrate the process of personalization in a microgenetic analysis of Nikki as she was completing an appropriateness judgment task during session 2 of the study. The authors analyzed in detail the cooperative interaction taking place between Nikki and the tutor as Nikki was attempting to decide whether to use *tu* or *vous*, and to explain her choice through the concepts, in the following situation:

> You're at the grocery store looking for some cheese for a small dinner party you're having with some friends. Unfortunately, you don't see the cheese you wanted. You decide to ask the clerk, a young woman in her mid-twenties.

The situation is rather ambiguous. Although the addressee is a near-peer (a factor conventionally favoring *tu* as an expression of social closeness), she is also a stranger and a store clerk (both factors conventionally favoring *vous* as an expression of polite or appropriate social distance). The ambiguity led to a lengthy discussion (~4.5 minutes) of the concepts of self-presentation (i.e. how Nikki wanted to be perceived), social distance (i.e. was the relationship close or distant), and power (i.e. which interactant, if any, could be perceived as being in a position of power relative to the other) in relation to the situation and *tu/vous* choice.

Van Compernolle and Kinginger note that Nikki needed to resolve the conflict between her desire to present herself as tee-shirt-and-jeans through the use of *tu* and the potential for that practice to be interpreted as an extension of her relative power over the sales clerk, which Nikki wanted to avoid. (Calling the sales clerk *tu* could be interpreted as positioning her in a position of lower power since the social convention would be for the clerk to call the customer *vous*.) In cooperation with the tutor, Nikki arrived at the following solution:

Excerpt 3.5

```
56  Nikki:  I would use ++ wait. + ugh. + like I don't necessarily
57          want to show that I have power over her. but like +++
58          I w- + I'd use vous.
59  Tutor:  okay,
60  Nikki:  cuz +++ I don't ++ want to +++ cuz
```

61	**Tutor:**	mhm,
62	**Nikki:**	cuz I <u>don</u>'t want a close relationship with this person.
63		so I'm like <u>dis</u>tancing myself from her.
64	**Tutor:**	okay,
65	**Nikki:**	but + and I <u>don</u>'t want to show that I have <u>pow</u>er,
66		over the person, but ++ so I wanna (3.5) use ++
67		I think we should use <u>vous</u> with each other. + like
68		to show that like ++ it's an equal relationship. but
69		distance equal? <u>dis</u>tant equal. =
70	**Tutor:**	=<u>ah</u>.

(van Compernolle & Kinginger, 2013: 297)

The authors argue that the importance of this excerpt is the synthesis of the concepts of social distance and power – that is, the emergence of the concept of *equal-distant relationships* (line 69) in reference to establishing a reciprocal *vous* relationship with one's interlocutor. Nikki did not simply use the concepts presented to her 'as is', but rather creatively personalized them as her own in response to the parameters of the situation described on the appropriateness judgment task and the tutor's questions, prompts and suggestions. As van Compernolle and Kinginger write, this interaction provides 'evidence of the microgenesis of a new and personally significant concept through which Nikki could think' (van Compernolle & Kinginger, 2013: 298). In short, there is evidence of inward growth (i.e. personalization of concepts as tools for thinking) and outward growth (i.e. ability to use personalized concepts for action). This is the transformative nature of the internalization/personalization process.

The role of human mediation

Understanding internalization as a process that involves personalization does not mean that learners ought to be left to their own devices to discover personally significant meanings. In fact, to withhold interventions by more expert or knowledgeable persons (e.g. teachers), or to expect learners to be capable of discovering what it is they need to know on their own, makes no sense within the SCT framework. This is because learners by definition do not already know what they need to learn – if they did, there would be no reason to engage them in educational activity. Indeed, learners depend on mediating agents such as teachers to support the internalization of psychological mediators (Kozulin, 2003).

As we saw earlier in the discussion of Davydov's position regarding personality development and education, teachers '*direct and guide* the individual activity of the students, but they do not force or dictate their own will to them' (Davydov, 1995: 13; italics in original). Human mediation therefore plays an important role in the personalization process: it aims to support the internalization of concepts while at the same time being sensitive to learners' individual particularities so that they may make the concepts their own. Part of the process of personalization entails confronting unsystematic knowledge of, or beliefs about, language and language use. Because language learners are people – people with diverse histories involving language use – they necessarily have attitudes regarding particular uses of language, and how such uses of language fit into ideological schema of meaning (Niedzielski & Preston, 2000). In fact, this is one of the core tenets of the concept of orders of indexicality proposed by Silverstein (2003) (see also Eckert, 2008; van Compernolle, 2011a; Chapter 2 of this book). However, learners often need support in rendering this knowledge open to conscious inspection and (re)interpreting it within the concepts at hand. This is a particularly important area for human mediation to direct and guide learners while recognizing and building on their uniqueness – notably, talking through salient experiences with language that learners orient to as relevant to understanding the concepts they are appropriating.

Excerpt 3.6 shows part of a dialogic verbalized reflection between Mary and the tutor during session 2 of the study that centered on the leading concept of orders of indexicality. Mary was having difficulty constructing an appropriate understanding of the contingent nature of meaning in language – that is, the idea that indexical meanings depend on both speaker intentions as well as interlocutor interpretations, which may or may not always align. Referencing her monologic verbalized reflection, which she had completed approximately 20 minutes earlier, Mary recounted a salient example from her past: a former professor who, according to Mary, always spoke in an overly formal academic register.

Excerpt 3.6

```
 1  Mary:   like ++ I kept thinking the whole time about this one
 2          professor I had here, + like oh my god. he would- like
 3          the way he spoke. like you couldn't even- it's like he
 4          wasn't even speaking English. like he would use every
 5          formal
 6  Tutor:  mhm
 7  Mary:   like. + language, construction, he would use + the
 8          fanciest words to talk about + just- you wouldn't even
 9          be able to understand him. and I felt like he was doing
10          that to say like look how smart I am.
```

11	**Tutor:**	ah. and so what was your interpretation=
12	**Mary:**	=that he has something to prove. + and I was like that's
13		annoying, like I know you're smart, you don't have to +
14		shove it in my face, like huhhuh I still respect you if
15		you're smart, but you don't have to + annoy me with
16		all these formalities,
17	**Tutor:**	so think about this. you can have your intention.
18		right,
19	**Mary:**	mhm.
20	**Tutor:**	but what else do you have to consider. (2.5)
21		((Mary makes 'I don't follow' face)) if you haven't-
22		you might intend + to do. one thing or another. right,
23	**Mary:**	mhm
24	**Tutor:**	but what's the other thing that you have to consider.
25	**Mary:**	oh how the other person is gonna +++ interpret that.

When prompted to consider her own interpretation of this professor's speech, Mary indicated that, for her, it was evidence that 'he has something to prove.' (line 12) and then continued to describe his speech and use of formalities as 'annoying' (lines 13–16). In response, the tutor led Mary to reconsider the relationship between a speaker's intention and others' interpretations of them. Mary demonstrated some difficulty here, following the tutor's question regarding other factors to consider in addition to intention (lines 21–22), as evidenced by the long pause and 'I don't know face'. The tutor reformulated his question in lines 22 and 24, which prompted Mary to recognize a new feature of the concept: that one also has to consider possible interpretations of one's speech. The evidence for considering this new or emergent knowledge on the part of Mary is the *oh*-prefacing of her response (line 25), indicating a change of (cognitive) state.

As we see in Excerpt 3.7, the tutor pursued the discussion further. Here, he attempted to guide Mary toward an understanding that multiple interpretations of speech styles are possible.

Excerpt 3.7

26	**Tutor:**	ah. and + is there just one interpretation?
27	**Mary:**	++ no I guess- that was something that I- that I was
28		saying- that I had a hard time thinking of examples.
29		where people use- specifically try to give off a certain +
30		um + impression. and someone takes it as- takes it
31		the wrong way.

```
32  Tutor:  ah
33  Mary:   I was having a hard time [thinking of   ] examples of that.
34  Tutor:                            [cuz you have ]
35                  well, just think about that pro<u>fess</u>or.=
36  Mary:   =<u>yeah</u>.
37  Tutor:  <u>you</u> interpret it as + kind of snobby or=
38  Mary:   =<u>yeah</u>.=
39  Tutor:  =(that) kind of <u>thing</u>. somebody <u>else</u> might interpret it as +
40                  a <u>good</u> thing. as a sign of intelligence. or something
41                  like <u>that</u>. right,
42  Mary:   yeah.
```

The tutor first prompted Mary to consider whether there is always a single interpretation of language use (line 26). In her response, Mary switched to past tense (lines 27–31) and described the difficulty she encountered during the independent verbalized reflection task, which is evidence that she was distancing herself from the task at hand (i.e. she did not respond to the question asked, but rather stated a problem she was having). The tutor's orientation to Mary's contribution at lines 27–31 suggests that he heard her switch to past tense and reference to the independent task as a request for assistance – namely, that an explicit explanation was necessary at this point because she was unable to articulate an appropriate response to the question asked. This provided an opportunity for the tutor to intervene by providing an explicit explanation of the appropriate interpretation of the concept, using Mary's professor as a concrete example (lines 35–42).

Mary's example illustrates two important dimensions of the role of human mediation in the appropriation of concepts. First, there was a clear intention to support Mary's developing understanding of the contingency of language. The tutor's role was to prompt Mary to think about aspects of the concept she had not considered (e.g. that there may be multiple interpretations of any use of language). The second dimension relates to the way in which the tutor co-constructed with Mary an appropriate understanding of the concept while at the same time refraining from being corrective: even though the tutor eventually provided an explicit explanation, he did not dictate to Mary how she should understand the example she provided, but rather indicated two potential options or interpretations of the professor's speech style. In other words, the point of human mediation in this example was to guide Mary toward a systematic understanding of the concept, but the choice to interpret her example in one way or another (e.g. snobby versus intelligent-sounding speech) remained hers alone.

Personalization and appropriateness

As we saw in Chapter 2, the SCT framework for L2 instructional pragmatics conceives of the notion of appropriateness in a fundamentally different way from more traditional approaches. Appropriate pragmatic actions are understood from an emic, or participant-relevant, perspective rather than equating the construct with stochastic, and often idealized, conventions of use. (See also Leung, 2005 and Dewaele, 2008 for similar arguments developed outside of the SCT tradition.) The internalization of holistic sociopragmatic concepts as orienting bases for action empowers learners to make meaningful choices, which may or may not always align with social conventions, but which must be understood as potentially appropriate. Because internalization is a process that involves the personalization of mediational means, different learners necessarily develop in different ways. Here, it is important to recall Chaiklin's (2001, 2002) comments regarding personality development in the SCT tradition (see above). In the SCT framework for instructional pragmatics, we are centrally concerned with the development of motives for societal practices – that is, the reasons underlying pragmatic choices, which are mediated by sociopragmatic concepts. There may be very different motives for engaging in the same societal practices (e.g. choosing the same forms) across individuals, just as different motives may lead to different choices. Thus, to judge any pragmatic action in terms of appropriateness requires an understanding of the motives underlying such action. By extension, this entails understanding the development of personalities as they are instantiated in the various subject positions, or identities, enacted to mediate between the Self and the world.

Appropriateness judgment tasks (see Chapter 5) are particularly revealing in this regard because they push learners to externalize their motives for selecting pragmatic forms in various real-life-like social-interactive situations. (Such is also true for the rehearsal, or planning, stage of strategic interaction scenarios, which will be discussed later in Chapter 6.) Excerpt 3.8 shows Susan's explanation for choosing the informal, or everyday, first-person plural pronoun *on* 'we' and verbal negation without *ne* (i.e. *pas* 'not' only) for an office hours meeting with a professor during the postenrichment session of the study.

Excerpt 3.8

1 **Susan:** ((explains that *vous* is appropriate to maintain distance))
2 and then just stick with [...] + I would stick with *on*.
3 and *pas* because I am + tee-shirt-and-jeans + I am a student.

Susan's choices are interesting in relation to personalization and appropriateness for two reasons.

First, the selection of the informal forms was mediated by her appropriation of the concept of self-presentation. For Susan, the context was one in which she would feel comfortable engaging in being Susan – a relaxed, informal, young student (i.e. tee-shirt-and-jeans). In other words, she had personalized the concept as a motive for being herself. The second interesting dimension of this example is that Susan also recognized that maintaining distance through the use of *vous* would normally be considered appropriate for the relationship, but that it is possible to do so without compromising her image of Self – mixing the *vous* form to create distance with *on* and the omission of *ne* accomplished both goals. In other words, she did not simply follow rules or use the content of the concepts mechanistically; rather, she had personalized them in a way that was significant and relevant to her. What is evident here is that Susan's choices were motivated by a particular sensitivity to expectations for social relationships and, at the same time, a desire to be herself in most contexts. These are integral aspects of her personality, which were made possible by the concepts she had appropriated.

Excerpt 3.9 displays Laurie's orientation to the same situation, which starkly contrasts with Susan's.

Excerpt 3.9

1	**Tutor**:	so- and you wanna do suit-and-tie, in that situation,
2	**Laurie**:	yeah. + I think so.
3	**Tutor**:	why.
4	**Laurie**:	cuz she's + my professor, and + um. yeah.
5		that's how I usually try to come off. with my professors,
6		in a more professional way.
7	**Tutor**:	oh. okay.

Laurie categorically chose to use the more formal suit-and-tie language forms (i.e. *vous, nous* and *ne...pas*) for the office hours meeting with her professor. Although Laurie typically chose more informal forms in many situations (including mixing *vous* with more informal forms, like Susan above), interactions with professors were a particular context in which more formal language was, according to Laurie, more appropriate. Laurie's explanation provides an interesting insight into her motives and how she had personalized the concept of self-presentation: for her, suit-and-tie indexed professionalism, which she desired in this context. It is important to note that Laurie certainly did not develop this desire during her participation in the study – it was likely already part of her personality. However, the appropriation of the concepts developed in Laurie a new framework for making and interpreting meaning in French as personally significant and relevant to her social practices.

From the perspective of the SCT framework for instructional pragmatics, both Susan's and Laurie's responses are appropriate because they represent thoughtful, motivated language choices that are mediated by personalized sociopragmatic concepts. The motives underlying each young woman's responses, though different, are integrated aspects of their personalities. Susan and Laurie are different people, people with unique histories and dispositions to language and to being in the world: Susan felt perfectly comfortable being more relaxed and informal with professors, while Laurie endeavored to present herself with an air of professionalism. What is important to recognize is how the concepts, personalized by Susan and Laurie in different ways, resulted in both young women assigning appropriate meanings and relevance to their pragmatic actions.

Emotion and Instructional Pragmatics

Thus far, this chapter has addressed the issues of personality, Self, identity and agency, and internalization as personalization in an attempt to understand learners as people. In this section, I take a look at an oft-ignored aspect of language learning in general and instructional pragmatics in particular: emotions. Emotions impact, and are impacted by, the activities in which we engage, including language learning. In other words, emotions influence language learning outcomes, but they are also in turn influenced by the processes and experiences involved in language learning. This is a dialectical relationship in which emotional and cognitive processes are unified. Vygotsky certainly recognized the inseparability of emotions and cognition when he referred to 'the existence of a dynamic system of meaning in which the affective and intellectual unite' (Vygotsky, 2000: 10). The point of this section is to highlight the interpenetration of emotional and intellectual processes that occur within the context of pedagogical interactions as means of furthering the understanding of learners as people.

(Re)cognizing emotional processes

In introducing her reinterpretation of an interaction between two university learners of French who were completing a dictogloss task, Swain makes the following observation:

> [L]earning another language is not just a cognitive process but an emotional one as well. Emotions are like 'the elephant in the room'. Everyone is aware of them but they reflect an unspoken truth: that they have a significant impact on what has happened in the past, what is happening

now, and what will happen in the future. In fact, emotions are an integral part of cognition. (Swain, 2013: 195)

Yet, as Swain goes on to argue, emotions have been largely ignored in the language learning literature, with the notable exception of anxiety (e.g. Horwitz *et al.*, 1986; MacIntyre, 2002): 'other emotions, such as enjoyment, relief, happiness, excitement, envy, admiration, hope, surprise, pride, gratitude, jealousy, love, hate, guilt, disgust, shame and boredom' (Swain, 2013: 195) are excluded because they are difficult to operationalize and measure (Imai, 2010).

Research that delves into language learners' and multilinguals' personal experiences through narratives, interviews, journals/diaries and/or questionnaires, however, has provided rich descriptions of emotional processes involved in learning and using languages beyond one's first (e.g. Dewaele, 2010; Kinginger, 2004, 2008; Pavlenko, 2005, 2006): learners often report experiencing emotions such as anxiety and excitement in face of new experiences, frustration, disappointment, hope and happiness when confronting and overcoming difficulties and challenges, to name just a few. Yet there is a limitation when it comes to understanding actual language learning processes: 'most research findings [in this tradition] are not so much the respondent's real-time emotional experience of the moment but rather an essentially abstracted representation of emotionally colored past memories' (Imai, 2010: 280). While such work is certainly important as a means of understanding language learning as an emotional experience from the perspective of the learners (i.e. what they say or report about their past emotions), it is also necessary to explore, and to understand, how emotions and cognition interact *in situ* – that is, how the emotional and the cognitive impact upon each other in real time. The emotional side of language learning is accessible not only through learners' retrospective accounts, but it can also be rendered visible in interaction.

Swain (2013) demonstrates how emotions and cognition are tied together by providing four interpretations of the following interaction (Excerpt 3.10) between Rachael and Sophie, as they confronted an L2 difficulty: the correct grammatical gender of the noun *menaces* 'threats':

Excerpt 3.10

1 **Rachel:** des nouveaux menaces [*some new threats*].
2 **Sophie:** Good one! {congratulating Rachel on finding a synonym for 'problèmes'}
3 **Rachel:** Yeah, nouveaux, des nouveaux, de nouveaux. Is it des nouveaux or de nouveaux↰

4	**Sophie:**	Des nouveaux or des nouvelles?
5	**Rachel:**	Nou ... des nou ... de nou
6	**Sophie:**	It's menace, un menace, une menace, un menace, une menace. Ay ay ay!
7	**Rachel:**	Je vais le pauser [*I'm going to pause it*] {i.e. the tape-recorder} {Sophie and Rachel look up 'menace' in the dictionary}
8	**Sophie:**	C'est des nouvelles!
9	**Rachel:**	C'est feminine ... des nouvelles menaces.

(Swain, 2013: 199)

Swain's first interpretation is grounded in cognitivist L2 acquisition: the interaction pushed the girls to notice and fill a gap in their linguistic competence (i.e. the grammatical gender of *menaces* 'threats'). The second, third and fourth interpretations are informed by SCT. Swain sees collaborative dialogue leading to the construction of new knowledge, private speech as Rachael and Sophie attempted to work things out for themselves and, finally, emotions that were inextricably linked to language learning processes. Regarding emotions, Swain writes:

> In turn 1, I see self-pride; in turn 2, I see pleasure, pride and admiration. During turns 3–6, I see trust in each other as each works on her own – trust that each is staying on task and moving it forward. In turn 6, Sophie is frustrated (perhaps an ideal 'teaching moment'). Turn 8 exudes excitement, exhilaration, joy. And in turn 9, a sense of satisfaction is apparent. (Swain, 2013: 203)[8]

Swain concludes that the interaction 'mediates the co-construction of a cognitively permeated set of emotional processes; or is it, perhaps, an emotionally permeated set of cognitive processes? The point, I think, is that it is both' (Swain, 2013: 203). In short, Swain argues that we not must only recognize, but re-*cognize*, the role of emotions in language learning: cognition is emotional, and emotions are cognitive.

An illustrative example

In the present study, it was often the case that learners experienced frustration when they encountered challenging concepts or tasks that pushed them to perform at, or beyond, the limits of their independent abilities. In many cases, the tutor clearly oriented to the learners' emotional processes as he moved to mediate their cognitive processes, thereby achieving not only those goals related to the intellectual development of the learners, but also emotional intersubjectivity – that is, 'joint emotional attention to specific objects or events' (Imai, 2010: 281).

As an illustrative example, let us return to the interaction between Nikki and the tutor analyzed by van Compernolle and Kinginger (2013) (see above). Although the authors do not explicitly discuss emotions, a reexamination of the data clearly shows the presence of emotional processes and their relevance to understanding the interaction. Excerpt 3.11 displays the opening of the interaction centered on choosing between the second-person pronouns *tu* and *vous* for the near-peer store clerk situation. (Transcripts have been modified from those presented in the van Compernolle and Kinginger study to highlight evidence of emotional processes, noted in double parentheses.)

Excerpt 3.11

```
1  Tutor:  umm okay. the fourth one¿
2  Nikki:  ((reads situation aloud)) um (3.5) I would¿ ++ use
3          (4.0) ((Nikki looks confused))
4  Tutor:  hmm. ((light chuckle))
5  Nikki:  ((smiles and laughs))
6  Tutor:  what are you thinking.=what's the-
7          what's giving you problems. don't think about the forms now.
8          just think about the situation.
```

Nikki was unable to respond at first, and her frustration was evident. She produced a number of uncertainty markers in lines 2–3, indicating that she did not know how to respond: for instance, the hesitation 'um', the incomplete utterance 'I would¿' with rising intonation, and a number of long pauses. In addition, Nikki's facial expression suggested confusion: her eyebrows were slightly furrowed as she stared blankly at the questionnaire during the 4.0-second pause at line 3. In response, the tutor oriented not only to Nikki's cognitive difficulty (i.e. responding to the task) but also to her emotional processes. In line 4, he produced a small 'hmm' followed by a light chuckle. This clearly had the effect of alleviating some of Nikki's frustration: she responded by smiling and laughing (line 5). In short, Nikki and the tutor had established emotional intersubjectivity – essentially, a mutual recognition that the task was difficult, and therefore frustrating. Given the emerging relationship between the tutor and Nikki as cooperative partners, it is likely that this emotional intersubjectivity also entailed an implicit understanding that they were to begin working together to resolve the problem, a type of mutual trust and confidence in each other (see Mahn & John-Steiner, 2002;

Swain, 2013). Such was certainly the case, as the tutor immediately began to mediate Nikki's performance in the task at line 6.

Nikki's eventual resolution of the problem – the cognitive process – was also emotionally permeated, to borrow Swain's (2013) terminology. Recall that through the cooperative interaction, Nikki was guided to a synthesis of the concepts of social distance and equal power, as achieved through reciprocal *vous* use, in what she coined as the concept of a distant-equal relationship (Excerpt 3.12).

Excerpt 3.12

```
1  Nikki:   I think we should use vous with each other. ((smiles))
2           + like to show that like ++ it's an equal relationship.
3           but distance equal? distant equal.=((looks at tutor))
4  Tutor:   =ah. ((smiles))
5  Nikki:   ((makes larger smile))
```

As Nikki recognized the solution to the problem (line 1), she smiled. This indicates a sense of satisfaction and happiness with having arrived at an appropriate response to a task that she was not initially able to accomplish on her own. Following her explanation of the synthesis of distance and equality (lines 2–3), the tutor produced an affirmation token (i.e. 'ah') followed by a smile (line 4), thereby confirming Nikki's response as an appropriate one and, at the same time, aligning with her emotional state. Nikki responded by producing a larger smile than she had already had. In short, she displayed an even greater sense of satisfaction once the tutor had not only confirmed the response as appropriate but also had established emotional intersubjectivity with her. Emotions were clearly integrated aspects of Nikki's intellectual achievement, and central to the qualities of the pedagogical interaction taking place between the tutor and her. In short, emotions mediated, and were mediated by, cognitive processes.

Emotional processes, and their relationship with cognition, are different for each individual. We should therefore not expect any two individuals to feel the same thing, just as we would not expect them to think the same thing, during the same or a similar task. This is part of understanding learners as people, as unique individuals. Nonetheless, it is important to recognize/re-*cognize* the role of emotions, and that of emotional intersubjectivity, in mediating L2 pragmatic development. Emotions permeate, and significantly impact upon, the qualities of developmental processes, including how learners orient to, and engage in, tasks as well as how teachers or other participants interact with learners during tasks.

Conclusion

This chapter has examined several ways in which the SCT framework for instructional pragmatics understands learners as people, and how the framework endeavors to embrace the uniqueness of individuals. This entails recognizing that learners – understood as unique individuals – ought to develop personally significant and relevant understandings of sociopragmatic concepts and the pragmalinguistic forms that instantiate them. Appropriateness must therefore be examined from the perspective of learners and in light of the motives and means that mediate their pragmatic choices. In this vein, I have discussed personality development, with particular focus on the concepts of Self, identity and agency, as well as the personalization of mediational means (e.g. concepts, forms) as a crucial component of the internalization process. I have also argued in the preceding section that emotional processes are intimately related to cognitive processes and the real-time unfolding of pedagogical interactions. Understanding that instructed pragmatic development is as much an emotional experience as it is a cognitive one helps us to humanize learners as people who feel as well as think during their interactions with teachers and engagement in pedagogical tasks.

One of the central themes running throughout this chapter is the importance of human mediation. To paraphrase Davydov (1995), human mediation has the goal of guiding learners in their development (i.e. supporting the internalization of psychological mediators), but it must also refrain from imposing a teacher's will on learners. In the SCT framework for instructional pragmatics, this entails a focus on guiding learners toward developing an appropriate understanding of sociopragmatic concepts and, at the same time, supporting the development of a personally significant and relevant relationship with concepts and the forms that instantiate them. The point is to support learners' internalization/personalization of psychological mediators (i.e. concepts) that will enable them to engage in new forms of agentive actions – that is, a sophisticated, systematic and mediated ability to enact desirable subject positions to mediate between the Self and the world. We have also seen that human mediation is itself mediated by emotional processes. Learners experience emotions as they engage in pedagogical tasks, and one of the aims of human mediation must be to recognize and align with those emotional processes. In other words, one of the primary objectives of human mediation should be to establish and maintain emotional intersubjectivity during cooperative pedagogical tasks. As we saw with Nikki, her sense of frustration was oriented to by the tutor, who moved to mitigate the frustration in the pursuit of co-creating with Nikki a cooperative interactive setting. We also saw clearly how Nikki's eventual resolution of the problem was emotionally permeated: a sense of satisfaction, and perhaps pride, was evident, especially once the tutor confirmed her response as an appropriate one. Clearly, emotional and cognitive processes are intertwined.

The insights developed throughout this chapter will be made especially clear in the next three chapters, which address the specific pedagogical tasks included in the SCT framework: verbalized reflections (Chapter 4), appropriateness judgment tasks (Chapter 5), and dynamic strategic interaction scenarios (Chapter 6). As we will see, developmental processes cannot be understood without reference to personalities, personalization and emotions.

Notes

(1) Recall that within the SCT framework, social appropriateness in language use is understood in relation to two criteria: (1) The degree to which a particular instance of language use – whether conventional or unconventional – is interpretable by one's interlocutor(s) or audience given the discourse situation in which language is being used; and (2) the degree to which a particular instance of language use – whether conventional or unconventional – is effective in reflecting and (re)shaping activity types, social relationships, and/or social identities.

(2) The concept of pragmatics as mediated action proposed in Chapter 1, and expanded on in Chapter 2, takes as axiomatic that sociopragmatic knowledge mediates pragmalinguistic choices, which in turn mediate the accomplishment of social actions. Therefore, understanding sociopragmatic knowledge is necessary for making judgments regarding the appropriateness of learners' use of language.

(3) Cultural-historical psychology certainly recognizes the importance of biologically determined abilities in all aspects of psychology. As outlined in Chapter 1, the point is to avoid both upward (behaviorism) and downward (innatism) reductionism (Valsiner & van der Veer, 2000). The integration of culturally constructed mediational means transforms lower biological functions into higher, specifically human forms of mental activity.

(4) This is not to suggest that children do not have personality characteristics prior to the development of conceptual thinking – they certainly do. On the one hand, there are neurobiological factors and, on the other, children are able to think in complexes and pseudoconcepts (Vygotsky, 1986), which mediate their behavior, including personalities. The point is that thinking through concepts is a qualitatively new, and more mature, form of personality.

(5) The study reported by van Compernolle and Williams (2012b) can be considered a predecessor of the SCT framework for L2 instructional pragmatics (see also van Compernolle & Williams, 2012c). However, this previous study did not follow the specific model of concept-based instruction illustrated in this book.

(6) Pavlenko and Lantolf (2000) examined autobiographical narratives of several late/adult bilingual authors who learned their second, and now dominant, language, English, as adults. Pavlenko and Lantolf argue that the authors' sense of Self was transformed as they appropriated English as their dominant language and the culture of their new homes as their own.

(7) These parameters were not meant to limit learners' choices in a negative way. Rather, they represented the parameters within which learners' choices could be oriented to and interpreted within the second languaculture they were appropriating.
(8) Unfortunately, Swain (2013) does not elaborate on her interpretation of the interaction in terms of the linguistic (or other) cues present in the data that suggest these particular emotions. Imai (2010), however, provides evidence of the linguistic basis for interpreting emotional processes.

4 Developing Awareness of Pragmatic Knowledge Through Verbalized Reflections

Introduction

This chapter considers the nature and function of verbalized reflection tasks in the development of concept-based pragmatic awareness or, more precisely – as the chapter title indicates – developing awareness of pragmatic knowledge. One of the central arguments of the sociocultural theory (SCT) framework for second language (L2) instructional pragmatics is that the development of pragmatic knowledge is a necessary, but not sufficient, condition for L2 pragmatic development. One must also develop awareness of such knowledge. With respect to concept-based L2 grammar instruction, Negueruela (2008: 194) points out that one of the goals of the approach is to promote 'awareness about awareness through concepts'. In this sense, awareness of pragmatic knowledge is metacognitive – it entails awareness of what one knows about the pragmatics of the L2 under study. In addition, metacognition entails awareness of what one does not know or fully understand (e.g. realizing that there are gaps in one's pragmatic knowledge). The metacognitive function of awareness therefore provides learners with a systematic orienting basis for using the L2 in agentive, controlled, thoughtful ways while simultaneously creating opportunities for further development.

Verbalized reflection tasks are a specific form of verbal activity designed to prompt learners to externalize (in speech), and to contemplate (through speech), their understanding of the concept they are appropriating.[1] The rationale for such tasks is grounded in Vygotsky's (1978, 1986) argument that language, while having a social (i.e. interpersonal) origin, can be inwardly directed to regulate one's own mental and physical behavior – that is, it can operate as a psychological tool (see also John-Steiner, 2007; Lantolf, 2003; Lantolf & Thorne, 2006; Wertsch, 1985). For example, people often talk to themselves when solving complex mathematical problems that they are not able to solve inside their heads. This self-directed talk (i.e. intrapersonal speech) is not random or inconsequential; rather, it represents the externalization of mental activity and serves to focus one's attention on the problem at hand (e.g. which step or operation comes next), much like a mathematics teacher might do with a student in the classroom through social speech. Verbalized reflections aim to capitalize on the mediational role of this type of language activity by means of an artificial, or intentional (Vygotsky, 1997), task – that is, intentionally prompting learners to externalize their thinking where they may not normally do so under non-elicited conditions. Verbalized reflections render learners' thinking processes visible to themselves and to others (e.g. a teacher). Consequently, learners' pragmatic knowledge is made open to conscious inspection and revision.

Excerpt 4.1, reported in van Compernolle (2011b: 3276),[2] provides an example of a monologic verbalized reflection. Jane – who was appropriating the concept of power hierarchies in relation to *tu/vous* use – was prompted to consider examples where one person might call another *tu* but expect to be called *vous* in return and what meaning would be produced by establishing an asymmetrical *tu/vous* relationship.

Excerpt 4.1

Jane: um ++ per<u>haps</u> two people of the same age <u>meet</u>? but they do <u>not</u> um +++ I'm not sure if I understand this one. ((rereads part of text and/or question but inaudibly/barely a whisper)) <u>OH</u>. <u>yeah</u>. So like an older- so like a person from a <u>higher</u> age group might+call a person of a <u>younger</u> age group um they might refer to them with a *tu* form. but would expect the younger person to use *vous* towards <u>them</u>.+um. and that <u>might</u> ++ <u>simply</u> just mean that there's a difference in+hierarchies as far as <u>age</u>. It may not necessarily mean much as far as <u>power</u>. + now if you're talking about people in a <u>work</u>- + on a <u>work</u> basis. ++ and one person uses *tu* and expect uh expects to be referred to as *vous*+they might be trying to um create a um <u>pow</u>er hierarchy.

Jane struggled to articulate her understanding, as evidenced by her self-assessment (i.e. 'I'm not sure if I understand this one.'). Consequently, she reread part of the text in front of her (presumably part of the concept explanation and/or the question). She then produced the change-of-state particle 'OH. yeah.', which suggests that she realized something at that moment (i.e. she understood the concept), before continuing her verbalized reflection and successfully responding to the prompt. The argument made in van Compernolle (2011b) is that prompting Jane to externalize her understanding of the concept through verbalized reflection allowed her not only to demonstrate her understanding (e.g. for a teacher) but, more importantly, to notice gaps in her own understanding, which she had to resolve in order to complete the task. Verbalized reflections therefore have significant developmental consequences (Negueruela, 2003; Swain *et al.*, 2009).

The data presented in this chapter come from two types of verbalized reflection tasks: (1) monologic tasks in which learners were instructed to explain to themselves (in the absence of the tutor) their understanding of the concepts and pedagogical diagrams provided to them (see Chapter 2); and (2) dialogic tasks in which the learners explained what they understood about the concepts and diagrams to the tutor, who in turn provided feedback, prompts, leading questions, and so on, in order to push learners toward a deeper understanding of the concepts. The focus of the discussion of verbalized reflection tasks is twofold. First, verbalized reflections assist learners in externalizing and rendering visible what they know, including unsystematic, and often invisible (i.e. nonconscious; see Chapter 1), everyday knowledge (e.g. rules of thumb). Second, verbalized reflections create opportunities for the processes of scientific concept formation and internalization.

Language as a Psychological Tool

Language occupies a central place in Vygotsky's theory of mind. As noted above, he argued that, while human language originally developed as a social/communicative tool, it also took on psychological status (Vygotsky, 1986, 1987). In the early stages of ontogenesis (i.e. the development of the person), a child's behavior is often mediated by an adult's directive language. For instance, an adult may assist a child in putting together a puzzle through social speech (e.g. 'Now, the purple piece goes here') as a means of regulating the child's actions. As children develop, and internalize social speech, they are increasingly able to talk themselves through tasks, in which case they produce egocentric speech (i.e. externalized/verbal speech that is directed to the self) as a means of regulating their own actions. Eventually, egocentric speech goes underground to become inner speech, or pure thought. However, as mentioned above, adults often reaccess earlier stages of development (i.e. the use of self-directed, or private, speech) when confronted with complex or difficult problems (see also Frawley, 1997; John-Steiner, 2007; Lantolf & Thorne, 2006; Wertsch, 1985).

It is important to point out that Vygotsky conceived of the psychological function of speech within his more general claim regarding the mediated nature of higher psychological functions. As discussed in Chapter 1, the incorporation of mediational means into mental functions produces a qualitatively different, culturally based psychological process.

> Vygotsky viewed the introduction of a psychological tool (language, for example) into a mental function (such as memory) as causing a fundamental transformation of that function. In his approach psychological tools are not viewed as auxiliary means that simply facilitate an existing mental function while leaving it qualitatively unaltered. Rather, the emphasis is on their capacity to transform mental functioning. (Wertsch, 1985: 79)

Speech, therefore, does not simply assist thinking but in fact transforms it into a specifically human capacity. This Vygotsky (1987) referred to as verbal thinking – that is, thinking mediated by language. The qualitative transformation of thinking entails a reorganization of mental processes that are not merely expressed in language but reshaped by it. As John-Steiner (2007: 137) points out:

> The internalization of communicative interaction, which becomes possible once children use language to express their needs, to describe their world, and to plan their actions with others, leads to the transformation of communicative language into inner speech and verbal thinking. But as [Vygotsky] further suggests, 'the structure of speech is not a simple mirror image of the structure of thought. It cannot, therefore, be placed on thought like clothes on a rack. Speech doesn't merely serve as the expression of developed thought. Thought is restructured as it is transformed into speech. It is not expressed but completed in the word'. (Vygotsky, 1987: 251).

In short, once children develop verbal thinking, thinking and speaking impact upon each other in a dialectical relationship: speech shapes thinking as much as thinking shapes speech.

In adults, verbal thinking is often invisible because it takes place internally through inner speech or, as Vygotsky (1987) put it, in the form of pure meaning. However, when faced with a difficult task, adults may externalize their thinking processes through verbalized self-directed speech. In discussing Frawley's (1997) reinterpretation of Vygotsky, Lantolf and Thorne (2006: 76) comment that self-directed speech in adults 'serve[s] to maintain the individual's focus on what is being done'. In other words, the function of self-directed talk is to mediate one's mental (or physical) behavior by keeping one's attentional resources on specific features of a task: 'it serves a planning function, in which speaking anticipates mental and physical action; in so doing, it enables the person to construct a mental image of a preferred future; and it inhibits us from acting impulsively, that is, non-thoughtfully' (Lantolf & Thorne, 2006: 79–80; paraphrasing Frawley, 1997).

The work summarized above provides a solid foundation for understanding the link between thinking and speaking, understood as a dialectic in which each exerts an influence on the other. Research into L2 development has explored the relationship between self-directed, or private, speech and language learning (e.g. Lantolf, 2003): self-directed speech can mediate L2 problems and promote further development. Elsewhere, researchers have investigated the role of collaborative dialogue (e.g. Antón & DiCamilla, 1998; Swain & Lapkin, 2002) in promoting L2 development. Together, this work supports the idea that the activity of talking oneself through (Swain, 2006) L2 learning tasks facilitates L2 development by externalizing internal thinking processes, thereby rendering them visible and open to conscious inspection. In a similar vein, concept-based L2 pedagogy, which draws on Galperin's (1989, 1992) model of systemic-theoretical instruction, proposes that verbalization tasks are a crucial component of the internalization process (Negueruela, 2003; Swain *et al.*, 2009). Galperin in fact advocated two forms of verbalization to assist in the internalization process: explaining the concept as such and explaining one's performance through the concept. In this chapter, I will focus exclusively on the former, reserving discussion of the latter for Chapters 5 and 6.

It is important to understand that Galperin did not intend verbalizations simply to be think-aloud protocols that provide teachers or researchers access to the qualities of learners' knowledge. Rather, verbalization tasks are opportunities for learners to talk themselves into an understanding of the concept to be appropriated (Lantolf & Thorne, 2006: 305). According to Galperin, verbalization pushes learners to represent actions in external speech, which allows learners to generalize the action beyond familiar contexts (i.e. abstraction of the concept as meaning) and to form new psychological functions (i.e. to restructure thinking processes through the concept). In short, verbalization does not simply lead to rote memorization of content or rules, but rather to the internalization of a psychological mediator (i.e. a concept).

As described in Chapter 1, the research of Negueruela (2003) and Swain (e.g. Swain et al., 2009) clearly shows that verbalization is a necessary condition for the internalization of L2 concepts.

Monologic Verbalized Reflection

In the SCT framework for L2 instructional pragmatics, monologic verbalization refers to tasks in which learners are asked to externalize their thinking as they attempt to understand the concepts of orders of indexicality, self-presentation, social distance, and so on, in the absence of a teacher. In the study from which data are taken for this book, monologic verbalized reflection tasks were done during sessions 2 and 4. The monologic verbalized reflection task in session 2 represented the initial presentation of the concept-based materials. For this task, the learners were instructed to read through the course book, which included written concept cards and pedagogical diagrams (see Chapter 2), and to externalize their understanding of the concepts in speech. To aid verbalized reflections, the materials also included think-aloud questions prompting learners to makes inferences about, and to expand upon, the content of the concept explanations, two forms of verbalization found to be beneficial to learners' development (Swain et al., 2009). For session 4, the students were instructed to verbally reflect on the pedagogical diagrams (e.g. to explain what the diagrams meant and how they worked in relation to French pragmatics). For both tasks, the tutor exited the room, leaving a video camera and digital audio recorder on to record the verbalizations.

The rationale for this methodology is grounded in an expansion of Negueruela's (2003) observation that both privacy and a social context are required for internalization to occur. The tutor's physical absence provided an environment in which there was enough privacy for the adult learners to feel comfortable externalizing their internal mental activity *for themselves*. At the same, the tutor's vicarious presence via the video camera and digital audio recorder created a social context that was intended to push learners to articulate their understanding of the concepts more fully *for a social other*.

Social and private dimensions of monologic verbalized reflections

As noted above, the monologic verbalized reflections were completed in a context that was simultaneously private and social. The qualities of the learners' verbalizations reflect the dual private and social dimensions of these tasks.

A principal feature of monologic verbalized reflections that reflects the social dimension of the task is the relative completeness of the discourse. Whereas true private speech – that is, speech produced for no one but the self – tends to be highly abbreviated, the discourse of monologic verbalized reflections is fully articulated as if designed for a social other. Excerpt 4.2 shows part of verbalized reflection from session 2 in which Nikki was responding to a think-aloud question asking what she could infer from the explanation of the concept of orders of indexicality. The question specifically referenced the ways in which speaker intentions and interlocutor interpretations of social meaning do not always converge.

Excerpt 4.2

1 **Nikki:** like what I in<u>fer</u>: from this explanation,
2   is that you need to be careful about +
3   what you say and <u>how</u> you say it,
4   depending on who you're <u>wi</u>th, because::
5   like if you're like with your <u>fri</u>ends,=
6   =your friends will know that you're <u>jo</u>king,
7   but like if you're with other <u>peo</u>ple? +
8   they might interpret it <u>wro</u>:ng:: an:: ++
9   they may think like you're <u>tea</u>sing er-
10   someone, an- + it just depends on who
11   you're with.

Although Nikki's verbalization certainly represents her thinking/understanding of the concept, it resembles a response to a survey-interview question (she was, after all, responding to a written question for a social other, i.e. the tutor). It should be borne in mind, however, that within Vygotsky's (1987) theory speech does not merely transmit thinking but impacts upon it in a dialectical unity (see also John-Steiner, 2007). As will be demonstrated below, the social nature of monologic verbalized reflections did not preclude individual, or private, developmental consequences.

In addition to social-like qualities of the speech produced during monologic verbalized reflections, there were other overt behaviors that indexed learners' orientations to the social nature of the task (i.e. the tutor's vicarious presence via the recording equipment). Excerpt 4.3, and the accompanying frame grabs shown in Figure 4.1, provide one such example. In this monologic verbalized reflection, Leon was attempting to respond to a think-aloud question about when and why one might choose to use different speech styles (e.g. informal versus formal registers).

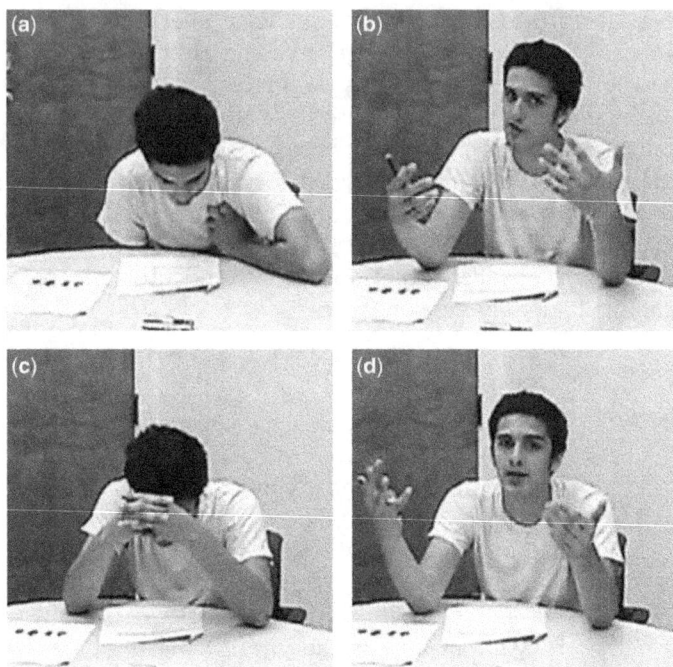

Figure 4.1 Leon looking at the camera during a monologic verbalized reflection

Excerpt 4.3

((*The following is produced in a very quiet, 'creaky' voice*))

1 **Leon:** I often don't (xxx) particular <u>lan</u>guage styles.
2   you know. + like (xxx) formal versus in<u>for</u>mal.
3   I would never say + um ++ **a <u>lot</u> of the things**
4   **I wouldn't** say (h)He (h)He (h) in front of
5   people who + um ++ who I don- + **whose**
6   re<u>spect</u> I'm <u>try</u>ing to + obtain.

Leon's verbalization is fully fleshed out discourse, like Nikki's in Excerpt 4.2, despite the fact the he spoke in a very quiet, 'creaky' voice, voice qualities often associated with private speech (John-Steiner, 2007; Lantolf & Thorne, 2006; Zinchenko, 2007). Leon also certainly recognized the social nature of the context itself: his gaze shifted several times between the concept-based pedagogical materials on the table in front of him and the video camera. As shown in Figure 4.1, Leon began his verbalized reflection while looking at the materials (lines 1–3; Figure 4.1a), then shifted his gaze to the camera as he said 'a lot of the things I wouldn't' (lines 3–4, in boldface; Figure 4.1b), looked back at the materials (lines 4–5; Figure 4.1c), and then once again looked up at the camera (lines 5–6, in boldface; Figure 4.1d). In short, Leon oriented to the camera as an interlocutor, suggesting that he also recognized that the tutor was vicariously present via the recording equipment and was going to watch the videos later (i.e. the social dimension of monologic verbalized reflections).

Nikki's and Leon's verbalizations illustrate the social dimension of monologic verbalized reflections, namely that the discourse tended to be fleshed out as if for a social other and that there were overt behaviors, such as talking to the camera, indexing a learner's recognition of the social nature of the task. However, private, or inwardly directed, features of discourse also emerged in and through the verbalization process. As noted above, private speech in adults serves to regulate one's mental (or physical) activity. In the case of monologic verbalized reflections, the learners used language to regulate their verbalization when they encountered difficulties articulating their understanding of a concept in speech. Thus, while the discourse of monologic verbalized reflections resembled social speech in many ways, the learners were able to mediate their performance in the task through private speech.

In Excerpt 4.4, taken from session 4 of the study, Susan was attempting to articulate her understanding of the pedagogical diagram depicting the concept of self-presentation (i.e. tee-shirt-and-jeans versus suit-and-tie; see Chapter 2). Susan was able to describe the basic meaning of the diagram in relation to the tee-shirt-and-jean versus suit-and-tie imagery (lines 1–3). However, she had trouble further elaborating her understanding of the diagram (lines 4–5).

Excerpt 4.4

1	**Susan:**	two:: is all about the way you speak.
2		do you wanna come off as:: +
3		tee-shirt-and-<u>jeans</u>, or:: suit-and-<u>tie</u>.
4		+ and you're gonna choose how you address
5		someone or how you:: **+ um:: like-**
6		**not add<u>ress</u> yourself + like your um- <u>OH</u>.**
7		you refer to yourself. using:: <u>formal</u> or informal:
8		+ language. based on what interpre↑tation you're
9		supposed to have::↑

In lines 5 and 6 (words boldface), Susan engaged in private speech aimed at regulating her performance in the verbalization. Specifically, she was not able to complete her thought initiated in line 5 (i.e. 'how you::'), which is evidenced by the brief pause followed by the hesitation marker 'um::'. Susan then initiated self-repair: 'like- not ad<u>dress</u> yourself + like your um-' (lines 5–6). This self-repair initiation functioned to maintain focus on the task at hand (i.e. explaining the diagram). The following '<u>OH</u>.' is critical to understanding this aspect of the discourse because it provides evidence that Susan had just realized, or remembered, something (i.e. a change of cognitive state), which was then followed by the completion of her verbalization (see also Gánem-Gutiérrez & Roehr, 2011 on discourse markers in private speech).[3] Thus, while the verbalized reflection included characteristics of social speech, Susan was also able to use language to mediate her own mental functioning during the task.

In addition to speech directed to the self, gestures may also function on the private plane as a means of regulating mental activity. Specifically, gesticulation – that is, gestures that synchronize with speech – function psychologically in what McNeill (2005) calls the growth point, which is where the psychological predicate (i.e. meaning) of the speaker is co-expressed analytically (in speech) and synthetically (in gesture). In the L2 field, it has been argued that 'gesture, like speech, can act as a means of thinking as part of the process of developing one's thoughts; moreover, it can function as a separate, spatio-motoric mode of thinking' (McCafferty, 2004: 149; see also Lantolf, 2010; van Compernolle & Williams, 2011b).

Excerpt 4.5 and Figure 4.2, in which Pierre was verbally reflecting on the self-presentation pedagogical diagram, provides an example of gesture activity that mediates thinking. Pierre was able to describe the meaning of one part of the diagram: tee-shirt-and-jeans and 'when to use: *tu* and *on* and uh: leave <u>out</u> the *ne*:' (lines 1–4). However, he encountered difficulty when articulating his understanding of the second set of pragmatic variants: *vous, nous* and *ne pas* (i.e. the suit-and-tie variants).

Excerpt 4.5

1	**Pierre:**	and then: + the se<u>co</u>nd one's abou:t +++
2		tee-shirt-and-<u>jeans</u>: an::d suit-and-tie:
3		and when to use: *tu* and *on* and uh:
4		leave <u>out</u> the *ne*: ++ and when to use
5		***vous*** ++ ***vous nous*** and ***ne <u>pas</u>***.

As Pierre uttered *vous* (line 5), he made a beat gesture (Figure 4.2a) and then moved his hand back toward his body (Figure 4.2b) during a silence. This suggests that Pierre knew that another variant needed to be listed, but that he had momentarily forgotten which one came next. He restarted the list by

Developing Awareness of Pragmatic Knowledge Through Verbalized Reflections 103

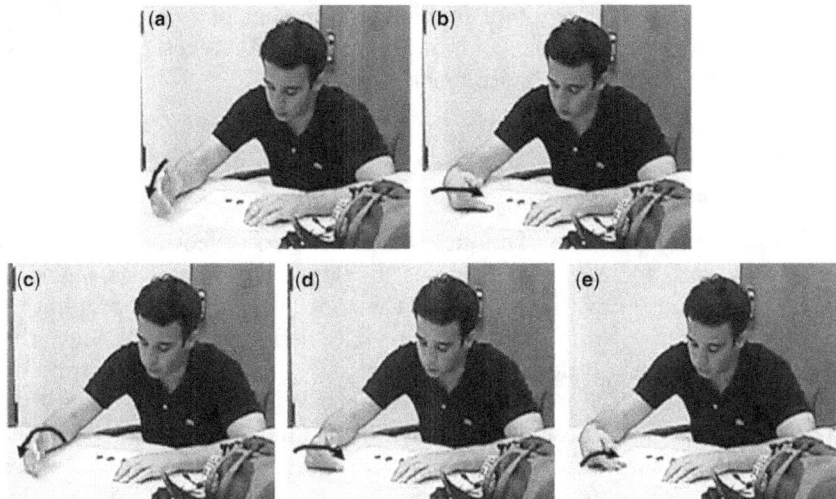

Figure 4.2 Pierre's self-regulating beat gestures

moving his hand back to its original position as he repeated *vous* (Figure 4.2c) and then produced two more beat gestures that synchronized with *nous* and *ne pas*. (Figures 4.2d, e), each of which moved slightly closer to his body. Pierre's gestures participated in externalizing his internal mental activity by creating an embodied list of suit-and-tie pragmatic variants, thereby helping to monitor (i.e. regulate) his verbal production (see McCafferty, 1998; Lantolf, 2010). In short, Pierre's beat gestures helped him to maintain focus on what he was verbalizing, a key aspect of the internalization process (Frawley, 1997).

The discussion of monologic verbalized reflections has thus far focused on the social and private dimensions of the tasks through description of discourse features that can be associated with social and private speech. On the one hand, verbalized reflection discourse resembles social speech in that it is complete and is intended for a social other (e.g. Nikki, Leon). At the same time, the learners were certainly aware of the tutor's vicarious presence and would at time direct their verbalizations to the camera (e.g. Leon). On the other hand, learners also used language (e.g. Susan) and gesture (e.g. Pierre) to mediate their own thinking when they encountered difficulties, behaviors that are decidedly private, or self-directed. In the following subsection, monologic verbalized reflections are discussed in relation to the main purpose of these tasks: rendering pragmatic knowledge visible to the learners and, therefore, open to conscious inspection. In this way, monologic verbalized reflections were a starting point for the development of awareness of pragmatic knowledge (i.e. the metacognitive function of awareness), a key dimension of L2 pragmatic ability within the SCT framework.

Rendering pragmatic knowledge visible and open to consciousness

The primary purpose of monologic verbalized reflections is to guide learners towards awareness of their existing pragmatic knowledge, including what they do not know, in relation to the concepts they are appropriating. In other words, the point is to render this knowledge visible to them so that they can consciously reflect on and, potentially, revise it. As illustrated in van Compernolle (2011b), monologic verbalized reflections can assist learners in getting in touch with what they know and in linking their existing functional, or rule-based, knowledge to the concepts. In many cases, learners draw on their previous L1 and L2 experiences (i.e. empirical, or everyday, knowledge; see Chapter 1) as a means of personalizing the concepts, which in turn helps them to reinterpret that knowledge (van Compernolle, 2012).[4] In short, everyday knowledge may support a learner's appropriation of concepts, but recursively everyday knowledge is transformed as the concepts are internalized. Verbalization therefore mediates between everyday and conceptual knowledge during the internalization process (Brooks *et al.*, 2010).

One of the initial objectives of the concept-based materials presented during session 2 of the enrichment program was to guide learners to an understanding of style-shifting (i.e. intrapersonal variation according to context and/or interlocutor) in relation to the leading concept of orders of indexicality. To do this, learners were prompted to consider examples from their L1, English. The idea was to introduce the concept through the linguistic practices that permeate their everyday lived worlds, but which are typically invisible to them, before showing learners how the concepts play out in the L2. In Excerpt 4.6, Stephanie was considering how, when and why she might vary her speech patterns in her L1.

Excerpt 4.6

1 **Steph:** and this explanation's just talking about like
2 adjusting the way you speak, like to either
3 con<u>form</u> or: go a<u>gainst</u>, people you're around?
4 ++ so:: I know for <u>me</u> + when I go home, ++
5 my Southern <u>drawl</u> comes out a lot more because
6 I'm around: people who are from like + <u>sou</u>thern

7	Virginia, and um +++ that makes it come out
8	worse. whereas when I'm in Pennsyl<u>va</u>nia, +
9	I <u>no</u>tice when I'm saying something like
10	*melk* (('milk')) or *hai::* (('hi')) + like with the
11	long *'I*'s or whatever. + um and I try not to do that
12	as much here. because + especially with my
13	roommate who's from <u>Jer</u>sey she will definitely
14	++ make fun of me for that.

A native of southern Virginia, Stephanie identified the Southern drawl as one recognizable pattern of her speech, which appears when she is at home (i.e. in Virginia) and around southerners, but which she tries to play down when in Pennsylvania (i.e. where she was living at the time of the study). Specifically, Stephanie noted the lowering of the vowel /i/ to /ɛ/ (such that *milk* is pronounced [mɛlk]) and the monophthongization of /ai/ (such that *hi* is pronounced [ha:]) as salient examples of her Southern speech style (line 10), which she reportedly tries to avoid in front of her roommate who makes fun of that accent (lines 11–14). Although the content of Stephanie's verbalization is interesting, the importance of it relates to the way in which the task provided an opportunity for her to think about, and to externalize, what she knew about her L1 practices in relation to the concept of orders of indexicality. The monologic verbalized reflection task created a context to bring to the level of awareness the kind of knowledge that is deeply ingrained, yet largely unarticulated, among native speakers.[5]

To be sure, this constitutes only a starting point for pragmatic development. Because learners are not trained linguists, they typically lack the capacity to make further sense of their experiences in relation to the concepts they are appropriating without assistance from a more competent person (e.g. a teacher). (We will return to this point in the discussion of dialogic verbalized reflections, below.) The following series of excerpts illustrates how monologic verbalized reflections can assist a learner (Leon) in reinterpreting his previously acquired empirical knowledge in terms of scientific concepts. As discussed in Chapter 3, learners' L2 socialization experiences are important sources of empirical knowledge. Although this kind of knowledge may be open to consciousness, it is not systematic since it is based on specific lived experiences, and learners do not always have a way of making sense of these experiences. Verbalized reflections enable learners to begin reinterpreting specific examples within a larger, systematic framework of meaning-making.

In Excerpt 4.7, Leon was commenting on differences between the French and English second-person pronoun systems. Specifically, his verbalization centered on the difficulties that one might encounter in

French when it is not clear whether to use the more informal *tu* or the more formal *vous*.

Excerpt 4.7

```
1   Leon:   °yeah.° + obviously English doesn't make a distinction
2           between you and you. (xxx) you means both the singular
3           and plural. + it can mean: + both the formal and the
4           informal. + um ++ an::d I guess typically I would use
5           tu:: with people (in) my age group, + um who I'm
6           comfortable with, + people who uh ++ or people who
7           are in my age group, or people I'm comfortable with.
8           um:: people I don't see an overt need to pay respect.
9           I mean not- not to say that tu is disrespectful, but it's
10          not overly respectful. um ++ whereas vous would be the
11          opposite. but again this is: + uh:: can- + uh yeah. + it can
12          definitely be very difficult. and (I've) + uh: various times
13          + I've had to:: ++ um + be explicitly told. or asked whether
14          um ++ je peux tutoyer? (('I can use tu')) uh + like my
15          teacher:,or uh:: if they can tutoyer:: er tutoie me, (('use tu'))
16          ++ um + which I think is pretty interesting.
```

Leon began his verbalization by noting the lack of a second-person distinction in English, which led to his listing of several examples or categories of persons with whom he would use French *tu* and *vous* (lines 1–8). However, he encountered some difficulty in line 9, where he backtracked to clarify that his intention was not to suggest that if *vous* were polite, then *tu* was impolite. This suggests that he recognized, at least in part, the inherent ambiguity of the French second-person address system, and the unsystematicity of textbook-style explanations of these pronouns (van Compernolle, 2010a). As he reformulated his explanation, Leon noted that he had been explicitly told or asked which pronoun to use on several occasions, specifically with one of his teachers (lines 12–15). He qualified this observation as 'pretty interesting' (line 16) but did not articulate why it was interesting, nor did he verbalize any understanding of its social significance. Although it is difficult to say whether Leon really did not know how to interpret this example, or whether he simply chose not to elaborate for whatever reason(s), the qualifier 'pretty interesting' suggests that he was at least not committed to a particular understanding of the experience. In other words, it was an experience worth noting, and relevant to the verbalized reflection task, but Leon had not attached a specific meaning to it.[6]

Approximately six minutes later, Leon revisited the example of his teacher telling him explicitly to use *tu* as he was contemplating the concept of self-presentation (Excerpt 4.8). The significance of this excerpt is that it represents an initial step towards linking Leon's empirical knowledge to, and reinterpreting it through, the concepts.

Excerpt 4.8

```
1    Leon:   °uh° + yeah. + uh although obviously yeah. sometimes
2            I'm like a + tee-shirt-and-tie, kind of guy, um ++
3            and it can be very difficult. for example in the classroom
4            where + you know. obviously I need to uh show my
5            teacher respect. but at the same time + um w-
6            we've become very familiar with each other::,
7            I can joke around with them, + we're:: + not friends.
8            at all. not friends per se. but + you know. + we uh:
9            ++ we're familiars. ++ um ++ and f- and for that reason.
10           I think that's why + like uh: + there can be confusion.
11           + and there has been. in the classroom. ++ where it needs
12           to be: explicitly said. you know. we can use:: + at least
13           the te. + uh the tu form.
```

Leon was responding to a think-aloud question prompting him to consider when it might be appropriate to mix more informal (tee-shirt-and-jeans) and more formal (suit-and-tie) personas. He commented that sometimes he was a 'tee-shirt-and-tie kind of guy' (line 2) (i.e. a mix of the two styles), which could be difficult in some contexts, specifically in the classroom (line 3). This led him to return to the example of his teacher with whom he used the more familiar *tu* pronoun. As Leon commented, there can be confusion in the classroom, where there needs to be an explicit request for one pronoun or the other (lines 10–13). The importance of this excerpt is in the link Leon was beginning to establish between a concept (i.e. self-presentation) and the empirical experience of his teacher requesting the *tu* form. Leon used the example to scaffold his understanding of the concept, but in turn the concept was also providing him with the means to talk about and interpret the experience. In short, the data in Excerpt 4.8 represent Leon's first attempt at making sense of the experience through the concepts he was appropriating.

Leon once again revisited the example of his teacher (about two and a half minutes later) as he encountered the concept of social distance. As shown in Excerpt 4.9, the concept clearly provided Leon with a framework for talking about, and understanding, the experience.

Excerpt 4.9

```
1   Leon:   you know. uh + um in high school for example.
2           I became very close, + uh with one of my teachers,
3           I had him for more than a year, he knew my family,
4           but still. he was one of my professors. so I continued
5           to use the vous form: + any time I spoke with him.
6           and eventually he just said. you know. Leon. +
7           tu peux me tutoy:+ yer, + tu peux me tutoyer.
8           (('you can use tu with me')) + and um: and after that.
9           it was + uh + it sort of + um + you know.
10          it didn't necessarily change everything. but it sort of:
11          + was an explicit reminder that + you know.
12          we do know each other very well. we are close.
```

The specific locus of interest here is in the emergence of closeness vocabulary. Previously (Excerpts 4.7 and 4.8), Leon had only talked about the experience in terms of familiarity, friends, politeness, and so on. In this verbalization, however, he reframed the experience in terms of becoming 'very close' with his teacher (line 2), which clearly comes from the explanation of social closeness and distance he had just read. The concept, which importantly included the alternative vocabulary, gave Leon a way of reinterpreting the experience as having to do with the quality of the social relationship: 'it didn't necessarily change everything. but it sort of: + was an explicit reminder that + you know. we do know each other very well. we are close.' (lines 10–12).

Leon's series of verbalized reflections centering on his experience with his high school French teacher show how previous socialization experiences, on the one hand, can scaffold a learner's understanding of concepts and, on the other, come to be reinterpreted through concepts. One of the most important aspects of the excerpts provided above is the incorporation of conceptual vocabulary into Leon's verbalization (Excerpt 4.9). This is important because the task pushed Leon to articulate what he understood (i.e. externalizing his internal mental activity) through speech, which recursively impacts upon thinking. The concept-based materials provided Leon with the appropriate metalanguage to talk about (externalization), and therefore understand (internalization), his experience (i.e. closeness).[7] Although Leon made only an initial step forward in the above excerpts, it was an important first step of rendering his knowledge visible and open to consciousness. As illustrated below, one of the primary functions of dialogic verbalized reflections was to further push learners to externalize their thinking using the vocabulary presented in the concept-based materials and to reinterpret their experiences and existing pragmatic knowledge in those terms.

Dialogic Verbalized Reflection

Dialogic verbalized reflection refers to tasks in which a learner explains his or her understanding of the concepts to another person – in the case of the present study, to the tutor. As shown above, monologic verbalized reflections created opportunities for learners to render their pragmatic knowledge visible to them. However, because they were not trained linguists, they were not always capable of constructing an appropriate meaning of the concepts they were appropriating. Dialogic verbalized reflections served to create a more social, collaborative frame for further pushing learners to consider the qualities of the concepts in greater depth and to (re)mediate their understandings of them and of their existing pragmatic knowledge and socialization experiences.

In the SCT framework for instructional pragmatics, dialogic verbalized reflections were modeled after the instructional conversation developed by Tharp and Gallimore (1988). Grounded in Vygotsky's (1986) claim that a great deal of mental development occurs through communicative interaction with more competent persons, instructional conversations aim to foster 'developmentally rich patterns of teacher-student interaction [in order to] assist learners' understanding of, and ability to communicate about, concepts and ideas that are central to their learning' (Hall, 2001: 83). Such interactions are characterized by a thematic focus (e.g. a concept), use of learners' background and relevant knowledge, promotion of more complex expression and argument support, connected discourse, and direct and explicit teaching when needed (Goldenberg, 1991; van Compernolle & Williams, 2012a; van Lier, 1996, 2004). The goal of this framework for pedagogical interaction is to create a zone of proximal development (ZPD) in which learners may construct an understanding of the theme of the instructional conversation that they would not be able to achieve independently. In other words, the idea is not merely to transfer knowledge from teacher to learner but to engage the learner in transforming the concept in a personally meaningful way, a point that articulates nicely with Vygotsky's conception of internalization as a process of making something one's own (Lantolf & Thorne, 2006; see also Chapter 1). Dialogic verbalized reflections therefore aim to promote learners' personalization of the concepts in cooperation with a more competent person (e.g. a teacher).

A collaborative frame for externalizing internal mental activity

Creating a collaborative frame for externalizing internal mental activity is a key component of dialogic verbalization. Although it may seem obvious that this entails the presence of a mediating agent (e.g. a tutor), it is important to consider the specific qualities of the collaborative frame because different participation frameworks, or contextual configurations, variably afford and constrain potential courses of action (Goodwin, 2007). As Aljaafreh and Lantolf (1994: 471) have noted, an initial shift from independent to collaborative frames involves a 'collaborative posture' in which the mediating agent is available as a 'potential dialogic partner'. Consequently, the qualities of dialogic verbalizations not only depend on the physical presence of a social other but are also influenced by the specific contextual configuration of the dialogic partners.

Figure 4.3 illustrates the contextual configuration for the dialogic verbalized reflections done in the present study.[8] The tutor and learner (Conrad) were seated close together at the rounded corner of a large oval conference table. In front of them were the concept cards and pedagogical diagrams. This configuration created two key affordances. On the one hand, it created a clearly demarcated social space between the two dialogic partners who were able to talk face-to-face rather than side-to-side. On the other, it afforded both interactants comfortable access to the physical artifacts that were relevant to the dialogic verbalizations (i.e. concept cards and pedagogical diagrams). In short, this contextual configuration was designed to allow the tutor and learners to work together cooperatively with a joint focus of attention.

The collaborative frame – like any participation framework – is not given, of course; rather, it is coconstructed by the interactants as they shift from one contextual configuration to another (Hellermann, 2007). Excerpt 4.10 illustrates the opening of a dialogic verbalized reflection between the tutor and Nikki.

Figure 4.3 The social frame for dialogic verbalization

Developing Awareness of Pragmatic Knowledge Through Verbalized Reflections   111

Excerpt 4.10

((*Nikki completes her monologic verbalized reflection, walks to the conference room door, and opens it to look for the tutor.*))

```
 1  Tutor:   ((from outside the conference room)) you done?
 2  Nikki:   yeah.
 3  Tutor:   okay.
 4           (5.0) ((Nikki walks back to her chair and sits down.
 5           Tutor enters the room))
 6  Tutor:   ((still standing)) okay. ((closes door)).
 7           what did you think.
 8  Nikki:   ++ um:: + it was long. + but it was very + informative.
 9  Tutor:   okay. ((sits down in collaborative posture))
10  Nikki:   I- I- I learned a few new things.
11  Tutor:   okay. + um:: + so let's just talk quickly about
12           these diagrams:: um just kind of- basically
13           based on what you've understood from: +
14           these explanations + um + can you- you just
15           wanna walk me through a little bit, + explain
16           how each diagram:: (works) + like what it means,
17           and how it relates to::=
18  Nikki:   =okay.=
19  Tutor:   =what you understood?
20  Nikki:   + um:: + the first diagram ((begins her dialogic
21           verbalized reflection))
```

After Nikki had completed her monologic verbalized reflection, she opened the door to tell the tutor she was finished.[9] As the tutor entered the room, he initiated some task-prefatory talk, asking Nikki what she thought of the materials (lines 5–10), thus signaling a transition from independent work to a social-interactive participation framework. In addition, at this time the tutor sat down with Nikki and assumed a collaborative posture (line 9), thereby creating with Nikki the collaborative frame for interaction. Once this was accomplished, the tutor transitioned to the task proper by outlining the purpose of the dialogic verbalized reflection (i.e. explaining the diagrams) (lines 11–19). This is important for creating a collaborative frame because it allows both participants to negotiate a shared goal for the forthcoming interaction. It also clearly established the tutor's status as a potential dialogic partner, specifically through his request to Nikki to 'walk him through' the diagrams (line 15).

As noted earlier, dialogic verbalized reflections were modeled after instructional conversations (Tharp & Gallimore, 1988). One of the principal features of this kind of interaction is that the teacher can help to promote more complex expression on the part of learners. In the present study, pushing learners to elaborate on their understanding of a concept was an initial step toward assessing the qualities of their knowledge. Excerpt 4.11 provides one such example.

Excerpt 4.11

```
 1  Con:    ((pointing to tee-shirt-and-jeans)) this is just-
 2           + yeah. + the:: tee-shirt-and-jeans:: is the informal,
 3           + whe::n you'd use the informal language. Like tu
 4           on and + u (h)m: + just pas,
 5  Tutor:  okay,
 6  Con:    ((pointing to suit-and-tie)) and this:: + the::
 7           suit-and-tie, ++ version of the scenario's the more
 8           formal. you use that in a more formal setting,
 9  Tutor:  okay. + well let's- let's talk about that diagram
10           a little bit. so is it just + um + tee-shirt-and-jeans,
11           is informal and suit-and-tie is formal? + what
12           was that explanation about.
13  Con:    we::::ll I mean i- that's just the rule. it's: obviously
14           not only (in that.) but um: + it's more just like
15           the relationship you have. I mean if you're in a:
16           a less formal situation ++ where it would be
17           acceptable to wear a tee-shirt-and-jeans::
18  Tutor:  okay
19  Con:    if you're just like hanging out with frien:ds,
20           you know. + like talking to classmates, then
21           you could use the less formal: um:: language.
```

Conrad's initial verbalization (lines 1–8) focused on a rather superficial description of the diagram in front of him. Such behavior is understandable, of course, given that many learners are more accustomed to providing a correct answer than to critically contemplating, and reflecting on, their knowledge when a teacher asks them to describe how they understand something. This is why the tutor prompted Conrad to delve further into the meaning of the concept, challenging Conrad's assumption that the diagram is simply about (in)formality: 'so is it just + um + tee-shirt-and-jeans, is informal and suit-and-tie is formal?' (lines 10–11). This led Conrad to articulate a different, and more complex (and appropriate), understanding of the diagram, which centered on social relationship qualities (lines 13–21).

Creating opportunities to work within the ZPD

The series of data excerpts presented below are meant to illustrate how dialogic verbalized reflections served to uncover, and as a result to work within, a learner's ZPD. As discussed in Chapter 1, the ZPD may be conceptualized as joint activity that is coproduced by a learner and a mediating agent, such as a tutor, that supports the internalization of mediational means (Holzman, 2009). In this sense, ZPD activity in dialogic verbalized reflections is not merely about supporting a learner's completion of a task (e.g. arriving at a correct interpretation of a concept), but instead centers on assisting the learner in developing a deeper, and more personally meaningful, understanding of the concept as part of the internalization/personalization process. This involves not only assessing the qualities of a learner's current understanding of a concept but supporting him/her in articulating more elaborate and systematic understandings as well as providing explicit explanations when necessary.

The specific exemplar case selected for analysis is Stephanie's first dialogic verbalization during session 2 of the study as she was explaining to the tutor how she understood the concept of social distance in relation to the second-person pronouns *tu* and *vous*. Stephanie, like several other students who participated in the study, initially conflated the concepts of social closeness and distance with categories of interpretations such as friendliness (e.g. closeness = friendly). What is lost in this understanding is the way in which creating closeness through *tu* can be interpreted as not friendly (e.g. a police officer who uses *tu* with a suspect is not being friendly, but rather extending constructs of power; see Ager, 1990), just as creating distance by using *vous* is not necessarily unfriendly, but can be interpreted as appropriate, polite or respectful (e.g. in the context of a job interview). Excerpt 4.12 shows the opening of the dialogic verbalized reflection between Stephanie and the tutor.

Excerpt 4.12

```
1  Tutor:  what about diagram three. ((social distance))
2  Steph:  I uh: I think they're creating a more friendly
3          situation by using tu ((points to closeness))
4          they're uh they're bringing a more laidback
5          aspe- I mean is he supposed to be dressed up⇗
6          and this person's not⇗=
7  Tutor:  =m:: don't worry about the dress.
8  Steph:  oh. okay.
9  Tutor:  is it- is it creating friendliness⇗ necessarily⇗
```

10	**Steph:**	um:: + I think so + since you're using *tu*.
11		that's showing closeness, versus if the other
12		person were to use *vous*.
13	**Tutor:**	so=
14	**Steph:**	=like this situation. ((pointing to distance))
15	**Tutor:**	so is that <u>un</u>friendly then,
16	**Steph:**	I don't know if it's necessarily un<u>fri</u>endly,
17		as it is maybe playing the hierarchy thing again?

Stephanie's initial response to the tutor's prompt to explain diagram three, which depicted the concept of social distance as the difference between two people standing close together (closeness, *tu*) versus far apart (distance, *vous*), revealed two points of confusion: Stephanie conflated closeness with friendliness (lines 2–3), as discussed above, and she also conflated the concept of self-presentation with social distance, as evidenced by her comment about being 'laidback' and her question regarding how the people in the diagram were dressed (lines 4–6). This is understandable because self-presentation (i.e. being more tee-shirt-and-jeans or more suit-and-tie) had just been discussed, and so it was likely on Stephanie's mind. Based on her response, the tutor was able to begin to co-construct Stephanie's ZPD: first, by indicating that the way the people in the diagram were dressed was not relevant here (line 7); and second, by prompting Stephanie to consider whether closeness was necessarily equivalent to friendliness (line 9). Although her response maintained the closeness-friendliness (*tu*) equivalence, Stephanie compared it to distance (*vous*) (lines 10–12). This provided an opportunity for the tutor to question Stephanie's equating of closeness with friendliness by pushing her to consider if distance (*vous*) were therefore unfriendly (line 15). During the remainder of the dialogic verbalized reflection centered on social distance (below), Stephanie and the tutor untangled the concept of social distance from interpretations of friendliness, working through Stephanie's ZPD to support her appropriation of the concept.

The data in Excerpt 4.13 show the tutor's initial move to orient Stephanie to the core meaning of the diagram under study (social distance). Specifically, he noted that friendliness may be an interpretation of some action (lines 23–24), but he attempted to focus Stephanie's attention on what *tu* and *vous* can do (lines 26–28, 30) – that is, the pronouns can participate in creating or maintaining social closeness or distance.

Excerpt 4.13

23	**Tutor:**	well: + and think about + more specifically that
24		<u>fri</u>endliness could be an interpretation of something.

25	**Steph:**	mhm
26	**Tutor:**	but what is this diagram telling you _tu_ can do,
27		and _vous_ can do. remember that this isn't just
28		a <u>rule</u>. but ++ these are + d<u>o</u>ings.
29	**Steph:**	mhm
30	**Tutor:**	right, + you're d<u>o</u>ing something.
31	**Steph:**	I mean I think it's pretty- it's + <u>show</u>ing that
32		like that you <u>need</u> the distance or you don't
33		need the distance.
34	**Tutor:**	right. + which in different con<u>tex</u>ts, [to different <u>peo</u>ple,
35	**Steph:**	[can be important
36	**Tutor:**	can be interpreted as friendliness or re<u>spect</u> or
37		politeness or what<u>ev</u>er.
38	**Steph**:	mhm. yeah.

Stephanie's response beginning in line 31 provides evidence of a shift in her thinking: she rearticulated her understanding of the diagram in terms of social distance (lines 32–33). Stephanie also appeared to recognize at this point that social distance can be important in different contexts (line 35), and as the tutor explicitly explained (lines 36–37), 'can be interpreted as friendliness or re<u>spect</u> or politeness'.

The tutor pursued the discussion of social distance by prompting Stephanie to consider examples of contexts in which closeness would not be appropriate or interpreted as friendliness (Excerpt 4.14). Although Stephanie initially misunderstood the question as focusing on when one would want to be unfriendly (line 43), the tutor recalled an earlier example she had discussed that involved a professor to whom she wanted to show respect (line 45). Stephanie had noted during the discussion of the concept of self-presentation that she preferred to present herself as more suit-and-tie to professors, at least in a formal educational context. Incidentally, one of the common features of dialogic verbalized reflections is the reuse of previously discussed examples that are relevant to further understanding the issue at hand.

Excerpt 4.14

39	**Tutor:**	right, + cuz you- can you think of maybe of
40		a context where cre<u>at</u>ing closeness + might <u>not</u>
41		be so friendly. or might not be interpreted as a
42		good thing. like friendliness.
43	**Steph:**	um:: + like when you wouldn't wanna be friendly¿

44		I guess is a::
45	**Tutor:**	well go back to your professor situation.
46	**Steph:**	well yeah. that's true. you wouldn't wanna
47		be like- you wouldn't speak to them the way
48		their <u>child</u> would or something like that.
49	**Tutor:**	and: probably + in a lot of situations + that
50		professor wouldn't see that as <u>frien</u>dliness,
51	**Steph:**	they would see it as disrespectful.
52	**Tutor:**	yeah. + because <u>closeness</u> for that relationship
53		is not maybe appropriate.
54	**Steph:**	mhm okay.

Mentioning the professor example was successful in pushing Stephanie to realize that closeness may not be seen as friendliness or appropriate behavior in all contexts. Specifically, she noted that one would likely not want to speak to a professor as a close intimate (e.g. a child) would (lines 46–48) because such behavior could be interpreted as disrespectful (line 51). This was confirmed by the tutor as an appropriate understanding of the concept (lines 52–53).

As a point of comparison, the tutor then asked Stephanie to consider the part of the diagram depicting distance (*vous*) (Excerpt 4.15).

Excerpt 4.15

55	**Tutor:**	right, + but whereas this ((pointing to distance))
56		+++ ((makes 'questioning' gesture))
57	**Steph:**	the *vous*?
58	**Tutor:**	u (h)Huh,
59	**Steph:**	um that would seem more appropriate.
60	**Tutor:**	and why.
61	**Steph:**	because it's like taking into account your social-
62		like what you're bringing to or like what you <u>want</u>
63		them to take away from the conversation and
64		the way you're speaking,
65	**Tutor:**	and what are y- yeah. and specifically what are
66		you <u>doing</u> by using *vous*.
67	**Steph:**	um: + you're establishing the relationship?
68	**Tutor:**	and what <u>kind</u>.
69	**Steph:**	in a formal way, in a distant way.
70	**Tutor:**	<u>distance</u>. right,

Stephanie's emerging understanding is apparent here. She noted that the *vous* would be more appropriate (in the context of a student–professor interaction) (line 59). When prompted to explain her response, however, she was relatively vague (lines 61–64), mentioning factors related to an interlocutor's interpretation of one's speech (e.g. 'what you want them to take away from the conversation and the way you're speaking'). Yet the tutor further pushed Stephanie to articulate her thinking by recalling the fact that using *vous* is an action (lines 65–66). Stephanie hesitated slightly, as indicated by the 'um:' and short pause, before offering a response in questioning intonation: 'you're establishing the relationship?' This was confirmed by the tutor as he prompted her to indicate the type of relationship *vous* could establish (line 68). Stephanie's (appropriate) response – that *vous* can establish a formal, distant relationship (line 69) – was accepted by the tutor, which constituted the closing of the discussion.

The brief segment of a dialogic verbalized reflection analyzed above has shown an initial shift in Stephanie's understanding of social distance. At first, she conflated the concept of creating closeness or distance with the everyday notion of friendliness. Through dialogue, Stephanie and the tutor were able to co-construct an opportunity to work within her ZPD. In this case, the interaction focused on disambiguating the concept of social distance from interpretations of friendliness since there is no one-to-one correlation between the use of *tu* or *vous* and friendliness. The tutor's role in the interaction was to push Stephanie to consider inconsistencies in her thinking and alternative understandings of closeness, distance and friendliness, which led to the co-construction of an appropriate understanding of the concept under study. This initial shift in thinking was subsequently built on over the course of the enrichment program, as the tutor pushed Stephanie to think through the concepts in a systematic fashion in making pragmalinguistic choices.

Conclusion

This chapter has described the nature and function of verbalized reflection tasks within the SCT framework for L2 instructional pragmatics. The rationale for such tasks is that speaking not only reflects, but impacts upon, thinking processes in a real-time dialectic. It is through speech that internal mental processes can be rendered visible and open to consciousness, thereby creating opportunities for development. As Galperin (1989, 1992) made clear, verbalization is a necessary condition for internalization: verbalization allows learners to generalize mental actions beyond familiar contexts, which leads to the formation of new psychological functions (i.e. internalization of new psychological mediators). Verbalized reflections therefore capitalize on the power of language as a psychological tool that mediates developmental processes.

Monologic verbalized reflections provide learners with an initial opportunity to get in touch with what they know and what they do not know as they work through, and respond to, concept-based materials (e.g. concept explanations and pedagogical diagrams). The nature of monologic verbalized reflection tasks includes social as well as private dimensions: learners are ostensibly verbalizing for a social other (i.e. a teacher) but, at the same time, they exhibit verbal behavior suggestive of inwardly directed, or private, speech. Through this form of verbalization, learners' internal knowledge is rendered visible to them, which makes it open to conscious inspection, even if they are not yet independently capable of making sense of the concepts they are appropriating. Dialogic verbalized reflections insert a more competent person (e.g. a teacher) into the verbalization process to support learners. The co-constructed collaborative frame for interaction promotes more complex expression and argument support. The teacher may push learners to further articulate their understanding of the concepts and to consider inconsistencies or gaps in their thinking as well as alternative understandings of the object of study. The goal of dialogic verbalized reflections is to create opportunities to work within a learner's ZPD. Through dialogue, the teacher may build on a learner's current understanding of the concept to push him or her toward a deeper, more systematic understanding of it.

Verbalized reflections are, therefore, important tasks that promote concept formation and development. However, an important issue to keep in mind is that conceptual knowledge alone is never enough. As Vygotsky (1986, 1997) emphasized throughout his writing on educational praxis, knowledge must not be detached from practical activity. As we will see in the following two chapters, a central concern of the SCT framework for L2 instructional pragmatics is to create pedagogical tasks that explicitly link conceptual knowledge with practical activity.

Notes

(1) Note that verbalized reflection tasks focus on learners' understandings of the concepts as such, which differs from other types of verbalization that center on planning and explaining one's performance on a task (i.e. applying the concepts), which will be discussed in Chapters 5 and 6.
(2) The data are extracted from a pilot study that aimed to test the effectiveness and comprehensibility of the pedagogical materials in which Jane, an intermediate-level US university learner of French, participated. She was not involved in the larger

study. The interested reader is referred to van Compernolle (2011b) for details regarding the pilot study and its findings.

(3) The discourse marker, or particle, *oh* is also used for launching self-attentive action in conversation. Bolden's (2006) analysis of *oh*-prefaced sequences shows that the practice signals to one's interlocutor that something concerning the present speaker has been 'just now remembered' (Bolden, 2006: 681). Recall that Vygotsky (1986) argued self-directed talk develops from social speech and thus retains the characteristics of social interaction. It is therefore reasonable to presume that Susan's *oh*-prefaced verbalization signaled (to herself) that she 'just now remembered' what had been on her mind.

(4) In van Compernolle (2012), I distinguished between three broad categories of pragmatic knowledge: functional knowledge, semantic knowledge and semiotic knowledge. Functional knowledge referred to context-bound rules of use or rules of thumb (i.e. when to use which form with whom). Semantic knowledge referred to static pragmatic meanings that emerge from a confusion of conventions of use and meaning potential (e.g. a form may be labeled formal or informal, polite). Semiotic knowledge referred to an understanding of the way in which language users actively design meanings (see Chapter 2), a view of language that privileges an emergent perspective on meaning creation rather than static pragmatic meanings. The analysis illustrated how monologic verbalization served to link these three types of pragmatic knowledge within a systematic framework of meaning-making. In this chapter, I am primarily concerned with illustrating how monologic verbalized reflections assist in making learners' pragmatic knowledge visible and open to consciousness, so I will not pursue an in-depth analysis of different types of knowledge. For such analyses, the reader is referred to van Compernolle (2011b, 2012).

(5) The interested reader is referred to Niedzielski and Preston (2000) and Preston (2003) for more information regarding folk linguistics and language attitudes, as well as to Guikema (2004) for a study of folk linguistics in second language learning.

(6) The point here is that this example suggests that Leon knew that the experience of his teacher telling him to use *tu* was potentially meaningful in some way, but that he did not have an appropriate framework for understanding it.

(7) One of the criteria for documenting concept formation and internalization is the use of vocabulary relevant to the concept (Negueruela, 2003; Swain *et al.*, 2009; van Compernolle, 2011b). This is not to say that use of appropriate vocabulary equates to internalization; however, given Vygotsky's (1986) analysis of the dialectics of thinking and speaking, the incorporation of new signs (e.g. vocabulary) into verbal thinking is at least an initial step toward reorganizing (i.e. remediating) one's internal mental functioning.

(8) A similar contextual configuration was created in all interactions between the tutor and learners. This concept will be revisited in later chapters, particularly in Chapter 5 when cooperative appropriateness judgment tasks are analyzed.

(9) The tutor explicitly instructed the learners at the beginning of the session to let him know when they had finished the monologic verbalized reflections so that they could continue the session collaboratively.

5 Developing Pragmatic Knowledge Through Appropriateness Judgment Tasks

Introduction

This chapter examines the processes by which the development of second language (L2) pragmatic knowledge may be assessed and further cultivated through engagement in appropriateness judgment tasks – that is, questionnaire-type tasks in which learners are asked to indicate which pragmalinguistic forms are appropriate for different social-interactive contexts and to explain their choices. Within the sociocultural theory (SCT) framework for L2 instructional pragmatics, appropriateness judgment tasks serve to link learners' emerging conceptual knowledge of indexical meanings, and the illustrative pragmalinguistic forms that can instantiate them, with concrete communicative contexts. It is not, however, the instrument itself that leads to development. Rather, it is the administration of the task where learners are engaged in cooperative interaction in which support is provided to them that is important. Through cooperative interaction, learners are pushed not only to apply their pragmatic knowledge but also to explore such knowledge further. Learners' internal mental activity (e.g. response processes, attention to sociolinguistic factors, intentions, goals) is externalized through verbalization (i.e. explaining choices through concepts) and therefore rendered visible and open to consciousness. This creates opportunities to uncover, and to work within, a learner's zone of proximal development (ZPD) in order to promote the continued growth of pragmatic knowledge (van Compernolle, 2013; van Compernolle & Kinginger, 2013).

We have already encountered a number of examples of interactions between the tutor and learners in the study as they worked together to complete appropriateness judgment tasks. In the tasks, the tutor supported learners as they attempted to select appropriate pragmalinguistic forms, prompting them to explain their choices, consider different dimensions of their choices, and/or to rethink their understanding of the concepts they were appropriating. For example, in Excerpt 5.1, the tutor pushed Susan to explain her understanding of distant relationships as it related to her choice of *vous* as the appropriate second-person pronoun to use with a near-peer interlocutor with potential friend status (i.e. the friend of a friend). Susan's response to the tutor's intervention suggests a slight, but highly consequential, shift in her thinking: from understanding social distance as preexisting the context, and therefore being something to react to, to understanding that her choice of language forms actively participates in creating the qualities of social relationships.[1]

Excerpt 5.1

1 **Tutor:**   o<u>kay</u>, + so why- you mentioned that it <u>is</u>
2   a distant relationship, + is it⸮
3 **Susan:**   well- + I'm- I <u>mean</u> + if <u>I've</u> never <u>met</u> him,
4   it's not that the relationshi- the relationship
5   doesn't ex<u>ist</u> already,
6 **Tutor:**   mhm
7 **Susan:**   so I'm cre<u>ating</u> a distant relationship⸮
8   because I <u>don't</u> know him.

As this and other examples provided throughout this book suggest, the cooperative dialoguing supported learners in making connections between the concepts, forms and the indexical meaning potentials that can be instantiated in concrete communicative activity.

In what follows, I expand the discussion of the administration of appropriateness judgment tasks in relation to the evaluation and continued growth of pragmatic knowledge. First, I outline a conceptual framework based on dynamic assessment (DA) principles. DA is grounded in Vygotsky's ZPD concept as a way of integrating assessment and instruction as a single, unified activity (Poehner, 2008). Second, I explore how dynamically administered appropriateness judgment tasks constitute a process of diagnosis through intervention, including how developmentally appropriate support aims not only to assist the learner in a task but, more importantly, in appropriating concepts as tools for thinking.

Dynamic Assessment and Pragmatic Knowledge

As noted above, DA derives from Vygotsky's ZPD concept, often described as the difference between what an individual is able to do alone and what becomes possible with various forms of support or mediation from others and/or cultural tools (see Chapter 1). The ZPD therefore encompasses those competencies that are in the process of formation but may not yet be under independent control. In DA, learners are provided with support as they attempt to complete tasks that are beyond their independent abilities (i.e. completed development) in order to uncover and to promote the continued growth of still-developing capacities (i.e. the ZPD). In this way, DA is an approach to integrating teaching and testing as a dialectically unified activity (Poehner & Lantolf, 2010).

ZPD and frames of interaction

Perhaps the most familiar – and certainly the most frequently cited – definition of the ZPD comes from Vygotsky's discussion of the concept in relation to intelligence testing in children. Vygotsky writes that the ZPD is 'the distance between the actual developmental level as determined by independent problem solving and the level of potential development as determined through problem solving under adult guidance or in collaboration with more capable peers' (Vygotsky, 1978: 86; see Chapter 1). This definition characterizes two important aspects of the ZPD. First, the ZPD may be thought of as latent or still-maturing competencies (i.e. those not yet under the child's independent control), which may point to what is in the child's immediate future developmental trajectory. Second, Vygotsky recognized the central importance of forms of social support in creating ZPD activity. That is, the ZPD comes into being through collaboration with others. (See Lantolf & Thorne, 2006: 263–290.)

Holzman (2009) argues, however, that while these two dimensions of the ZPD have had an important impact on educational psychology, an alternative reading of Vygotsky's work – and one she argues to be more in the spirit of Vygotsky's overall theory – implies understanding the ZPD as a form of collective, transformative activity. Such a view of the ZPD resonates especially with interactionist approaches to DA (Lantolf & Poehner, 2004) wherein human mediation is dialogically negotiated on the basis of the mediator's and the learner's mutual attunement to each other's interactional practices (see Poehner & van Compernolle, 2011).[2] What is meant by this interpretation is that ZPD activity involves much more than measuring developmental potential as a property of the learner or assisting the learner in accomplishing some task that he or she is unable to do alone. Rather, it entails creating the conditions for the qualitative transformation of the learner's knowledge or skills. In relation to DA, this implies treating assessment and instruction as a dialectical unity in which elements of instruction are not simply present during a test but rather form the basis of assessments, or diagnoses, of learner capacities, with the aim of simultaneously evaluating these capacities and promoting their continued growth (see also Lantolf & Poehner, 2011; Poehner & Lantolf, 2010). In this regard, and following Holzman's argument, Poehner and van Compernolle (2011: 187) write that:

> assessment and teaching are understood as an ongoing, integrated activity of diagnosis through intervention. This stands in stark contrast to portrayals of DA as essentially an alternative procedure for administering assessments that includes teaching, or intervention. (e.g. Haywood & Lidz, 2007)

The authors continue by arguing that DA is achieved through the co-construction of, and shifts between, what they term collaborative and cooperative frames of interaction. Collaborative frames include segments of DA interactions in which the focus of activity is on the appropriate completion of the task while cooperative frames go beyond the task at hand to address more general difficulties a learner may be experiencing.

To make their case, Poehner and van Compernolle (2011) examined several excerpts of a dynamically administered multiple-choice test of L2 French reading comprehension. In their examples, collaborative framing took the form of instructional support aimed at guiding the learner to select and understand the correct response to a particular test item through such moves as providing prompts, asking questions and narrowing the scope of the task. Cooperative framing, by contrast, was characterized by a shift away from working on the task proper (i.e. responding to the test item) to address the source of a learner's struggle on a more general level (e.g. understanding a particular grammatical feature). Although the sources of difficulty in learners' performances were certainly relevant to completing the task at hand, the cooperative interactional frame focused on creating opportunities for the learner to further develop a non-task-specific understanding of the problem. This interactional frame, Poehner and van Compernolle argue, has the potential to help learners move toward greater independence in future tasks (see also Poehner, 2007; Poehner & van Compernolle, forthcoming). It is important to note, however, that collaborative and cooperative frames of interaction are not conceptualized as two different approaches to doing DA, but rather as two distinct, yet dialectically united, foci of interaction during DA. In other words:

> it is precisely through the mediator's efforts to co-construct collaborative and cooperative interactional frames with learners that new learner understandings emerge. In other words, it is the shifting from one frame to another and back again – a process that requires careful attention to learner needs, frustrations, and efforts – that marks DA as developmental, diagnostic activity. (Poehner & van Compernolle, 2011: 184)

Thus, although collaborative and cooperative frames of interaction have distinct functions from moment to moment (i.e. supporting task performance, on the one hand, and supporting further maturation of learner abilities, on the other), together they participate in unifying assessment and teaching – diagnosis *through* intervention – in DA.

The value of understanding collaborative and cooperative frames of interaction in DA is in recognizing that such mediator–learner interactions simultaneously involve instructed assessment and assessed instruction (Poehner & Lantolf, 2010). Instruction during DA provides the basis for evaluating learners' knowledge and/or abilities as revealed by their responsiveness to mediation. For example, a learner who is able to complete a task with only a few low-level hints would be considered further along developmentally than a peer who requires more frequent and/or explicit support to complete the same task, even if the two perform similarly on a test of independent performance. At the same time, instruction is assessed on the basis of learner responsiveness to mediation. The mediator may need to adjust the frequency and/or qualities (e.g. explicitness) of support provided so that it is continuously attuned to the needs of the learner (Poehner, 2008) – that is, to the emergent ZPD. This is precisely the dialectic between assessment and teaching in DA – diagnosis and instruction lead (to) each other in an ongoing, integrated manner. In addition, the scope of the assessment is not limited only to the collaborative accomplishment of the task at hand, but it may through cooperative interaction extend beyond the bounds of the task to promote further maturation of those capacities not yet under independent control, or even to introduce new concepts or skills as needed (Poehner & van Compernolle, 2011). This last point is especially important in the context of the SCT framework for instructional pragmatics because, as is fleshed out below, appropriateness judgment tasks were administered not simply as assessments of learners' knowledge, but as opportunities to co-construct the ZPD in order to promote further conceptual development.

DA and appropriateness judgment tasks

As noted above, the dynamic administration of appropriateness judgment tasks aims not only to diagnose learner abilities, but also to provide an interactional context in which the ZPD – conceived of as collective, transformative activity – can be talked into being in order to promote learners' continued growth. This stands in stark contrast to the use of similar tasks (e.g. discourse completion) in the general L2 pragmatics literature, where such tasks are used primarily to assess learners' independent knowledge of pragmatic conventions and/or their ability to produce pretheorized appropriate speech acts (see van Compernolle, 2013; van Compernolle & Kinginger, 2013). This is not to minimize the importance of assessments of independent knowledge, which are certainly useful for a number of purposes. However, within the context of DA, cooperative interaction around appropriateness judgment tasks has as its objective to link and further cultivate learners' emerging conceptual knowledge of sociopragmatic meaning potentials in relation to pragmalinguistic forms in specific contexts of use.

Figure 5.1 displays the appropriateness judgment task used during the pre-enrichment and post-enrichment sessions of the study reported in this book. Learners were instructed to indicate which of the pragmalinguistic

Directions: Please indicate which of the following language forms – *tu* or *vous* 'you', *on* or *nous* 'we', and *ne...,pas* or *Ø...pas* for negation – you would use in each of the situations described below. You will also be asked to explain your choices.

Situation	*tu* or *vous* 'you'	*on* or *nous* 'we'	*ne...pas* or *Ø...pas*
You are at a local café one evening and a friend of yours, Jean, comes in. He walks over to your table and greets you.			
Just before you and your friend order your drinks, your friend's girlfriend, Sophie, enters the café, sees the two of you, and comes over. You've never met her before.			
You're walking down the street with some of your friends on a Saturday afternoon when you run into one of your favorite teachers, M Robinet. He's about 40 years old.			
You have a question about your course schedule so you go to the main office of the department. There, the administrative assistant – a woman in her 50s – greets you. You've never talked to her before, but you know that she is relatively formal with students.			
You are going to see your professor, Mme Triolet, during her office hours because you have a question about an up-coming French culture exam. You haven't scheduled a meeting so you don't know if she's available right now.			

Figure 5.1 Appropriateness judgment task

forms targeted for instruction would be most appropriate in five situations representing a variety of social contexts and interlocutor relationship qualities. They were also instructed to explain their choices. The initial design of the task, therefore, articulates with other instruments and procedures that are widely used in the L2 pragmatics literature – for example, discourse completion tasks combined with verbal protocols (see van Compernolle, 2013). Conventions based on relative status or power, social distance and formality of context vary across the situations. In some cases, however, one or more of these factors may in fact be ambiguous or at least highly variable across individuals' interpretations. Table 5.1 displays information about these factors for each situation based on (perhaps idealistic) sociolinguistic conventions.

Situations 1 and 2 both represent relatively informal social-interactive contexts in which the use of everyday, informal French (e.g. *on* 'we', Ø...*pas*) would most likely be expected. However, since situation 2 involves a first meeting, the degree of distance between Sophie and the participants is somewhat ambiguous, or at least subject to variable interpretations. This is especially true for learners who may not be familiar with the sociolinguistic conventions of native speaker communities (e.g. use *tu* with friends of friends who are peers) because Sophie is stranger, a context requiring *vous* according to learner textbooks. Situation three, too, is not completely straightforward. First, the appropriate level of style/register is subject to variable interpretations (e.g. more informal because the setting is an everyday, noninstitutional context or more formal because the interaction takes place between a student and professor). Second, although there exists the convention to use *vous* with teachers/professors, M Robinet is described as a favorite teacher who is very friendly with his students, which could lead at least some less experienced language learners to deem *tu* appropriate. Situations 4 and 5 are clearly contexts in which *vous* is the conventionally appropriate form of address, based on the amount of social distance and/or relative status. However, the formality of, or expected level of style for, situation 4 is ambiguous: some speakers may favor a more formal style because

Table 5.1 Situation information

Situation	Power	Distance	Context
Situation 1: Jean (friend)	No	No	Informal
Situation 2: Sophie (friend's girlfriend)	No	Variable	Informal
Situation 3: M Robinet (professor)	Yes	Yes/variable	Variable
Situation 4: Administrative assistant	Variable	Yes	Variable
Situation 5: Mme Triolet (professor)	Yes	Yes	Formal

of the age difference and the institutional setting of the situation while others may find a more relaxed, everyday style to be perfectly appropriate.

It is important to note that DA does not rely on any one type of specially designed assessment task. Rather, it is an approach to administering assessments in which support is provided during the task. As such, the SCT framework for L2 instructional pragmatics – though novel in its orientation to pedagogy – can certainly integrate mainstream or traditional assessment instruments as long as their administration articulates with Vygotsky's theory. With regard to DA, this entails going beyond independent performance coupled with verbal protocols in order to include collaborative and cooperative frames of interaction (Poehner & van Compernolle, 2011) that support the learner during the task as well as create opportunities for his or her continued growth. It should also be borne in mind that the appropriateness judgment task shown in Figure 5.1 is only one possibility – other formats or instruments (e.g. oral, written or multiple-choice discourse completion, appropriateness ratings) may also be useful, and teachers and researchers should be encouraged to design tasks that align with their own goals.

Another important feature of the dynamic administration of appropriateness judgment tasks is the focus on cognitive development in relation to the use of sociopragmatic concepts as tools for thinking. Although the instrument is – at least ostensibly – centered around the selection of appropriate pragmalinguistic forms in particular contexts, this serves only a pretext for exploring the ways in which the various concepts can play out in communicative activity. In other words, DA principles extend beyond the mere scaffolding of the task, or assisted performance (i.e. selecting appropriate forms), in a particular context in order to create the conditions for real development: the appropriation of concepts. Poehner (2007) is clear on this point in his discussion of transfer, or transcendence. In his study, DA interactions assisted an L2 learner of French – Donna – not only in using appropriate past tenses in an oral narrative task but also, and more importantly, in appropriating the concept of verbal aspect (e.g. foregrounding and backgrounding states and events, communicating punctuality versus durativity through the use of perfective and imperfective aspect). This resulted in Donna developing a systematic, meaningful framework for choosing tenses (forms) that she could apply, extend and modify in novel contexts. In short, the concept enabled Donna to transcend the demands of a specific task (see also Poehner, 2008). The same is true in the SCT framework for instructional pragmatics. It is not enough to simply scaffold a learner's selection of a pretheorized or idealized appropriate pragmalinguistic form in a specific context. What is needed is cooperative interaction focused on the relevance and significance of sociopragmatic concepts (meaning potentials) in order to create conditions for the formation of new, systematic ways of thinking (i.e. the internalization of scientific concepts) and creating meaning through language use.

Dynamically Administered Appropriateness Judgment Tasks as Transformative, Developmental Activity

The data excerpts and analyses presented in this section aim to illustrate how DA interactions around appropriateness judgment tasks function as transformative, developmental activity. Eliciting verbalizations (e.g. verbalized response processes) and engaging learners in dialogue during these tasks supports learners not only in the accomplishment of the task at hand, but more importantly in appropriating sociopragmatic concepts. It should be borne in mind that, as discussed above, DA is predicated on a dialectical view of assessment and instruction in which diagnoses of learner knowledge and abilities are forged through intervention as a single, unified activity. This starkly contrasts with assessments of pragmatic competence that integrate verbalizations (i.e. concurrent and/or retrospective verbal protocols) as a means of diagnosing learners' knowledge or understanding their response processes (e.g. Woodfield, 2010) without engaging them in cooperative pedagogical activity (see van Compernolle, 2013, for discussion).

Eliciting verbalizations is an important component of DA interactions because learner verbalizations provide a basis for a teacher's, or mediator's, decision to intervene in developmentally appropriate ways (Poehner & van Compernolle, 2011). In other words, eliciting verbalizations during an assessment task is the start, not the culmination, of the process of diagnosing learner knowledge and abilities by intervening in the assessment task. In what follows, I present data to demonstrate this process. Each subsection focuses on a single case analysis of an individual learner interacting with the tutor. The first subsection focuses specifically on the notion of diagnosis through intervention. The second subsection then addresses the ways in which DA interactions – situated as they are within a larger, cohesive pedagogical program – may also foreground instructional activity, with specific reference to orienting learners to the concepts as tools for thinking. To recall Poehner and van Compernolle's (2011) discussion of collaborative and cooperative frames of interaction, it is the shift from foregrounding diagnosis at one moment to foregrounding instruction at another and back again that marks DA as transformative, development-oriented activity. The third subsection examines ambiguity and learner struggle as drivers of development during dynamically administered appropriateness judgment tasks.

Diagnosis through intervention

As described above, DA – conceived of as transformative, development-oriented activity – is a process of diagnosis *through* intervention. This requires a qualitatively different understanding of assessment – and its relationship with instruction – from more mainstream educational and psychological traditions. As Poehner writes:

> In lieu of understanding assessment as the observation and recording of individuals' behaviors for the purpose of inferring underlying abilities, assessment in the dynamic sense involves transformation of those abilities through dialogic collaboration between learners and assessor-teachers, or *mediators*. (Poehner, 2007: 324)

With regard to dynamically administered appropriateness judgment tasks, there is no clear separation between the assessment of pragmatic knowledge and engagement in pedagogical activity. It is through the tutor's interventions – and the learner's responsiveness to intervention – that emerging capabilities are simultaneously diagnosed (assessment) and supported (teaching) in order to foster their continued maturation.

The following series of data excerpts illustrate the process of diagnosis through intervention during dynamically administered appropriateness judgment tasks. The excerpts are taken from an interaction between Stephanie and the tutor as they worked together to choose between the use of the second-person pronouns *tu* and *vous* with a near-peer grocery store clerk on the second appropriateness judgment task of the study (session 2, immediately following the presentation of the concepts and verbalized reflections; see Chapter 4). To recall discussions of this situation presented in earlier chapters, it is somewhat ambiguous because, although the clerk is a near peer (a factor favoring the use of *tu*), she is also a stranger and the context is a service encounter, which are both factors that conventionally favor the use of *vous*. As we will see, although Stephanie did initially choose a conventionally appropriate pragmalinguistic form (*vous*), the tutor nonetheless pursued Stephanie's understanding of the relevance and significance of her choice in relation to the concepts she was appropriating. This served as a means of simultaneously diagnosing Stephanie's pragmatic knowledge and creating an opportunity to co-construct Stephanie's ZPD through intervention – that is, to create conditions for development. Excerpt 5.2 displays the opening of the interaction.

Excerpt 5.2

```
1   Tutor:  so + what about the + grocery store.
2           the fourth situation.
3           (6.5) ((Stephanie silently reads the situation))
4   Steph:  um + I would use + vous¿ + cuz + we-
5           she's just a clerk. + er- that sounds terrible.
6   Both:   ((laughter))
7   Steph:  ((laughing)) she's not like + your best friend.=
8   Tutor:  =okay,=
9   Steph:  who happens to work there. you know. +
10          like you don't kno:w her + um:
11          it's just being¿ respectful::
12  Tutor:  okay. but why is it respectful.
13  Steph:  because:: + just + you don't just yell at somebody
14          when you're at the grocery: + hey you. get me some
15          cheese. + like it's not what you'd do. + you'd say
16          excuse me: + do you know where:: ++
```

Stephanie's initial response, though conventionally appropriate, suggested uncertainty, as evidenced by the hesitation marker 'um', multiple pauses, and rising, interrogative intonation on '*vous¿*' (line 4). She continued by providing a rationale for her choice in relation to the specific type of relationship between the clerk and Stephanie (i.e. 'she's just a clerk,' 'she's not like + your best friend' and 'you don't kno:w her'; lines 5, 7, 10). Her conclusion, then, was that *vous* would be the respectful choice (line 11). As presented in Chapter 2, while this understanding is not necessarily wrong, it is incomplete since respect and politeness are interpretations of pragmatic actions; pragmalinguistic forms are not inherently imbued with such meanings. At line 12, the tutor intervened, thus shifting from the role of *observer* to that of *cooperative interactant*. His intervention specifically aimed to push Stephanie to reflect on, and to explain, why *vous* may be respectful in this situation. Stephanie's response indicated a lack of a systematic understanding of respect. Rather than explaining how respect may be communicated by the use of *vous*, she provided a context-bound explanation of – and essentially a judgment about – conventional proper social behavior (lines 13–16).

Indeed, it is clear that the tutor interpreted Stephanie's response as evidence that she needed further support in relation to linking the concepts to pragmalinguistic practices – that is, he diagnosed Stephanie's current level of

Developing Pragmatic Knowledge Through Appropriateness Judgment Tasks 131

control over the concepts through intervention. This is played out in excerpt 5.3, where the tutor pursued the discussion of respect, this time narrowing the scope of the task for Stephanie by asking a yes-no question, rather than a more open-ended question (cf. Excerpt 5.2, line 12): 'but is *vous* respectful' (line 17).

Excerpt 5.3

17	**Tutor:**	but is *vous* re<u>spect</u>ful.
18	**Steph:**	I see it as respectful. ++ I don't know if it's supposed
19		to be seen that way:¿ but that's-=
20	**Tutor:**	well it's presented like that all the time.
21	**Steph:**	mhm
22	**Tutor:**	that *vous* is respectful.
23	**Steph:**	polite. yeah.
24	**Tutor:**	but <u>is</u> it. + really. think about- think about <u>this</u>
25		kind of thing. ((pointing to distance diagram))
26		cuz that's really what you're- that's <u>really</u> what
27		you're doing. + closeness or distance.
28	**Steph:**	mhm
29	**Tutor:**	and it's in<u>ter</u>preted as politeness or respect or whatever.
30	**Steph:**	mhm

In response to the tutor's question, Stephanie asserted that, in her view, *vous* was respectful (line 18). However, she also began to question this assumption: 'I don't know if it's supposed to be seen that way:¿' (lines 18–19). Although the tutor acknowledged that *vous* is often presented as respectful (e.g. in learner textbooks) (lines 20, 22), he moved to orient Stephanie's attention to the concept diagrams, specifically the diagram depicting social distance, and to rethink her initial understanding of *vous* (lines 24–26). In fact, the tutor explicitly told Stephanie that it was a question of either closeness or distance, which could then be interpreted as politeness or respect (lines 27, 29).

As we see in Excerpt 5.4, the tutor continued his intervention by providing a counter-example to Stephanie's earlier assertion that *vous* was respectful, simultaneously pointing to the social distance diagram again (lines 31–32). This functioned to push Stephanie to reflect on the meaning potential of *vous*: as she stated, using *vous* with a friend would be 'kind of weird' (line 33), explaining that it could signal anger toward a friend.

Excerpt 5.4

| 31 | **Tutor:** | cuz <u>think</u>. + <u>*vous*</u> ((points to distance)) with your |
| 32 | | best friend. + is that respectful¿ |

33	**Steph**:	no. it's kind of weird. + it'd be like you're in an
34		argument and you want to show that like you're mad.
35	**Tutor**:	right. so: *vous* isn't respectful by itself.
36	**Steph**:	mhm. + but I'd also: + like I wouldn't wanna be like
37		<u>best</u> <u>friends</u> with the cheese girl. like-
38	**Tutor**:	exactly.
39	**Steph**:	so: +
40	**Tutor**:	so what are you <u>doing</u>.
41	**Steph**:	I don't know. + I'd use *vous* to create distance,
42	**Tutor**:	right. and it could be interpreted as appropriate
43		respect. or something like that.

The tutor acknowledged Stephanie's statement as appropriate and further explained that '*vous* isn't respectful by itself.' (line 35). This explicit teaching moment was not, however, the culmination of the task. Rather, because DA is a process of diagnosis through intervention, what must be determined is what a learner is able to do with the intervention, or support. In Stephanie's case, it is clear that the tutor's interventions pushed her to orient to the concepts as tools for constructing an appropriate understanding of the use of *vous*. The evidence for this is at line 41, where – after a slight hesitation ('I don't know') – Stephanie concluded that she would 'use *vous* to create distance'. Incidentally, another important feature of this excerpt is the shift from generic-indefinite references (e.g. 'you're in an argument and you want to show that like you're mad'; lines 33–34) to first-person (e.g. 'I wouldn't wanna be like <u>best friends</u>'; line 36–37), which suggests that Stephanie was personalizing the concept – and its relevance and significance – as her own (see Chapter 3).

It is important to note that Stephanie's pragmalinguistic choice did not change over the course of this interaction. Instead, what changed was Stephanie's understanding of the relevance and significance of her pragmalinguistic actions in relation to the concepts, or meanings, that she was appropriating. By intervening in the response process, the tutor was not only able to gauge Stephanie's current understanding but also, and more importantly, to effect a qualitative change in her thinking. Specifically, given the understanding that *vous* was not necessarily respectful but rather was a way of creating distance (that is, the intervention from the tutor), Stephanie was able to reinterpret her choice to use *vous* in this situation. This certainly represents only an initial developmental shift in Stephanie's thinking. But it is an important one that arose in and through cooperative dialogue with the tutor during the diagnosis-through-intervention process.

Orienting to concepts as tools for thinking

As noted above, a crucial dimension of the dynamic administration of appropriateness judgment tasks is that support ought to aim not only to assist learners in arriving at an appropriate pragmalinguistic choice, but also – and more importantly – in achieving an appropriate understanding of the relevance and significance of the concept or set of concepts that learners are appropriating as tools for thinking. Indeed, as Stephanie's case illustrated, learners may already have some conception of appropriate or proper social behavior that is not guided by a systematic orienting basis for action (i.e. a scientific concept), which may not work in all situations (e.g. the hypothesis that *vous* is polite or respectful does not apply to interactions between friends). Consequently, it is necessary to guide learners to orient to the concepts as tools for thinking as they attempt to respond to appropriateness judgment task items.

Although much of this book has been dedicated to discussions of the qualities of learners' emerging conceptual knowledge, it is also important to highlight the core basic mechanisms by which learners are guided toward using the concepts as tools for thinking. The following excerpts illustrate one case, Conrad, as he worked with the tutor on two appropriateness judgment task items during session 2 of the study. What emerges on the part of Conrad is a certain resistance to using the concepts at first, because his preexisting everyday knowledge did in fact allow him to select appropriate pragmalinguistic forms in a rather unambiguous, or straightforward, social-interactive context. Nonetheless, the tutor led Conrad to the conclusion that the concepts were indeed relevant and useful for understanding the meaning potential of his pragmalinguistic choices. Excerpt 5.5 shows the opening of the interaction around the selection of a second-personal pronoun for the first item of the task (inviting a peer/classmate, and potential new friend, to a party).

Excerpt 5.5

```
1                ((Conrad is looking at item 1))
2                (6.5)
3    Con:        um.
4                (4.5)
5                I'd use tu.=
6                =I mean he's my age + so + I mean=
7    Tutor:      =is it because he's your age?
8    Con:        well, and also.
9                (.)
10               I me- I me- I mean I've known him.
```

11		for a few months. so=
12	**Tutor:**	=okay,

Conrad's initial response – that he would use the pronoun *tu* – was appropriate according to social conventions for student peers. However, his reasoning centered on rules of thumb related to his interlocutor's age and existing relationship status (that Conrad has known him a few months; line 11). These factors were certainly relevant to the situation, yet they were not evidence of a systematic framework for choosing pragmalinguistic forms. As such, the tutor questioned Conrad's rationale for selecting *tu* (line 7 and Excerpt 5.6, below) in an attempt to diagnose through intervention the extent to which Conrad might be able to use the concepts as tools for thinking. As is evident in Excerpt 5.6, the tutor moved to orient Conrad to the meaning potential of his choice – that is, the relevant concepts.

Excerpt 5.6

13	**Con:**	i- it's +++ I'm just thinking like- (1.0)
14	**Tutor:**	but what's the <u>mean</u>ing.
15		you keep going back to these + rules,
16		but that's + you've gotta keep track of so many lists:
17		when in fact, + for *tu* and <u>*vous*</u>, ++
18		you've got three things + only ((gestures toward diagrams))
19		that you need to think about.
20		(2.5)
21	**Con:**	right. + se- well see +
22	**Tutor:**	so what are you d- when y- + you're using *tu*. okay¿
23		++ what's the <u>mean</u>ing though.
24		++
25	**Con:**	that we are like- + equal. that like I don- I don- I don-
26		I don't see him + I'm not like trying to like- +
27		cut myself off from him. [like] I'm o:pening up that (.) path=
28	**Tutor:**	[okay,]
29	**Con:**	=for our relationship. because I see + you know.
30		he's + I've known him for a few months,=
31	**Tutor:**	=mhm,=
32	**Con:**	=you know. he's a classmate. and in general,
33		if I was talking with a classmate, i'd use + *tu*.
34		+ yeah- I- so I see him y- +

The tutor's intervention (lines 14–19) included three key features. First, the tutor insisted on questioning the meaning of Conrad's choice (line 14).

Figure 5.2 Tutor orienting Conrad to the diagrams

Second, he explained that the concepts were in fact a simpler way of thinking than relying on lists or rules (lines 15–19). Third, the tutor physically oriented Conrad to the diagrams by gesturing toward the diagrams (line 18 and Figure 5.2). In essence, the tutor showed Conrad where the answer to the question could be found without being corrective from the outset. Although Conrad did momentarily appear to consider the diagrams (e.g. his gaze shifted to the diagrams when the tutor gestured toward them, as depicted in Figure 5.2), he still struggled to integrate them into his thinking. Specifically, he demonstrated difficulty in articulating a rationale based on relationship status (lines 25–29). Conrad eventually abandoned the concepts and reverted to his existing everyday knowledge of conventions (e.g. 'I've known him for a few months', line 30; 'he's a classmate', line 32). This suggests that although he recognized that the tutor was providing support, Conrad was not yet able to benefit from it, meaning that more explicit instructional support was still required.

Indeed, the tutor pursued the provision of support by narrowing the focus of the task for Conrad (Excerpt 5.7). In particular, the tutor returned to the question of meaning, but this time explicitly stated that 'the types of people' (i.e. categories such peer, friend, stranger) were not the main issue (lines 35–36).

Excerpt 5.7

```
35   Tutor:   but again, why.=what's that mea:ning. + it's not the examples,
36            it's not the types of people, right? +
```

37	**Con:**	it's + th[e type of ( )] relationship.
38	**Tutor:**	[( )]
39		literally + all you have to do really, is follow ++ ((points to diagrams))
40		first whadda y- + what's the choices. + that you have to make.
41		+ first of all, +
42	**Con:**	um=
43	**Tutor:**	=how do you wanna be around <u>this</u> guy. +
44	**Con:**	right. + so um + I'm deciding that I wanna be +
45		um + more friendly around him? +
46	**Tutor:**	or: just tee shirt and jeans type, +
47	**Con:**	right.=
48	**Tutor:**	= cuz you don't have to, if you don't want to,
49	**Con:**	right. right.
50	**Tutor:**	right?
51	**Con:**	so then I'm um +
52	**Tutor:**	okay. and so the se[cond,
53	**Con:**	[it's also + by doing that ((pointing to closeness))
54		I'm also deciding that + I'm being more + close with him,
55	**Tutor:**	right,
56	**Con:**	and then I'm also deciding that we are like +
57		on equal + ground. ((pointing to same status/reciprocal *tu*))
58	**Tutor:**	right. yeah.

Conrad acknowledged that 'the type of ( ) relationship' (line 37) was important, presumably in contrast to categories of persons. In response, the tutor once again oriented Conrad to the diagrams (line 39 and Figure 5.3). The tutor first asked Conrad to consider how he would want to present himself

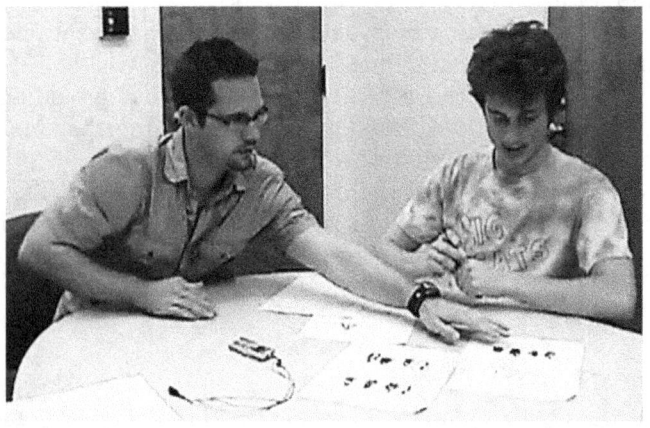

Figure 5.3 Tutor orienting Conrad to the diagrams for the second time

in the situation (lines 43–50). Conrad then recognized how the concepts were useful: as the tutor began to reference the next diagram (distance versus closeness), Conrad overlapped him, thus taking the floor in order to explain that his decision was to show closeness through the use of *tu* (lines 52–54). Then, without the tutor prompting him to do so, Conrad continued to explain – in reference to the concept of power hierarchies – that *tu* use signaled equal status (lines 56–57). In other words, Conrad benefited from the support provided by the tutor this time inasmuch as he recognized how the concepts could be used as tools for thinking through the (meaning of the) selection of pragmalinguistic forms.

Conrad demonstrated more control over the concepts on the following item, a situation involving a telephone interview with a work-study program director in France. As the data presented in Excerpt 5.8 show, Conrad continued to require some prompting. However, he was able to make sense of the situation through the concept of social distance with much less support than was needed for the preceding situation.

Excerpt 5.8

```
1    Con:     this is very formal. I'm trying to be very
2             business like. + I'm trying to impress them.
3    Tutor:   okay,
4    Con:     um + so I'd use vous.
5    Tutor:   okay,
6    Con:     and nous + and ne pas.
7    Tutor:   okay, + and what else is vous doing in that case.
8             (3.5)
9             besides just + showing + some kind of formality
10            or whatever.
11            (2.0)
12   Con:     yeah. + so it'd be putting them, + like above me¿
13   Tutor:   it could. yeah it could. + but more specifically
14            so you already decided + the kind of suit-and-tie
15            type thing.
16   Con:     mhm
17   Tutor:   and what's it doing for your relationship.
18            (4.0) ((Conrad is looking at the diagrams))
19   Con:     cutting them off¿ ((said very slowly/hesitantly, looks confused))
20   Tutor:   how's it cutting them off.
21   Con:     ((smiles)) cuz you're creating distance ((points to distance diagram))
```

Conrad immediately identified the formality of the context as an important factor, indicating a preference for the second-person pronoun *vous* as well as the conventionally more formal sociostylistic variants *nous* 'we' and *ne*'s presence in verbal negation (lines 1–6). Conrad's choices were certainly conventionally appropriate, yet the tutor prompted him to elaborate his rationale (lines 7–10). This is because, as noted earlier, dynamically administered appropriateness judgment tasks are not only concerned with evaluating responses (i.e. selection of pragmalinguistic forms) but, more importantly, in diagnosing underlying response processes. Conrad first mentioned that *vous* could signal that his interlocutor had a higher status (line 12), likely in reference to the concept of power hierarchies. The tutor then pushed him to consider the issue further, specifically in relation to the quality of the social relationship (line 17). Here, Conrad turned his gaze to the pedagogical diagrams, which is evidence that he knew that the diagrams were appropriate tools for thinking through and responding to the question. Hesitantly, he stated that *vous* would 'cut off' his interlocutor (line 19), which the tutor questioned (line 20). Conrad then recognized how the concept of social distance was relevant: he smiled, suggesting satisfaction with having just now realized something, and noted that by using *vous* 'you're creating distance' while pointing at the diagram depicting distance (line 21 and Figure 5.4).

The excerpts presented above have provided an illustrative example of the way in which one learner, Conrad, began to appropriate the concepts as tools for thinking during a dynamically administered appropriateness judgment task. To be sure, this represented only an initial step in Conrad's conceptual development, but it was an important one. It is not enough to know about the concepts (i.e. content knowledge alone); learners must also be guided through an understanding of how they are relevant for thinking

Figure 5.4 Conrad pointing to distance

through issues related to their communicative intentions. The tutor's role in the preceding excerpts was to push Conrad to use the concepts, rather than his everyday knowledge, to reason through his pragmalinguistic choices, and in so doing to support him in gaining greater practical control over the concepts as relevant tools for pragmatic action.

Ambiguity and learner struggle as drivers of development

The two illustrative case analyses presented above demonstrated two key features of dynamically administered appropriateness judgment tasks. First, following DA principles, human mediation, or support offered during the task, aims to diagnose learners' pragmatic knowledge through intervention. Importantly, as illustrated by Stephanie's case, human mediation is not co-equivalent with scaffolded performance in selecting appropriate pragmalinguistic forms but goes beyond this to support the learner's understanding of the relevance and significance of the concept he or she is appropriating. Second, as Conrad's case demonstrated, much of the human mediation occurring during dynamically administered appropriateness judgment tasks focuses on orienting the learner to the concepts as tools for thinking. In this subsection, I turn to a third important feature of appropriateness judgment tasks: ambiguity and learner struggle as drivers of development.

A study by van Compernolle and Kinginger (2013), discussed in Chapter 3, illustrated the developmental consequences of ambiguous appropriateness judgment task items, defined in terms of two or more sociopragmatic rules of thumb being in conflict (see also Chapters 1 and 2). Situation 4 of the second appropriateness judgment task administered in the present study (i.e. a near-peer service encounter at a grocery store; see also Stephanie's case, above) was particularly important: while the hypothetical interlocutor was a peer (a factor favoring *tu*), she was also a stranger and a grocery store employee (factors favoring *vous*). In the van Compernolle and Kinginger study, this situation pushed one participant, Nikki, to transcend (Poehner, 2007) her understanding of the concepts as such in order to consider when the demands of one may outweigh the demands of the others. In Nikki's case, the difficulty was in resolving her desire to present herself as tee-shirt-and-jeans but to avoid an unequal, or asymmetrical, power relationship, which would occur if she were to use *tu* with the store clerk and receive *vous* in return. With support from the tutor, Nikki arrived at a synthetic concept combining social distance and reciprocal *vous* use: that maintaining distance with *vous*, and receiving *vous* in return, could create what she labeled a distant-equal relationship.

The following excerpts showcase Leon's struggle over a similar issue in relation to the grocery store situation. It is noteworthy that Leon used the concepts he was appropriating to complete the first three, relatively unambiguous task items without support – the tutor only prompted him to explain his choices, which Leon did using the concept diagrams. This suggests that Leon did have some control over the concepts and was able to apply them in contexts that did not include any kind of conflict. However, situation 4 proved more difficult because of the ambiguity of the interlocutor's status relative to Leon, and his performance faltered. The opening of the interaction, including Leon's initial selection of and rationale for using *tu*, is presented in Excerpt 5.9.

Excerpt 5.9

1	**Tutor**:	so would you use *tu* or *vous*.
2	**Leon**:	I would use the *tu* form.
3	**Tutor**:	okay. + let's talk about that for a second.
4	**Leon**:	okay.
5	**Tutor**:	so what are you doing by using *tu* with her.
6		+ and think about the relationship that
7		you guys have.
8	**Leon**:	okay. + um +++ I mean I don't know this woman.
9	**Tutor**:	okay,
10	**Leon**:	we don't nec- I guess we don't know yet. +
11		I guess we don't have a relationship. + at all.
12	**Tutor**:	well no. you do. because there's- I mean=
13	**Leon**:	= I mean [( )] I mean there's a-
14	**Tutor**:	[there is a-]
15	**Leon**:	there is like a + I'm interacting with her for my-
16		for the first time,
17	**Tutor**:	okay,
18	**Leon**:	uh she's someone who works here, + uh and I'm asking
19		her to help me out.

Leon's initial choice of *tu* is unconventional: reciprocal *vous* use is often preferred – at least at first – in customer–employee interactions, even among younger, student-age interlocutors who might otherwise call each other *tu*.[3] Rather than being corrective from the outset, however, the tutor moved to elicit Leon's rationale for the choice: he signaled a cooperative frame ('let's talk about that for a second', line 3) and then prompted Leon to consider the qualities of the social relationship between the clerk and him and what *tu* may accomplish in that situation (lines 5–7). Leon demonstrated some uncertainty here. Although he pointed out that he did not know the woman and that they were interacting for the first time, he was not able to articulate a coherent understanding of the context or their relationship (lines 8–19).

The tutor's next move was to focus Leon's attention on the type of interaction depicted in the situation, as shown in Excerpt 5.10.

Excerpt 5.10

```
20  Tutor:  so what kind of like- what kind of interaction is this.
21          between you and her.
22  Leon:   I guess this is + um + hmm. + yeah. it's that I- I-
23          I am + I am asking for her help. + she's like +
24          in this case like + I + you know. not like uh
25          obviously not like being- emphasizing like she-
26          in this case she's like someone + superior. she's more
27          knowledgeable, she's-
28  Tutor:  how's she-=
29  Leon:   =not like superior. + that's not- I don- I don- I don't like know
30          what word to use. but + she is + in this case. she is like
31          someone who + is going out of her way to help me.
32          um. so I don't know.
33  Tutor:  is she going out of her way?=she works=
34  Leon:   =she works there. yeah. ((laughs))
35  Tutor:  ((laughing)) it's kind of her job.
36  Leon:   exactly.
```

Leon interestingly oriented to the fact that the clerk was assisting him as a relevant aspect of the interaction (line 23), concluding – inaccurately – that 'she's like someone + superior. she's more knowledgeable' (lines 26–27). When the tutor began to challenge this assertion, however, Leon revised his statement, this time noting that the clerk was 'going out of her way to help' him (line 31). This, too, was a somewhat inaccurate understanding of the context, as the tutor led Leon to notice: as an employee of the store, it is the clerk's job to help Leon (lines 33–36). This was a critical step in reorienting Leon toward a more appropriate understanding of the context and, by extension, which concepts were relevant, as shown in the last two excerpts.

The tutor's next move (Excerpt 5.11) was to push Leon to contemplate his position in relation to the store clerk (lines 37–38). Leon was then able to conclude that the store clerk was obligated to assist him (line 39), which created an opportunity for the tutor to mediate Leon's understanding of the concept of power hierarchies and how this was relevant to the task at hand.

Excerpt 5.11

37	**Tutor:**	think about- think about <u>your</u> position. ++ who are <u>you</u>.
38	**Leon:**	um + I am ++ yeah. I'm the customer.
39	**Tutor:**	uhhuh,
40	**Leon:**	she needs to be helping <u>me</u> out.
41	**Tutor:**	ah. + so think about your earlier ans- answer about <u>*tu*</u>.
42	**Leon:**	mhm,
43	**Tutor:**	if <u>you're</u> the <u>customer,</u> + in a customer employee, + interaction¿
44	**Leon:**	uhhuh, + I guess it's like +
45	**Tutor:**	who- who <u>could</u> be- conceivably have some kind of power.
46	**Leon:**	uh + certainly + <u>me</u>. the customer.
47	**Tutor:**	and so + look at your diagram. look at that um
48		look at diagram four. ((power diagram))
49	**Leon:**	yeah. that's what I was just thinking about.
50		so uh I guess +++ um if +
51	**Tutor:**	if you use-=
52	**Leon:**	=yeah. I'm trying to downplay- cuz if I use the *tu* form,
53	**Tutor:**	what could tha=
54	**Leon:**	=no matter what she woul- she would <u>still</u> + possibly still
55		feel obligated to use the *vous* form.=
56	**Tutor:**	=ah.=
57	**Leon:**	=and then that would have the effect that + we're not
58		on equal footing.
59	**Tutor:**	and you can do that. that's fine. but=
60	**Leon:**	=yeah. but I don't want to be a jerk or anything. ((laughs))

The tutor prompted Leon to recall and contemplate his original choice to use *tu* (line 41), but this time to consider how the customer–employee interactional context related to the concept of power (lines 43–45). Leon responded that he, the customer, had a higher power status (line 46). In response, the tutor explicitly oriented Leon to the power diagram, indicating its relevance to the situation. Leon was then able to begin to articulate an appropriate understanding of the context: he recognized that the clerk would likely be obligated to use *vous* with him (lines 54–55), which would create an imbalance of power in the relationship if he were to use *tu* (lines 57–58: 'and then that would have the effect that + we're not on equal footing'), something he was inclined to avoid so as not 'to be a jerk or anything' (line 60).

Leon's realization of the potentially negative or unwarranted consequence of using *tu* represented an important shift in his thinking. As the tutor continued to pursue the topic (Excerpt 5.12), Leon demonstrated a new understanding of the relevance and significance of the concept of power in relation to *tu/vous* choice in this rather ambiguous situation.

Excerpt 5.12

61	**Tutor:**	((laughs)) cuz essentially what would- what's the effect.
62		or what's a potential interpretation.
63	**Leon:**	that um that if I'm- if I'm using *tu* then she's still going to
64		use *vous* and therefore you know. I'm higher up. I expect
65		you to do things for me.
66	**Tutor:**	mhm
67	**Leon:**	I'm not necessarily being a nice guy, I'm being pretentious.
68	**Tutor:**	and so if you want to avoid being a jerk,
69	**Leon:**	then I would use *vous*. because + I can't be sure that she's, +
70		I don- I don't know and in fact I may + know for a fact
71		that she won't be comfortable calling me *tu*.
72	**Tutor:**	mhm
73	**Leon:**	so I guess I would use *vous* in tha- in that case.

When asked to explain the consequences of using *tu* with the store clerk and receiving *vous* in return, Leon appropriately concluded that it would make the power difference salient inasmuch as he would be seen as 'higher up' (lines 63–65). He also expressed his interpretation of an asymmetrical relationship in terms of 'not necessarily being a nice guy' or 'being pretentious' (line 67), which is evidence of an initial step toward personalizing the concept as relevant and significant to his goals and communicative intentions (see Chapter 3). Picking up on this statement, the tutor prompted Leon to complete the task item: 'and so if you want to avoid being a jerk,' (line 68; cf. Leon's comment regarding being a 'jerk' in Excerpt 5.11, line 60). Leon revised his response, opting to use *vous* in recognition of the fact that the clerk would also most likely use *vous*. This is a qualitatively new form of thinking through the concepts for Leon: it is not enough to *apply* the concepts as such and in relation to his own communicative intentions, but he must also consider how they work together and in relation to potential social obligations on the part of his interlocutor.

Leon's case, like that of Nikki presented by van Compernolle and Kinginger (2013), highlights the importance of ambiguity and struggle in driving development. More straightforward situations may provide ideal contexts for learners to be guided to an understanding of how to apply the concepts as they are presented by a teacher and/or in pedagogical materials. Ambiguous situations, however, require learners to go beyond a superficial understanding of the content of the concepts (e.g. simple declarative knowledge) to forge deeper understandings of them and their relationships to each other and to pragmalinguistic practices. This is certainly not meant to suggest that only ambiguous situations are useful. Rather, both straightforward and ambiguous situations work in tandem to create opportunities to develop orientations to the concepts as tools for thinking (e.g. Conrad) as well as deeper, more systematic understandings of them (e.g. Stephanie & Leon).

Pre-enrichment and Post-enrichment Appropriateness Judgment Tasks

In this section, we will turn our attention to development over time as evidenced by a comparison of pre-enrichment and post-enrichment appropriateness judgment tasks. Detailed results are reported elsewhere (van Compernolle, 2012), so there is no need to repeat them here. Instead, I will focus on a limited number of principal findings and discussion of illustrative examples.

As noted in Chapter 1, the same appropriateness judgment task was administered during session 1 (pre-enrichment) and session 6 (post-enrichment) in order to directly compare learner responses before and after their participation in the enrichment program Figure 5.1, presented earlier in this chapter, displays the actual task with full situation descriptions. As a reminder to the reader, the task included the following situations:

(1) talking with a friend, Jean, at a café;
(2) meeting a friend's girlfriend, Sophie, for the first time;
(3) running into a favorite teacher, M Robinet, at the weekend;
(4) asking a university administrative assistant for course scheduling help;
(5) meeting a professor, Mme Triolet, in her office.

Learner responses

Table 5.2 provides a snapshot of each learner's pre-enrichment and post-enrichment appropriateness judgment task responses. Figure 5.5 is a plot chart representing combined sociostylistic variant (*nous/on* and =/– *ne*) and *tu/vous* scores for each situation during pre-enrichment and post-enrichment. The scores range from 0 to 1, with 0 being total agreement on the use of informal sociostylistic variants (*y* axis) and *tu* (*x* axis), whereas 1 indicates total agreement on the use of formal sociostylistic variants and *vous*. For example, the data shown in Table 5.2 indicate that all the participants selected *tu* as the appropriate second-person pronoun, and all but one (Conrad) selected the

Developing Pragmatic Knowledge Through Appropriateness Judgment Tasks   145

Table 5.2 Responses to pre-enrichment and post-enrichment appropriateness judgment tasks

Pseudonym	Situation 1		Situation 2		Situation 3		Situation 4		Situation 5	
	Pre	Post	Pre	Post	Pre	Post	Pre	Post	Pre	Post
Nikki	TF	TI	TF	TI	VF	VI	VF	VI	VF	VI
Susan	TF	TI	VF	TI	VF	TI	VF	VF	VF	VI
Leon	TF	TI	TF	TI	TF	VI	VF	VF	VF	VI
Pierre	TF	TI	VF	TI	VF	VI	VF	VF	VF	VI
Mary	TF	TI	TF	TI	VF	VI	VF	VI	VF	VI
Stephanie	TF	TI	VF	TI	VF	VI	VF	VF	VF	VI
Laurie	TF	TI	VF	TI	VF	VI	VF	VF	VF	VF
Conrad	TI	TI	TI	TI	VF	VI	VF	VI	VF	VI

Note: T/V, *tu/vous*; I/F, informal (i.e. *on*, absence of *ne*)/formal (i.e. *nous*, presence of *ne*).

formal sociostylistic variants on the pre-enrichment task. Therefore, the pre-enrichment *tu/vous* score is 0 and the sociostylistic variant score is 0.875. The corresponding data point in Figure 5.5 appears in the upper left corner of the chart, indicating a high sociostylistic formality score but a strong preference – in this case, total agreement – for *tu*.

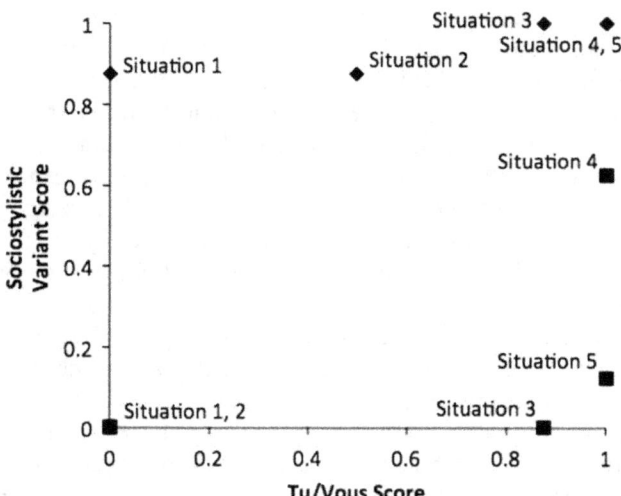

Figure 5.5 Plot chart of pre-enrichment and post-enrichment appropriateness judgment task responses
Note: ♦, pre-enrichment; ■, post-enrichment.

Overall, there the data indicate a shift toward selecting informal sociostylistic variants during the post-enrichment phase of the study. In the pre-enrichment task, only Conrad selected informal variants for situations 1 and 2. However, this was an artifact of the task itself. Because of the format of the task, Conrad was able to accurately surmise that *on* was a less formal alternative to *nous* (see Excerpt 5.13), which also led him to assume that *ne*'s absence was a less formal way of expressing verbal negation.

Excerpt 5.13

```
 1  Con:    ((reads situation 1 silently)) I feel like this is suggesting that
 2          + they all have to do with + different levels of + um +++ like
 3          +++ of- of- you know. different levels of relationships.
 4          for instance. + so.
 5  Tutor:  okay.
 6  Con:    I- I would use tu for this.
 7  Tutor:  okay. why would you use tu with Jean.
 8  Con:    because it's a friend. so like I'm very familiar with this person.
 9  Tutor:  okay.
10  Con:    I guess then I would use on. because I feel like + this is implying
11          that on is the more familiar version of nous.
```

In the post-enrichment task, however, all the students agreed that situations 1, 2 and 3 warranted the use of informal sociostylistic variants, and all but one (Laurie) agreed that it would be appropriate to use the informal variants in situation 5. There was less agreement for situation 4: five students (Susan, Leon, Pierre, Stephanie & Laurie) selected the formal variants, while the remaining three (Nikki, Mary & Conrad) opted for the informal variants.

The figures also show that the students were already able to choose between *tu* and *vous* in conventionally appropriate ways during the pre-enrichment task. Therefore, their *tu/vous* scores did not change significantly between pre-enrichment and post-enrichment. This is not to say, of course, that their reasons for selecting *tu* and *vous* did not change – there were important differences between pre-enrichment and post-enrichment response processes. One important difference in responses, however, is evident in a comparison of pre-enrichment and post-enrichment results for situation 2 (meeting a friend's girlfriend, a peer, for the first time). During the pre-enrichment task, the learners were evenly divided: Nikki, Leon, Mary and Conrad indicated that *tu* was appropriate because the interlocutor was a peer, while Susan, Pierre, Stephanie and Laurie opted for *vous* because the interlocutor was a stranger they were meeting for the first time. On the post-enrichment task all eight learners chose *tu*, indicating that in this context the desire to create closeness – and thus signal potential friend status – through the use of *tu* outweighed any rules of thumb related to the use of *vous* for first meetings. More about this will be said in the following subsection.

A final important observation is the lack of 100% correspondence between *tu/vous* and sociostylistic variants on the post-enrichment task. Specifically, while the learners all agreed that *vous* was the more appropriate second-person pronoun for situations 4 and 5, this did not necessarily lead them also to select the more formal sociostylistic variants *nous* and *ne...pas*. In other words, their choices were informed by the meanings, the concepts, they had appropriated rather than a simplistic either/or, formal versus informal, distinction. Conrad, for instance, noted that for situation 4 (Excerpt 5.14), it was appropriate to use *vous* to create a respectful distance, but at the same it was acceptable to use the more informal sociostylistic variants as an expression of his relaxed persona.

Excerpt 5.14

1	**Con**:	((reads situation silently)) I would- yeah
2		I would use the same thing as the + um as the past one.
3		so I would use <u>vous</u> and <u>on</u> and *pas,*
4	**Tutor**:	okay
5	**Con**:	<u>vous</u> again for that same + level of respect + ful <u>dist</u>ance.
6		that we talked about. for my teacher.
7	**Tutor**:	okay.
8	**Con**:	and um. + yeah. *on* and *pas*. for um +
9	**Tutor**:	cuz you just wanna be you, ((laughs))
10	**Con**:	yeah. I'm me. ((laughs))

This is evidence of the internalization – personalization – of the concepts as tools for thinking, as discussed below in greater detail.

Evidence of internalization

In what follows, we will consider two examples of learners' (Susan and Leon) pre-enrichment and post-enrichment responses for evidence of the internalization of concepts. Both cases involve a change in *tu/vous* choice in relation to the concept of social distance. For Susan this entails a shift from *vous* to *tu* for situation 2, while for Leon this involved a shift from *tu* to *vous* for situation 3 (see results above).

As the reader will recall, the choice between *tu* and *vous* for situation 2 (meeting a friend's girlfriend, a peer, for the first time) presented some difficulty to learners during the pre-enrichment stage. Nikki, Leon, Mary and

Conrad all selected the conventionally appropriate *tu* form, while Susan, Pierre, Stephanie and Laurie decided that *vous* would be the appropriate pronoun to use with Sophie. On the post-enrichment task, however, all eight participants agreed that *tu* would be the appropriate pronoun to use, one indication that the enrichment program helped learners to disambiguate the indexical meanings of the second-person pronouns *tu* and *vous*. Susan, for example, commented during the pre-enrichment task that *vous* would be appropriate in order to show respect toward someone she had never met before, despite the fact that Sophie was a peer and the girlfriend of a good friend.

Excerpt 5.15

1	**Tutor:**	What about the second one. +++ Jean's girlfriend Sophie.
2	**Susan:**	I would pro<u>b</u>ably say *vous*. just because I haven't met her before,
3		+ and its goes back to the whole re<u>spec</u>t thing, I think, +
4		and <u>even</u> <u>though</u>, + she's my age, and + the girlfriend of <u>my</u> friend,
5		+ I still just + be<u>cause</u> I'm meeting her for the first time, +
6		I feel like I <u>would</u> just default to *vous*,
7	**Tutor:**	okay.
8	**Susan:**	to be re<u>spec</u>tful,

Susan's reasoning changed on the post-enrichment task, however. Specifically, she noted that because of the similar social status, and the fact that Sophie is her friend's girlfriend, *tu* would be appropriate since there is no reason to create social distance through the use of *vous*.

Excerpt 5.16

1	**Tutor:**	and the second one?
2	**Susan:**	okay. ((silently reads situation)) umm + I guess,
3		for <u>that</u> one, cuz I know there was one like that before.
4		and I think I said *vous* to maintain a distant relationship,
5		+ <u>BUT</u> I <u>would</u>n't + <u>actu</u>ally. because I went and thought about it.
6		and I was like if it's my <u>friend</u>'s girlfriend, + she's clearly kind of like
7		+ I don't wanna say on our level, + but almost like +
8		kind of <u>on</u> our level. [...] so I would just use *tu*. +
9		and hope she wouldn't get offended by it.
10	**Tutor:**	and what would that <u>do</u>.
11	**Susan:**	umm + like create a relationship that like +
12		you don't have to be distant. like you're my friend's girlfriend,
13		+ like there's no reason for us to be like mmmm
14		((moves back in chair as if distancing herself from someone))
15		I don't wanna talk to <u>you</u> ha ha,
16	**Tutor:**	yeah.

Together, these two excerpts provide evidence that Susan's thinking shifted from a rule-of-thumb-bound system (i.e. default to *vous*) to a conceptually based system (i.e. avoiding social distance) following her participation in the enrichment program. It is also telling that Susan appeared to recall and reinterpret her pre-enrichment response through the concept of social distance: 'I think I said *vous* to maintain a distant relationship' (line 4). In point of fact, Susan said nothing about distance in the pre-enrichment task, but instead mentioned the fact that she had never met the friend's girlfriend and therefore wanted to use *vous* to show respect. Yet, because she had internalized the concept, she was thinking through it, even when recalling a past task performance.

Another example that illustrates the internalization of concepts as tools for thinking is evident in Leon's changing response to situation 3. On the pre-enrichment task, Leon noted that because M Robinet was a favorite teacher, he would likely use *tu* with him despite the fact that M Robinet was older and a teacher, both factors that typically call for the use of *vous* (Excerpt 5.17).

Excerpt 5.17

1	**Leon:**	((silently reads situation)) so <u>again</u>.
2		this is (xxx) he's one of my <u>favo</u>rite teachers,
3		+ even though he may be <u>for</u>ty years old, um +
4		if I've had him for like a while, I feel like I'm familiar with him,
5		there's a very good chance I'd actually use the *tu* form,
6		+ even though often + um teachers use the *vous*,

However, on the post-enrichment task, Leon reinterpreted the category *favorite teacher*. He commented that *favorite teacher* did not necessarily mean *close relationship*, and as such he would use *vous* to create and maintain a sort of professional distance, at least initially.

Excerpt 5.18

1	**Leon:**	((reads situation aloud)) hmm + so in this case,
2		this person's ol- I guess ++ a teacher of <u>mine</u>,
3	**Tutor:**	mhm,
4	**Leon:**	uh + <u>again</u>. it depends. cuz like often- I guess typically.
5		with my teachers. they've told me whether or not + um
6		I should like. <u>use</u> the *tu* form or not,
7	**Tutor:**	okay.
8	**Leon:**	um so because there is no other information,
9		I would jus- I would start out using <u>*vous*</u>, um

10	**Tutor:**	okay.
11	**Leon:**	because although he's- he's one of my favorite teachers.
12		it doesn't necessarily mean like that we're + very <u>close</u> or
13		+ there's still that sort of like ++ um pro<u>fess</u>ional distance,
14	**Tutor:**	mhm,
15	**Leon:**	he's my teacher and I'm the student.
16	**Tutor:**	sure.

In other words, Leon not only shifted to a more conventionally appropriate choice of second-person pronoun, but more importantly he was able to reflect on the qualities of the relationship through the concept of social distance, which led him to make an informed decision without direction from his interlocutor (cf. his comment at lines 5–6: 'my teachers. they've told me whether or not + um I should like. <u>use</u> the *tu* form or not,').

Conclusion

This chapter has explored the role of dynamically administered appropriateness judgment tasks in the assessment and the development of pragmatic knowledge. The modifier *dynamically administered* is meant to index the process of diagnosis through intervention that occurs in DA (Poehner, 2008; Poehner & van Compernolle, 2011). Collaborative and cooperative interaction with the tutor served not only to support learners' performance on appropriateness judgment tasks (i.e. selecting pragmalinguistic forms), but to mediate their interactions with, and by extension the appropriation of, sociopragmatic concepts.

Three key features of the dynamic administration of appropriateness judgment task were examined in some detail in the first analytic section of the chapter. The case analysis of Stephanie illustrated the diagnosis-through-intervention process, whereby the tutor offered support during the assessment of Stephanie's pragmatic knowledge. In particular, he pushed Stephanie to think critically about her responses and to consider aspects of the concepts that she had not yet fully grasped, which resulted in her developing a more appropriate understanding of social distance. In Conrad's case, emphasis was on orienting him to using the concepts as tools for thinking. Although Conrad's existing everyday knowledge allowed him to choose a conventionally appropriate pragmalinguistic form in one situation, the tutor guided him toward an understanding of the relevance of the concepts as tools for thinking. The analysis of Leon's interaction with the tutor as he attempted to respond to a difficult item highlighted the importance of ambiguity and learner struggle in driving pragmatic development. It was in Leon's struggle to reconcile conflicts and negotiate the ambiguities of a near-peer service encounter in cooperation with tutor that a deeper, more systematic understanding of the concepts of social distance and power, and their relationship, emerged. Together, these examples illustrate the transformative, development-oriented nature of dynamically administered appropriateness judgment tasks.

The second analytic section of this chapter offered a comparison of learners' pre-enrichment and post-enrichment responses to an appropriateness judgment task. The findings revealed a number of important changes. First, learners shifted toward a general preference for the more informal sociostylistic variants *on* and the absence of *ne* during the post-enrichment task. Second, while *tu/vous* choices did not change significantly (learners already made conventionally appropriate choices during the pre-enrichment stage), their response processes were dramatically altered on the post-enrichment task. This was especially evident in the examples taken from Susan's and Leon's pre-enrichment and post-enrichment tasks, which offered some evidence of the internalization of the concept of social distance. A third finding was that learners were not limited to making pragmalinguistic choices according to a binary formal-informal. Rather, there was evidence of thinking in terms of a flexible, or malleable, sociolinguistic system in which, for instance, one could use *vous* as a means of maintaining an appropriate social distance, but at the same time opt for the more informal sociostylistic variants in order to project a more relaxed, tee-shirt-and-jeans persona.

Dynamically administered appropriateness judgment tasks serve as an important link between learners' emerging knowledge of the concepts as such, initially developed through verbalized reflections (see Chapter 4), and concrete communicative practices – that is, the selection of pragmalinguistic forms in specific social-interactive contexts. This simultaneously functions to apply the concepts but also to foster their further growth. However, to recall the discussion of Vygotskian educational praxis (e.g. Davydov, 2004; Galperin, 1989, 1992; see Chapter 1), conceptual knowledge alone is not sufficient. As we will see in the next chapter, it is also necessary to engineer opportunities to link conceptual knowledge to practice. In the case of the SCT framework for instructional pragmatics, this entails dynamically administered spoken-interactive tasks, modeled after Di Pietro's (1987) strategic interaction approach, that allow learners to plan their performances in relation to the concepts and pragmalinguistic forms they are appropriating and then to carry out their plan with support from the tutor.

Notes

(1) A detailed analysis of Susan's appropriateness judgment tasks appears in van Compernolle (2013), which focuses on Susan's appropriation of the concept of social closeness as indexed in the *tu/vous* system. With respect to the data in Excerpt 5.1, van Compernolle (2013) documents how the tutor also intervened to guide Susan toward an understanding of the unconventionality of her choice, as a 20-something young woman, to use *vous* to create distance with a near-peer with potential friend status. In fact, the study documents in great detail how Susan personalized the concept, eventually deciding that creating closeness through the use of *tu* in this and other similar situations as more desirable because it aligned with her vision of self.

(2) This is not to dismiss or minimize the contribution of other approaches to DA and understandings of the ZPD discussed elsewhere (e.g. Haywood & Lidz, 2007; Poehner, 2008). As will be fleshed out below, however, within the context of the SCT framework for instructional pragmatics outlined in the present work, and especially with regard to the use and purposes of appropriateness judgment tasks, Holzman's (2009) proposal to read Vygotsky's writings about the ZPD as collective, transformative activity is most useful. There are certainly other approaches to DA of L2 pragmatics that may be insightful in different circumstances and for different purposes (see Chapters 6 and 7).

(3) There is certainly variability in second-person address practices in service encounters. *Tu* can be perfectly acceptable, or even expected, in places that cater to a young, hip clientele (e.g. clubs, bars, youthful clothing stores) precisely because it is interpreted as informality, youthfulness, closeness, solidarity, and so on.

6 Developing Performance Abilities Through Strategic Interaction Scenarios

Introduction

This chapter addresses the development of second language (L2) pragmatic performance abilities as it occurs in and through engagement in dynamically administered strategic interaction scenarios (SIS). As we saw in the preceding chapter, the dynamic assessment (DA) of appropriateness judgment tasks helped to link learners' emerging concept-based pragmatic knowledge to particular contexts of communication and to foster the continued growth of such knowledge. Dynamically administered SISs go one step further in order to push learners to put their knowledge into practice in real-life-like communicative interaction. As will be fleshed out below, one of the primary goals of SISs was to support learners' developing control over pragmalinguistic features in performance through DA procedures – that is, to create opportunities to unite knowledge (concepts) and practice (pragmalinguistic performance) in the zone of proximal development (ZPD).

Dynamically administered SISs draw from Di Pietro's (1982, 1987) Strategic Interaction approach (see also Negueruela, 2003 for SISs in concept-based language instruction). The approach centers on the performance of scenarios, 'a strategic interplay of roles functioning to fulfill personal agendas within a shared context' (Di Pietro, 1982: 41). A key component of scenarios, which distinguishes them from role-plays, is the tension created by providing each participant with a specific agenda without sharing all of the information with others. In other words, while the participants share some information regarding the context of the scenario, they are not aware of each other's specific agendas, which are designed to introduce some (potential) conflict. For example, in one of the scenarios performed in the present study, the tutor and participants played the roles of future roommates searching for apartments. The unshared information, which created the tension, included budgetary constraints regarding the maximum monthly rent and preferred proximity to the university campus. The goal of such scenarios is to push learners to strategically negotiate the conflict. As an extension of this idea to the domain of pragmatics, the scenarios used in this study also aimed to push learners to project, and potentially reshape, particular qualities of social relationships and identities through the use of the pragmalinguistic options available to them.

Although critiques have been leveled against tasks that require learners to suspend reality to participate in an imaginary role as being too cognitively demanding (Kasper, 2001), scenarios are well suited to the pedagogical goals of the sociocultural theory (SCT) framework for instructional pragmatics. This is particularly evident when one considers that, unlike traditional role-plays, scenarios consist of three stages:

(1) a rehearsal stage in which a provisional plan for language use is made;
(2) a performance stage in which the plan is executed, and potentially modified;
(3) a debriefing stage where the performance is discussed and evaluated.

The rehearsal stage also provides an opportunity for learners to ask questions to clarify their role, scenario and objectives for the interaction, as well as to create a plan for the performance in cooperation with the tutor. In the study reported here, planning questions prompted learners to consider the qualities of the relationship between the interlocutors in the scenario, how they wanted to present themselves in the scenario, and how language could be used to accomplish these goals. Thus, in cooperation with the tutor, the learners were able to develop a plan of action prior to the execution of the scenario. The learners were, however, free to change their plan depending on how the scenario unfolded. This planning stage articulates nicely with concept-based approaches to instruction, which emphasize the orientation function of mental actions as guiding material activity (Davydov, 2004; Galperin, 1989, 1992; see Chapter 1).

It should also be noted that scenario performances involve cooperative interaction between the tutor and the learners. In cases where the learners' performance faltered, the tutor intervened to mediate their performance through prompts, leading questions, hints, and so on. This approach derives from the interactionist approach to DA (Lantolf & Poehner, 2004; Poehner, 2008; Poehner & van Compernolle, 2011), which encourages mediators not only to assess but also to support problems in performance as they arise. Excerpt 6.1 shows one such example. For this scenario (attempting to find an apartment to rent), Leon had planned to use negation without *ne*. However, his performance faltered in line 3, where he initially used *ne* twice before self-correcting. The tutor intervened (line 4) to ask Leon what he had wanted to say, which elicited a repetition of the appropriate form from Leon (line 5), which he then used again as he and the tutor continued the scenario (line 7).

Excerpt 6.1

1	**Tutor:**	est-ce qu'y a quelque chose qui est + peut-être
		is there something that is maybe
2		un peu moins che:r, + mais=
		a little less expensive but
3	**Leon:**	=um, + je ne + uh je ne pouvais- + je pouvais pas
		um I [neg] uh I [neg] could I could not
4	**Tutor:**	what do you want to say, + wha- =
5	**Leon:**	=je pouvais pas.
		I couldn't
6	**Tutor:**	okay, + je pouvais pas,
		I couldn't
7	**Leon:**	je pouvais pas + #uh# trouver un autre
		I couldn't uh find another

As further elaborated below, this type of cooperation helped learners not only in their current performance, but in developing better control and consistency in future performances as well.

The remainder of this chapter has three principal aims. First, I outline the approach to dynamically administered SISs in terms of the theoretical and empirical framework, the interpsychological (interpersonal) distribution of control over performance, and the neurolinguistic basis for the approach. Second, I present data that illustrate the role of human mediation (i.e. support in performance) in diagnosing and promoting the development of pragmatic performance abilities, with specific focus on the emergence of controlled pragmalinguistic performance. The third objective of the chapter is to demonstrate the three stages of mental actions: orientation, execution and control (Galperin, 1989, 1992). I present data to illustrate gains in learners' abilities to plan and execute their performances with greater control.

Dynamic Assessment and Pragmatic Performance

As discussed in the preceding chapter, DA is an approach to administering assessment tasks in which the assessor, known as the mediator, intervenes to support a learner's performance and to foster the continued growth of the learner's abilities. In other words, it is a process of *diagnosis through intervention* (Poehner & van Compernolle, 2011) that unites assessment and instruction as a single, unified activity (Poehner & Lantolf, 2010). DA therefore articulates with Vygotsky's (1978) proposal that, in order to understand learners' abilities, it is necessary not only to evaluate their current, or actual, developmental level as revealed through independent performance, but also to identify and support those abilities that are still in the process of formation – that is, the ZPD.

DA and L2 speaking abilities

In Chapter 5, we explored how the dynamic administration of appropriateness judgment tasks functioned to diagnose and promote the growth of learners' emerging conceptual knowledge. In this chapter, we will see how dynamically administered SISs serve to link conceptual knowledge to concrete communicative activity. This constitutes a different orientation to DA, one that focuses more on supporting the application of theoretical knowledge (i.e. performance abilities) than on developing theoretical knowledge as such.

Poehner (2008: chapter 8) points out that DA – conceived of as transformative, development-oriented activity – is uniquely positioned as an approach to administering assessments of L2 speaking abilities that articulates with Galperin's (1989, 1992) theory of the formation of mental actions. This is because DA aims not only to evaluate task performance (execution), but also to uncover, diagnose and intervene in learners' orientations to language use (plan of action) and control over performance as revealed through intervention on the part of a mediator. Poehner's study focused on L2 French learners' appropriation of the concept of verbal aspect and their ability to use past tenses appropriately in oral narrative tasks. The author illustrates how the elicitation of verbalizations from learners when they encountered difficulties provided diagnostic insights into their orientation (i.e. the meaning they were trying to convey) and, therefore, created opportunities for the mediator to intervene in order to assist in the orientation process and to support learners' control over past tenses in performance. Thus, as Poehner demonstrates, responsibility for the task is distributed *inter*psychologically at all three stages of the formation of mental actions. The goal of DA is to support learners in taking on more individual responsibility for the orientation, execution and control functions so that they depend less on external forms of mediation – that is, the intent is to foster development rather than to simply assist performance *in situ*.

Dynamically administered assessments of L2 speaking abilities therefore starkly contrast with other current approaches to providing instructional feedback during performance. Form-focused approaches in the interaction hypothesis tradition (e.g. Gass & Mackey, 2006), for example, aim to correct learners' performance errors through such instructional practices as recasts, prompts, repetition of errors with interrogative intonation, and metalinguistic feedback. In other words, feedback is corrective from the outset, and it targets only linguistic performance (as evidence of a learner's underlying and developing interlanguage system), or the executive function in Galperin's terms. This is not to say that instructional moves like recasts and prompts are not incorporated into L2 DA procedures – they certainly are in many cases. The difference is that DA does not simply aim to correct the execution of linguistic performance, but to understand and further cultivate the orientation and control functions – that is, to engage learners in transformative, development-oriented ZPD activity. Sensitivity to the ZPD is paramount. While any form of feedback has the potential to be beneficial for development, it must be attuned to the learner's current and emerging abilities (Aljaafreh & Lantolf, 1994; Nassaji & Swain, 2000; see also Lantolf & Thorne, 2006: 276–282).

In any early study of corrective feedback from the vantage of ZPD activity, Aljaafreh and Lantolf (1994) note that *graduation of assistance* and *contingency of feedback* are important aspects of effective support. Lantolf and Thorne (2006: 277) summarize the position as follows:

> Assistance should be *graduated* – with no more help provided than is necessary, for the assumption is that over-assistance decreases the student's agentive capacity. At the same time, a minimum level of guidance must be given so that the novice can successfully carry out the action at hand. Related to this is that help should be *contingent* on actual need and similarly removed when the person demonstrates the capacity to function independently.

Thus, the goal of DA is not simply to produce a correct linguistic form, but to position the learner to contribute maximally to the task at hand. This entails, in many cases at least, guiding the learner toward the identification of the problem and supporting him or her in the process of resolving it (Poehner, 2008; Poehner & van Compernolle, 2011; van Compernolle, forthcoming). As we will see below, four basic processes are involved in dynamically administered SISs: (1) recognition that a problem has occurred; (2) identification of the locus of difficulty; (3) diagnosis of the source of difficulty; and (4) identification of an appropriate solution to the problem.

Dynamically administered SISs

As noted at the beginning of this chapter, Di Pietro (1987) conceived of SISs as having three basic stages: a *rehearsal*, where learners may think about, plan and practice their language use for the scenario to be performed; a *performance*, where what was rehearsed may be implemented and/or modified in response to changing communicative circumstances; and a *debriefing*, where a teacher and other learners may evaluate the performance and provide feedback. This is an ideal spoken performance task for the SCT framework for instructional pragmatics since the three stages correspond to the processes involved in the formation of mental actions (Galperin, 1989, 1992): orientation, execution and control (see also Negueruela, 2003). In what follows, I sketch out the procedure for dynamically administering SISs in the current study.

During the rehearsal, or orientation, stage, the learner was presented with a scenario description card, an example of which is provided in Figure 6.1. The scenario description card included relevant information about the context, the learner's relationship with the interlocutor (in the current study, performed by the tutor), the learner's goal for the interaction, and three planning questions designed to prompt learners to use the concepts they were appropriating in order to choose appropriate pragmalinguistic forms. The concept diagrams were also available to learners if they wanted to refer to them. In collaboration with the tutor, the learners responded to the questions as a way of planning their pragmalinguistic performance. Importantly, the tutor did not impose a pretheorized or idealized set of appropriate pragmalinguistic forms, but instead guided and supported learners in arriving at a plan of action – based on the concepts – for creating

---

You recently met an exchange student from France. He doesn't know many people at the university because he's only been here for a couple of weeks. The two of you have gotten together a couple of times for lunch and seem to get along well. You and your roommate are having a party at your place on Friday and want to invite him, so you call to invite him.

(1) What do you think about the relationship between each person in this scenario?
(2) In your opinion, what's an appropriate or desired way to present yourself in this scenario?
(3) How can the language you use help to show the relationship between the two people in this scenario and how you want to present yourself?

Figure 6.1 Scenario description card

the meanings they wanted to create. In essence, the tutor followed the same DA-inspired procedures during the rehearsal stage of SISs as he did during appropriateness judgment tasks (see Chapter 5). This resulted in variable judgments regarding the appropriateness of pragmalinguistic forms across learners, especially for the scenarios reflecting conventionally more formal contexts where some students chose to use *vous* to create distance with the interlocutor but at the same time to use the more informal sociostylistic variants (i.e. *on* instead of *nous* 'we' and *ne* omission in negation) to give off a more relaxed, informal persona.

During the performance stage, the tutor had dual roles: first, to perform the part of the learner's interlocutor as described in the scenario; and, second, to intervene as a mediator if the learner's performance faltered (e.g. if the learner began to diverge from his or her plan of action, as decided during the rehearsal/orientation stage). As demonstrated in van Compernolle (forthcoming), intervention therefore involved a change in footing, or role, on the part of the tutor, from scenario-defined interactant to teacher, effectively putting the task on hold in order to resolve the problem at hand. In order to be sensitive to the learner's ZPD, the tutor negotiated the quality of mediation with the learner along the lines outlined in Aljaafreh and Lantolf (1994), discussed above. In other words, the tutor's support was graduated (i.e. just enough help to allow the learner to regain control without over-assisting or being corrective from the outset) and contingent upon the learner's at-the-moment needs. To recall the discussion of DA in the context of L2 spoken performance, the goal was twofold: to understand the source of the difficulty and to position the learner to take on as much responsibility for resolving the performance difficulty as possible. In this way, the control function – to borrow from Galperin – was in fact distributed between the learner and the tutor. The ultimate aim was to support the learner in developing the ability to control his or her own performance without support from the tutor (cf. the concept of contingency).

The final stage, debriefing, allowed the tutor and the learner to evaluate the performance immediately following its execution. No formal procedure was used for this stage. Instead, the tutor initiated an open discussion of the performance. This left open the possibility for the tutor to comment on any issues he noticed during the performance and for the learner to ask the tutor any questions related to the performance of the scenario or to elicit additional support. In addition, the debriefing stage was intended to provide supplementary speaking practice focused, for example, on particular lexico-grammatical structures that presented difficulties for the learner. The debriefing stage therefore represented another opportunity to work on control over performance.

Insights from neurolinguistics

Support for DA procedures – in particular, emphasis on conscious learning and control over performance – can be found in Paradis' (2004, 2009) neurolinguistic account of bilingualism and the declarative and procedural determinants of second languages. Paradis (2004: 30) points out that '[s]peakers who have learned a second language after acquiring their native language will compensate for gaps in their implicit competence by relying more extensively on the other components of verbal communication, namely metalinguistic knowledge and pragmatics'. His argument, elaborated in Paradis (2009), is that once a person has acquired a first language, it becomes increasingly difficult to acquire languages beyond the first (in the sense of incidentally acquiring implicit linguistic competence). Yet, adult learners may develop what he calls speeded up (i.e. accelerated) access to explicit metalinguistic knowledge, which may in some cases be functionally equivalent to implicit linguistic competence during language use (i.e. the L2 can be produced fluently and effectively although it is controlled by the declarative rather than the implicit system). Repeated use of the L2, according to Paradis, may even result in the acquisition of some components of the L2 as implicit competence.

Paradis (2009) argues that gaps in one's implicit L2 linguistic competence are compensated for by one's available metalinguistic knowledge. Importantly, the model implies a continuum of reliance on metalinguistic knowledge or implicit linguistic competence rather than an interface between the two in which metalinguistic knowledge becomes implicit linguistic competence. The two systems remain distinct because their operations are subserved by different neurological components, but an L2 user can rely on both systems in parallel during communication. Thus, while there is no interface between metalinguistic knowledge and implicit linguistic competence, L2 users may switch between the two, most notably when a gap in implicit linguistic competence necessitates the use of metalinguistic knowledge.

Adult L2 learners in formal (structured) educational contexts do not have a lifetime to acquire an additional language incidentally through repeated exposure to and use of a language, that is, the manner in which one typically acquires one's first language (Paradis, 2009: 96). To compensate, adult L2 learners rely more heavily on their metalinguistic knowledge and declarative memory, which entails primarily those (not necessarily accurate) rules, conventions and pragmatics that they have consciously learned through explicit teaching, noticing, deduction, and so forth, and that they are able to control to varying degrees. It is neurophysiologically impossible to transform explicit metalinguistic knowledge into implicit linguistic competence, except indirectly through repeated use of the L2 (Hulstijn, 2007; Paradis, 2009). In other words, for Paradis (2009), it is the implicit tallying up of patterns derived from actual L2 use that has the potential to lead to implicit competence acquisition. This is not to say, however, that adult L2 learners can never attain a high or even near-native level of proficiency in an additional language. In fact, '[e]xplicit learning may lead to speeded-up controlled use of a second language (and may even, with repeated practice, *indirectly* lead to the internalization of some components of L2)' (Paradis, 2009: 8). As Paradis argues in a later passage, while the so-called '*normal* acquisition of language, which results in implicit linguistic competence' (Paradis, 2009: 117) appears to be determined by age, 'language can also be learned, using cerebral mechanisms other than those used to acquire implicit linguistic competence, and resulting in conscious knowledge about form, namely metalinguistic knowledge that can be mastered to a high degree of proficiency. Its controlled use can be sufficiently speeded up to be perceived as native-like' (Paradis, 2009: 117–118).

Within the SCT framework for instructional pragmatics, dynamically administered SISs aim to support the acceleration of learners' access to conscious pragmatic knowledge (i.e. concepts and relevant forms) though intervention from a mediator. In other words, there is no claim that implicit acquisition results from mediation. Instead, the objective is to promote consciously controlled performance, or access to declarative pragmatic knowledge, which may eventually be accelerated enough to be functionally equivalent to implicit competence. Figure 6.2 displays a heuristic representation of this process.

As discussed in the preceding section, control over performance in dynamically administered SISs is distributed between the tutor and the learner. Taking account of Paradis' (2009) argument, this is fundamentally about control over *conscious* pragmatic knowledge – the concepts, or meanings, and pragmalinguistic forms that instantiate them. At first, the locus of control is predominately with the tutor, who mediates the learner's performance by intervening when he or she encounters difficulties. With proper graduated and contingent support, however, the locus of control moves to the learner over time. The two curved arrows in Figure 6.2 represent the shift from tutor-controlled to learner-controlled performance (i.e. access to conscious pragmatic knowledge): essentially, as the learner is increasingly capable of accessing his or her pragmatic knowledge in performance, support is withdrawn. As we will see below, this shift is also marked by gains in accuracy and speed of production, which is evidence of Paradis' concept of speeded-up access to conscious metalinguistic knowledge.

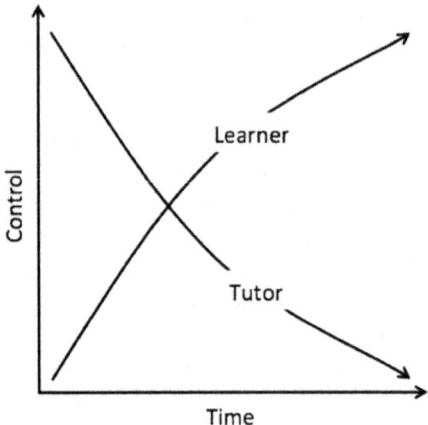

Figure 6.2 Shift in locus of controlled access to pragmatic knowledge during performance

Human Mediation and the Emergence of Controlled Performance

The excerpts of dynamically administered SISs shown in this section illustrate how intervention from the tutor – or human mediation – supported learners in gaining control over pragmalinguistic forms in spoken performance. The availability of human mediation plays a crucial role in the development of performance abilities because it effectively distributes the locus of control over access to conscious pragmatic knowledge between the tutor and the learner (see above). Graduated, contingent assistance that is sensitive to the learner's ZPD enables the learner to take on greater responsibility for performances over time. Development is therefore marked not only by the emergence of independent control, but also – and importantly – by shifts in the amount and quality of support needed during performance.

Diagnosing learners' difficulties and supporting emerging autonomy

The analysis presented below centers on a case study of Mary's developing control over *ne*-absent negative structures during speech production. This case study illustrates how cooperative interaction with the tutor assisted Mary in incorporating the *ne*-absent structure into her productive repertoire and in increasing her control over her performance.

During session 3, Mary elected to use *tu*, *on* and negation without *ne* for the informal scenario in which she and the tutor would be adopting the roles of soon-to-be roommates debating the pros and cons of four apartments they have found. Although Mary had learned that *ne* could be omitted during the previous session (i.e. introduction of concepts and the second appropriateness judgment task of the study), this was the first time she had the opportunity to omit the negative particle during spontaneous speech production. Excerpt 6.2 displays the first negative utterance produced by Mary (line 6), which included *ne* and thus diverged from her plan to omit it, and the resulting opportunity for mediated development. (Mary's negative utterances are set in boldface.)

Excerpt 6.2

1	**Mary:**	+ um. cet + ce + cet appartement est
		um this this this apartment is
2		+ um + le plus loin.=
		um the farthest
3	**Tutor:**	=ah.=
4	**Mary:**	=de campus.
		from campus
5	**Tutor:**	donc euh + on peut pas marcher?
		so uh we can't walk
6	**Mary:**	um ah non. **on ne peut pas** marcher.
		um ah no we cannot walk
7	**Tutor:**	wait- do you want to say on ne peut pas,
		we cannot
8		+ what do you want to say.
9	**Mary:**	<u>oh</u>. + um (5.5) I guess I wan-
10		I'm just saying like we can't walk.=
11	**Tutor:**	=okay,=
12	**Mary:**	=there?
13	**Tutor:**	so what d- so think about that, + a little bit,
14		+ what did you just say,
15	**Mary:**	OH. **on ne pouvons pas**.
		oh we cannot
16	**Tutor:**	mmm,
17	**Mary:**	+++ <u>oh</u>. + **ON** + **peut pas**.=
		oh we can't
18	**Tutor:**	=ah. there you go. + right, + **on peut pas**.
		we can't

19	**Mary:**	**on peut pas**.
		we can't
20	**Tutor:**	on peut pas.
		we can't
21	**Mary:**	okay. so **on peut pas** + uh marcher.
		we can't uh walk
22		+ mais il y a un + what's bus stop?
		but there is a
23	**Tutor:**	un arrête de [bus?
		a bus stop
24	**Mary:**	[un arrête de bus.
		a bus stop

Mary's first negative utterance appears in line 6. Here, she has responded to the tutor's utterance *on peut pas marcher?* 'we can't walk?' (line 5) by repeating a similar structure that differs in two ways. First, it is designed as an answer to a question, signaled by final falling intonation (cf. the tutor's final rising intonation). Second, she includes *ne* where the tutor had omitted it. Although it is clear that Mary has understood the question, as evidenced by her orientation to the preceding utterance as a question and the delivery of an appropriate response, her use of *ne* diverges from her plan to omit it as she had indicated during the rehearsal stage of this scenario.[1]

The mediated learning opportunity began at line 7. The tutor stopped Mary (*wait*) and then asked her if she wanted to say *on ne peut pas*, with slightly rising final intonation, signaling that there was a potential problem with her utterance. After a brief pause (line 8), the tutor rephrased the question as *what do you want to say*. Mary responded by explaining *what* (i.e. the content) she was trying to say (lines 9–12), which is evidence that she had not noticed her use of *ne* but rather oriented to the tutor's question as an indication that there was a problem with the content of her response. In turn, the tutor prompted Mary to consider what she had said in the form of a clarification request (*what did you just say,*; line 14). At this point, Mary recognized that there was an issue with language form (line 15): she produced a change-of-state particle (*oh*) and then reformulated her utterance by changing the verb ending, producing the ungrammatical construction *on ne *pouvons pas*. This is ungrammatical because she used the first-person plural form of the verb with a third person singular pronoun.[2] In line 16, then, the tutor once again signaled that there was a form-related problem by a simple *mmm*, articulated with slightly rising intonation, to which Mary oriented by producing the target form: *on peut pas* (line 17). It should be clear that Mary understood where the problem was because she again produced the particle *oh* – an indication that she had realized something – and then produced emphasis on *on*, a slight pause where *ne* previously was, and then *peut pas*. The appropriateness of this construction was confirmed by the tutor in line 18, where he repeated the phrase, prompting Mary to do the same.

This interaction is important because it served as the initial opportunity for Mary to develop control over her use of verbal negation in French. It should be noted that the assistance provided by the tutor in this excerpt was strategic rather than directive: it pushed Mary to make successive attempts at resolving the problem (i.e. content > verbal morphology > *ne*). Mary's eventual production of the appropriate form was not attributable to Mary alone, but rather to the cooperative interaction[3] between her and the tutor (i.e. *inter*psychological functioning). In other words, Mary was offered just enough support to allow her to assume most of the responsibility for working through the problem.

Excerpt 6.3 provides evidence that Mary began to develop increasing control over *ne*'s presence versus absence following the mediated learning opportunity shown above. The following exchange took place as Mary used verbal negation for the second time (just under two minutes after the first negative construction was used). The tutor, in his role as a future roommate, had suggested finding a third roommate for one of the apartments (lines 1–3), but Mary seemed to hesitate (line 3), to which the tutor oriented by asking if she did not like this idea (line 4). In line 5, then, Mary began to respond with the utterance *je ne suis pas* 'I am not', which included the negative particle *ne*.

Excerpt 6.3

1	**Tutor:**	mais tu sais, + il y a <u>trois</u> chambres. on pourrait peut-être
		but you know there are three bedrooms we could maybe
2		trouver une autre per<u>sonne</u>. + pour partager le loyer.
		find another person to share the rent
3	**Mary:**	oui. um.
		yes um
4	**Tutor:**	tu veux <u>pas</u>¿ ou=
		do you not want to or
5	**Mary:**	=um ++ **je ne suis pas** + umm
		um I am not umm
6	**Tutor:**	hm¿ ((with raised eye brow))
7	**Mary:**	++ ((nods head)) **je suis pas** um I don- I'm not + against¿
		I'm not um
8	**Tutor:**	contre¿
		against
		I'm not

9	**Mary:**	**je suis pas** contre, + um trouver + uh
		I'm not against um finding uh
10		un autre camarade de chambre,
		another roommate
11		mais ++ **je sais pas**. + uh quelqu'un.
		but I don't know uh someone

Evidence for Mary's increasing control over the variation comes in her response to the tutor's *hm¿*, which co-occurred with a raised eyebrow as Mary and the tutor made eye contact (line 6). Mary paused for a moment, then nodded her head once as if to say 'right' or 'oh yeah', before reformulating her utterance as a *ne*-absent structure.

In contrast to the interaction in Excerpt 6.2 (above), here Mary immediately oriented to *ne*'s presence as the problem source in her utterance. Although the tutor still needed to signal that there was a problem, Mary demonstrated increasing self-regulation. More importantly, after receiving lexical assistance with the word *contre* 'against' (lines 7–8), she completed her full response (lines 9–11), which included both a repetition of *je suis pas* 'I am not' (line 9), as well as a new negative construction that excluded *ne*: *je sais pas* 'I don't know' (line 11). Although her choice of verb was inappropriate in this instance (the verb *connaître* 'to know/be familiar with' should have been used), this example nevertheless provides evidence that Mary was increasingly coming to control her use/omission of *ne* in spontaneous speech. In addition, Mary produced another six tokens of *ne*-absent negation during the remainder of the scenario, but zero instances of *ne* presence. In the formal scenario that followed, Mary planned to use *ne*, which she did without hesitation the two times she produced a negative utterance, which provides further evidence of her developing control over the variation. In other words, the data point to an emerging ability to control both the presence and omission of *ne*.

The scenarios that occurred two weeks later (session 5) simultaneously show Mary's continued ability to use and omit *ne* as well as her loss of control when things became complicated. In the informal scenario, Mary produced only one negative utterance, from which she omitted *ne*, yet in the more formal scenario (arranging an office hours meeting with a professor) Mary demonstrated some variation. She had planned on omitting *ne*; however, she twice produced a *ne*-present construction. Excerpt 6.4 shows the first of these examples.

Excerpt 6.4

1	**Tutor:**	oui¿
		yes¿

2	**Mary:**	j'ai des questions um. ++ uh pour + l'ex- l'examen?
I have some questions um for the exam
3	**Tutor:**	ah d'accord. d'accord. euh ++ bon j'ai pas beaucoup de temps
ah okay okay uh right I don't have a lot of time
4		+ maintenant, euh + mais euh est-ce que vous pouvez revenir
right now uh but uh can you come back
5		peut-être euh + aujourd'hui à deux heures? + parce que j'ai
maybe uh today at two o'clock because I have
6		mes heures de permanence de deux heures à trois heures.
my office hours from two to three
7	**Mary:**	(4.5) ((silently rereading scenario description))
8		um + **je ne suis pas-** + er **je suis pas** + libre?
um I am not er I'm not free

Mary and the tutor were attempting to arrange a meeting that fit into their respective schedules (indicated on the scenario descriptions). The tutor explained that he held office hours that day from 2:00 to 3:00 in the afternoon (lines 3–6). Mary turned to her scenario description card to reread part of it (most likely her schedule) (line 7), and then in response began to tell the tutor that she was not free at the available time (line 8). Mary's first negative utterance included *ne* (i.e. *je ne suis pas-*); however, she stopped and corrected herself, producing the construction *je suis pas + libre?* 'I'm not free'. Although she initially used *ne*, this example does show that Mary was capable of self-regulating her performance, or at least of noticing when she diverged from her planned performance and repairing the problem.

The next example, however, shows where Mary's independent control began to falter. In the lines preceding this fragment of the interaction, Mary had demonstrated difficulty in remembering her schedule and other pieces of information provided on the scenario description card (see also Excerpt 6.4, above). In line 2 of Excerpt 6.5, below, she was looking at the description of her role as she responded to the tutor's question from line 1.

Excerpt 6.5

1	**Tutor:**	est-ce que vous pouvez venir me voir euh =
can you come see me uh
2	**Mary:**	=ah oui. oui. + **je n'ai pas** de + <u>classe</u>. +++
ah yes yes I do not have class
3		je suis libre + tout ((looking at scenario description))
I'm free all
4	**Tutor:**	mhm, + go back,

5	**Mary:**	++ <u>oh</u>. **j'ai pas** + de classe.
		oh I don't have class
6	**Tutor:**	so j'ai pas de classe. say it,
		I don't have class
7	**Mary:**	**j'ai pas** de classe. =
		I don't have class
8	**Tutor:**	= j'ai pas de classe.
		I don't have class
9	**Mary:**	um je suis libre + um tout le jour.
		um I'm free um all day

Mary demonstrated some difficulty delivering her response in line 2, as indicated by the multiple pauses in this turn. However, this was likely not a linguistic problem as much as it is one related to cognitive overload or the division of her attention: she was consulting the scenario description as a means of remembering her schedule, which was the content of her response.

The result was that she momentarily lost control over her use/omission of *ne* when she uttered *je n'ai pas de* + *classe*. 'I do not have class' (line 2), a *ne*-present structure. During the long pause that followed, the tutor can be seen on the video looking at Mary with a raised eyebrow to bring her attention to this; however, Mary continues to consult the scenario description and to complete her utterance, at which point the tutor verbally intervened (line 3). Mary clearly required very little support from the tutor, who only needed to say *mhm,* +*go back,* (line 3). Mary hesitated slightly (cf. the pause in line 4), but then recognized where the problem was and revised her utterance. This excerpt therefore illustrates the extent to which Mary controlled the variation: although she could omit *ne* consistently (as demonstrated during other scenarios), this control faltered with increasing cognitive demands related to the task itself, where she reverted to the more habituated forms present in her repertoire (i.e. in this case, *ne*-present negation). This finding articulates with Paradis' (2009) theory of the procedural and declarative determinants of adult SLA in that Mary relies heavily on her declarative memory capacities (e.g. remembering to omit the *ne*) during performance. When other cognitive demands were present, she reaccessed an earlier, and more habituated, learned form (see also Tarone, 1988; van Compernolle & Williams, 2012b).

Learners' awareness of performance difficulties

Another consequence of dynamically administered SISs for learners is awareness of their own performance difficulties. This is perhaps unsurprising given DA's focus on supporting the development of performance abilities, or the executive function, by mediating the orientation and control processes involved in performance (Poehner, 2008). It is also congruent with Paradis' (2009) claim that adult L2 learners rely heavily on declarative memory systems: L2 performance development is marked by faster access to, and more systematic or accurate use of, conscious knowledge the language learners are appropriating. Within the SCT framework, we would expect to find evidence not only of conscious knowledge of pragmatics, on the one hand, and ability for use in performance, on the other, but of an emerging unification of the two. While the unification of knowledge and ability for use may be largely internal, and therefore inaccessible from the outside, evidence of it may manifest when a learner's performance falters – for instance, when a learner produces an infelicitous pragmalinguistic form. This is apparent in Excerpt 6.6, where Susan's performance (i.e. use of second-person pronouns) does not align with her orientation in the final SIS of the present study.

Excerpt 6.6

1 **Tutor**: ah bonjour Susan. comment allez-vous.
oh hello Susan how are you [vous]
2 **Susan**: ehh + pas mal. **et toi** ¿
not bad and you [tu]
3 **Tutor**: ((looks at Susan with raised eye brow))
4 **Susan**: mm et <u>vous</u>. ((in a low, serious tone))
mm and you [vous]
5 **Both**: ((laughing))
6 **Susan**: <u>GEEZ</u>.
7 **Tutor**: uhhuh, ((laughing))
8 **Susan**: <u>AHHH</u>.
9 **Tutor**: ((laughs)) donc. + moi ça va, merci. ((scenario moves forward))
so me fine thanks

The tutor, playing the role of a work-study program director in Montpellier, France, asked Susan how she was doing, using a *vous* form in his question (line 1). In her response, Susan produced the tag *et toi¿* (line 2), which was both incongruent with the tutor's initiation of *vous* and divergent from Susan's own orientation to the scenario. Following the tutor's glance at Susan with a raised eyebrow (line 3), she recognized that she had diverged from her stated plan and, in a low, serious tone, corrected herself, this time using the *vous* form of the tag question (line 4). During the debriefing that followed the performance, Susan immediately addressed this example.

Excerpt 6.7

1	**Susan:**	okay. so I <u>screwed up</u> right in the beginning. I was like *et <u>toi</u>?* ((laughs))
2	**Tutor:**	uhhuh ((laughs)) you don't get the job.
3	**Susan:**	<u>crap</u>. um probably you get so used like <u>drilled</u> in your <u>head</u>.
4		like *ça va? ça va bien. et <u>toi</u>?* (('how are you?' 'fine' 'and you?'))
5	**Tutor:**	mhm
6	**Susan:**	so it was just like it wasn't + that I wasn't <u>think</u>ing about it,
7		it was out of habit. it just + <u>came out</u>.
8	**Tutor:**	right.
9	**Susan:**	so <u>that</u>'s + going to be something I have to think about.
10		[...] I'm <u>so so so</u> used to being like *et toi?* (xxx)
11		I've been used to saying that.

Susan's account of why she produced the *tu* form rather than the *vous* form pointed to her previous experience learning French, where the tag form *et toi?* is much more frequent than its *vous* alternative, most notably in greeting sequences. Thus, while more novel (i.e. less autonomous) sequences may be consciously controlled, there is evidence that other sequences remain more habitual, despite gains made in conceptual knowledge. Nonetheless, the fact that Susan was becoming aware that certain sequences might be habitual in her own discourse constituted a step toward progressively coming to control them.

Leon similarly commented on the relative ease with which he was able to control the various pragmalinguistic forms during the debriefing of an informal SIS during session 5 of the study (Excerpt 6.8). During the performance, he had been successful in using *tu* consistently as well as in systematically omitting the *ne* from verbal negation. His performance faltered, however, the first time he attempted to use a first-person plural pronoun – that is, he used *nous* rather than *on* as he had planned.

Excerpt 6.8

1	**Tutor:**	so. ++ what did you think.
2	**Leon:**	uh + I guess, I don't know. the <u>*tu*</u> is like again. very easy for me to use
3	**Tutor:**	uhhuh
4	**Leon:**	and I think <u>*pas*</u> even is like I'm like slowly beginning
5		to be able to drop that like pretty easily.
6	**Tutor:**	mhm
7	**Leon:**	but again like the *on* versus *nous*, it's still like the-
8		<u>*nous*</u>'s like <u>still</u> very much ingrained in my head.

Leon's awareness of his performance difficulties – which were in fact accurate self-assessments – was related to his developing ability to control his performance. Control requires consciousness, and an awareness of what one is doing (execution) and why one is doing it (orientation). As we see in Leon's debriefing, he was aware that *on* was more difficult to control because *nous* was the more 'ingrained' form. Thus, like Susan's use of the tag *et toi?*, Leon's faltering performance was due to his reaccessing a more habituated form, and his awareness of this fact was evidence of increasing control over the link between his conscious pragmatic knowledge and actual performance. It is important to note that, after the infelicitous use of *nous*, Leon's performance was remediated by the tutor. Leon then went on to produce three more tokens of the *on* variant without support, suggesting that he was in fact able to control his performance when attention was brought to his performance difficulty.

Orientation, Execution and Control

In the preceding section, I focused on the qualities of human mediation (i.e. support from the tutor) and the emergence of controlled pragmalinguistic performance in dynamically administered SISs. In this section, I now turn to an overview of the learners' abilities as a group, and the relationship between the orientation, execution and control functions.

Orientations to scenarios

As a reminder to the reader, participants discussed with the tutor their understanding of the relationship between the interlocutors depicted in the scenario, a desired way to present themselves in the scenario, and how these could be shown/accomplished through language during the rehearsal stage of SISs. In short, this rehearsal stage aimed to allow the participants to develop a plan of action for their use of sociopragmatic and sociolinguistic variants. Table 6.1 displays a brief description of the context of each scenario performed during the study. Tables 6.2 and 6.3 provide each participant's planned performance (i.e. orientation) for the informal and formal scenarios.

As these data indicate, the participants categorically agreed on the appropriateness of *tu* in informal scenarios and *vous* in formal scenarios for all strategic interactions, including prior to the start of the enrichment program (session 1). None of the participants indicated a preference regarding the pronouns *on* and *nous* or verbal negation during the first session. This should not be a surprise given the lack of awareness about this type of variation as evidenced by the preenrichment LAIs and AJQs analyzed above. Beginning in session 3 (the first pair of scenarios after the introduction of

172 Sociocultural Theory and L2 Instructional Pragmatics

Table 6.1 Brief description of scenarios

Session	Formality	Context
Session 1	Informal	Inviting a new acquaintance (peer) to a party
	Formal	Office hours meeting with a professor
Session 3	Informal	Roommates discussing the pros and cons of several new apartments
	Formal	Calling a travel agent in France
Session 5	Informal	Friends deciding where to eat lunch
	Formal	Office hours meeting with a professor
Session 6	Informal	Inviting a new acquaintance (peer) to dinner
	Formal	Telephone job interview

Table 6.2 Planned performance in informal scenarios

	Session 1			Session 3			Session 5			Session 6		
	T/V	O/N	Ne	T/V	O/N	Ne	T/V	O/N	Ne	T/V	O/N	Ne
Nikki	T	?	?	T	O	—	T	O	—	T	O	—
Susan	T	?	?	T	O	—	T	O	—	T	O	—
Leon	T	?	?	T	O	—	T	O	—	T	O	—
Pierre	T	?	?	T	O	—	T	O	—	T	O	—
Mary	T	?	?	T	O	—	T	O	—	T	O	—
Stephanie	T	?	?	T	O	—	T	O	—	T	O	—
Laurie	T	?	?	T	O	—	T	O	—	T	O	—
Conrad	T	?	?	T	O	—	T	O	—	T	O	—

Note: T, *tu*; V, *vous*; O, *on*; N, *nous*; —, *ne* omission; +, *ne* presence; ?, no response.

Table 6.3 Planned performance in formal scenarios

	Session 1			Session 3			Session 5			Session 6		
	T/V	O/N	Ne	T/V	O/N	Ne	T/V	O/N	Ne	T/V	O/N	Ne
Nikki	V	?	?	V	O	-	V	O	-	V	N	+
Susan	V	?	?	V	O	-	V	O	-	V	N	+
Leon	V	?	?	V	O	-	V	O	-	V	N	+
Pierre	V	?	?	V	N	+	V	O	-	V	N	+
Mary	V	?	?	V	N	+	V	O	-	V	N	+
Stephanie	V	?	?	V	O	-	V	O	-	V	O	-
Laurie	V	?	?	V	N	+	V	N	+	V	N	+
Conrad	V	?	?	V	N	+	V	O	-	V	N	+

Note: T, *tu*; V, *vous*; O, *on*; N, *nous*; —, *ne* omission; +, *ne* presence; ?, no response.

the concept-based materials), however, the participants all judged the use of *on* and absence of *ne* to be appropriate for the informal scenarios. The formal scenarios proved to be somewhat more ambiguous. For instance, the participants were equally divided with regard to stylistic appropriateness during session 3 (calling a French travel agent to make a hotel reservation), while session 5 (meeting a professor during office hours) was overwhelmingly judged to be at least moderately informal and session 6 (telephone interview for a work-study program) was overwhelmingly judged to be formal.

The reasons for this variability were many, but they all essentially related to the participants' interpretations of the scenarios, including the quality of the relationship between the interlocutors, the type of activity they are to engage in and how they wanted to present themselves in such situations. Leon, for example, explained that informal variants were appropriate in session 3 (calling a travel agent) because the scenario represented a type of activity in which he was comfortable presenting himself as 'some informal random guy' while at the same time maintaining a degree of social distance through the use of *vous*.

Excerpt 6.9

```
1  Leon:   in terms of the other ones though. ((on/nous, ne))
2          I don- I don't know- I don't think that there's like
3          a + huge need to be like + overly formal. and use ne,=
4  Tutor:  =so what do y- so how do you want to come off.
5  Leon:   well + I guess uh just like. you know. = s- s-
6          a + nice + just kind of some informal. random guy.
7          who's calling. I don't know.
8  Tutor:  okay.
```

By contrast, Mary decided to use the more formal variants based on her understanding of the potential negative consequences of the *tee-shirt-and-jeans* style of self-presentation in such a situation, namely being duped into something because she could be perceived as naïve.

Excerpt 6.10

```
1  Tutor:  do you want to be tee-shirt-and-jeans? or suit-and-tie.
2  Mary:   + um ++ WELL I guess I wouldn't want to be taken
3          as someone who like could be duped into + like +
4          I don't want to sound um naïve,
5  Tutor:  okay,
6  Mary:   by sounding too casual, + or too young, + or too +
7  Tutor:  okay.
```

For session 5, Laurie was the only participant who believed that more formal variants were most appropriate, the others deciding that an office hours meeting was more casual, despite the distance and power factors related to using the *vous* form of address. As Laurie explained:

Excerpt 6.11

1	**Laurie:**	((reads scenario)) um + with the professor
2		I woul- it's a suit-and-tie situa¿=I would want to
3		come off as a suit-and-tie situation¿
4	**Tutor:**	okay
5	**Laurie:**	um + to show re<u>spect</u> + and just + um yeah.
6	**Tutor:**	okay
7	**Laurie:**	so I would use <u>*vous*</u>, *ne* <u>*pas*</u>, and + <u>*nous*</u>. I guess.
8	**Tutor:**	okay.

Laurie's orientation therefore reflected her interpretation of an office hours meeting as a situation in which she preferred to present herself as *suit-and-tie* (i.e. more formally).

As noted, all of the participants except Stephanie judged session 6 (job interview) to be formal. She explained that, while *vous* was certainly appropriate for creating social distance, she would opt for the more informal stylistic variants, *on* and *ne*'s absence, to sound more welcoming, an important aspect of her own personality and, in her view, a trait desirable for the job positions available (i.e. waiting staff in a restaurant or front desk receptionist at a hotel).

Excerpt 6.12

1	**Steph:**	I don- cuz at the <u>same</u> time I would want to <u>show</u>
2		my perso<u>na</u>lity¿=cuz like it's a + it's a program +
3		it's like a <u>wai</u>tress and a or a front desk¿
4		so you're gonna need to be like + welcoming¿
5	**Tutor:**	okay.
6	**Steph:**	so I wouldn- I wouldn't wanna necessarily use
7		*nous* and *ne* *pas*.=cuz that would be like + too stiff.
8		and like for me. if I were + (xxx) in this <u>role</u>. I
9		wouldn't wanna be like + I would wanna show that
10		I'm more laid back, I'm not like + <u>uppity</u> or whatever.
11		so prob- so <u>I</u> would probably use *on* and *pas*.
12	**Tutor:**	okay. + so *vous* for the + relationship. [distance.]
13	**Steph:**	[mhm]
14		and then *on* and *pas* to show like + my personality.

15   I guess.
16 **Tutor:** okay.

The variation in interpretations of appropriate levels of discourse is therefore indicative of each individual's unique perspective on which meanings they wanted to produce in interaction. Therefore, while some choices may have broken with conventional patterns of use, the participants' decisions were grounded in a real understanding of the meaning potential of the pragmalinguistic variants. In what follows, we will explore the extent to which these orientations were successfully executed and controlled.

Execution of the orientation

Group results regarding performance (i.e. execution of the orientation) during scenarios are presented below. The figures provide a snapshot of the group's development across time. Overall, the results indicate that the learners became increasingly able to control their use of both informal and formal language variants according to their orientations to the scenarios. Most notably, the figures indicate a rise in the use of conventionally informal sociostylistic variants (i.e. *on* 'we' and negation without *ne*), which aligns with these learners' orientations to the scenarios displayed above.

To tally the number of occurrences of each language variant produced by the learners in the scenarios, the following methods were used:

(1) All morphologically marked tokens of *tu* and *vous* produced by learners were identified in the corpus. These included (see Kinginger, 2008; van Compernolle *et al.*, 2011):

Subject pronouns
Examples: *si **tu** veux venir* 'if you want to come ...'; *qu'est-ce que **vous** avez dit?* 'what do you say?'.

Direct/indirect object pronouns
Examples: *je voulais **t'**inviter à notre fête* 'I wanted to invited you to our party'; *j'ai besoin de **vous** parler* 'I need to speak to you'.

Strong forms used in
  Tags
  Examples: *et **toi**?* 'and you?'; *et **vous**?* 'and you?'.

  Subject doubling/dislocation
  Examples: ***toi** tu préfères celui-là?* 'you you prefer that one?'; *vous voulez voyager ensemble **vous** et votre amie?*'you want to travel together you and your friend?'.

Prepositional phrases
Examples: *c'est un ami **à toi**?* 'is it a friend of yours?'; ***chez vous**?* '(at) your place?'.

Determiner phrases
Examples: ***ton/votre** ami* 'your friend'.

Imperative verb forms
Examples: ***regarde** celui-ci* 'look-[*tu*] at this one'; ***revenez** me voir demain après-midi* 'come back-[*vous*] to see me tomorrow afternoon'.

(2) All instances of the pronouns *on* and *nous* were identified in the corpus. However, only subject pronouns with first-person plural reference (i.e. tokens in which the two pronouns are in fact variable; see van Compernolle, 2008b) were included in the analysis. That is, tokens of *nous* used as object pronouns and strong pronouns or in prepositional phrases were excluded from the analysis, as were tokens of *on* having an indefinite third-person referent (i.e. the equivalent of English *one*).

(3) All instances of negation were identified in the corpus. However, only verbal negation (i.e. negation of a verb phrase) is considered here, since *ne* can variably be present or absent only in this context (see van Compernolle, 2008a). In other words, tokens of elliptical negation (i.e. negative utterances not including a verb phrase such as *pas vraiment* 'not really') were excluded from the analysis.

Because the scenarios were dynamically administered, a certain number of tokens of interest produced by learners were excluded from the final analysis. While giving assistance, the tutor often modeled the utterance for the learners to repeat. These repeated tokens produced by learners following the researcher's model have been excluded from the figures presented below. Thus, tokens included in the final analysis include only those produced during the execution of the scenario itself, which excludes inserted pedagogical sequences in which learners are instructed to repeat a phrase modeled by the tutor (see van Compernolle, forthcoming, on the concept of mediation sequences in dynamically administered SISs).

Table 6.4 provides total figures for appropriate *tu/vous* use. The term appropriate is used here to refer to the use of *tu* in informal scenarios and *vous* in formal scenarios. Appropriateness judgments are possible because of the categorical agreement among participants across time about which pronoun should be used as evidenced by their planned performance (see above). It is also noteworthy that the participants' appropriateness judgments during the rehearsal stage all happened to align with the sociolinguistic conventions of European French.

Table 6.4 Group results for appropriate *tu/vous* use in scenarios

	Informal (T)		Formal (V)		Total	
Session	n	%	n	%	n	%
Session 1	66/72	91.7	16/21	76.2	82/93	88.2
Session 3	25/25	100.0	22/28	78.6	47/53	88.7
Session 5	21/21	100.0	17/18	94.4	38/39	97.4
Session 6	53/53	100.0	10/12	83.3	63/65	96.9

As these figures show, the participants demonstrated some difficulty in using the appropriate pronoun consistently during session 1, where there were several instances of mixed *tu/vous* use. However, following the start of the enrichment program, the participants moved to categorical consistency in the use of *tu* in informal scenarios. The use of *vous* in more formal scenarios, however, proved to be more difficult. Although the data indicate increasing stability after the start of the enrichment program, there were still a number of infelicitous uses of *tu* forms. The inappropriate *tu* form in session 5 and the two in session 6, where we see the greatest consistency of appropriate *vous* use, were used in the tag question *et toi?* 'and you?' Recent corpus-driven research (van Compernolle et al., 2011) has suggested that certain supraword constructions such as tags may be memorized by rote as (semi)autonomous sequences, which aligns with the results of this study. A number of the participants in fact noted that the tag *et toi?* 'and you?' came to them more automatically, even though they knew that the alternative *et vous?* 'and you?' was appropriate.

Table 6.5 provides group figures for the use of *on* in variation with *nous* 'we'. Observed frequencies (*n*) and percentages (%) refer to the number of *on* tokens used out of the number of contexts in which either *on* or *nous* could have been used for first-person plural reference. Table 6.6 displays group figures for the absence of *ne* in verbal negation. Observed frequencies and percentages refer to the number of times *ne* was omitted from negation out of the number of contexts in which *ne* could have been present or absent (i.e.

Table 6.5 Group results for *on* use in scenarios

	Informal		Formal		Total	
Session	n	%	n	%	n	%
Session 1	0/17	0	0/19	0	0/36	0
Session 3	35/39	89.7	19/48	39.6	54/87	62.1
Session 5	15/16	93.8	3/4	75.0	18/20	90.0
Session 6	18/23	78.3	1/8	12.5	19/31	61.3

Table 6.6 Group results for *ne* absence in scenarios

Session	Informal		Formal		Total	
	n	%	n	%	n	%
Session 1	1/8	11.1	0/13	0	1/21	4.8
Session 3	34/45	75.6	6/18	33.3	40/63	63.5
Session 5	23/30	76.7	10/16	62.5	33/46	71.7
Session 6	10/14	71.4	2/15	13.3	12/29	41.4

negative verb phrases). It should be kept in mind that all eight participants indicated that informal variants were appropriate for the informal scenarios during sessions 3, 5 and 6, whereas appropriate judgments regarding the formal situations were variable: participants were evenly split between formal and informal variants during session 3, while session 5 was overwhelmingly judged to be more informal and session 6 to be more formal (see above for the analysis of orientations to the situations).

The results for the informal scenarios show a dramatic shift in performance starting in session 3, where *on* was used in the vast majority of contexts where either *on* or *nous* could have been used, and *ne* was omitted at very high rates from negated verb phrases. This trend continued for the remainder of the study as indicated by the high rates of *on* use and *ne* omission in sessions 5 and 6. Nonetheless, there was still some variation – in all sessions, there is at least one instance of *nous* and *ne* presence despite planned performance. This is indicative of increasing controlled use of the informal variants, but that the more formal, standard variants that were taught as invariable forms most likely remain more habitual for these learners (see also van Compernolle & Williams, 2011a, 2012b) and required mediation during the performance of the scenario.

In the formal situations, there was also an increase in the total number of *on* tokens and *ne* absence across time. Although individual results will be discussed in detail below, it is appropriate to tease out some of these patterns here since there was variation in orientations to the more formal scenarios, which resulted in variable appropriate performance (i.e. in line with planned performance) among the participants. As noted above, the participants were evenly split in appropriateness judgments during session 3, with Nikki, Susan, Leon and Stephanie opting to use the more informal stylistic variants and Pierre, Mary, Laurie and Conrad deciding that the more formal variants were appropriate to use. Pierre, Mary, Laurie and Conrad categorically produced the more formal *nous* ($n = 26/26$; 100%) and *ne...pas* ($n = 11/11$; 100%). Such consistency should not be surprising since the more formal, standard variants were the ones with which the learners were most familiar. However, Nikki, Susan, Leon and Stephanie were also consistent in their use of the informal variants *on* (*n* = 19/22; 86.4%) and Ø...*pas* (*n* = 6/7; 85.7%). Taken together with the results of the informal scenarios, it appears that even after only one enrichment session, the learners were able to control their use of both formal and informal language variants. This conclusion is supported by the relatively consistent use of informal variants in session 5 and formal variants in session 6, which were overwhelmingly judged to be more informal and more formal, respectively.

Control over executive function

As the figures presented above have indicated, the learners increasingly incorporated informal sociostylistic variants into their speech over time, and they also demonstrated greater control over their performances. Support provided during dynamically administered SISs assisted learners in executing their orientations to the scenarios – that is, putting their plan of action into practice and controlling (i.e. monitoring and evaluating) their performances in relation to the orientation.

Figures 6.3, 6.4 and 6.5 display control scores for learners' performances in informal scenarios, formal scenarios, and informal and formal scenarios combined, respectively. Control scores represent the degree to which learners' performances aligned with their orientations, calculated as a simple ratio:

$$\text{Score} = \frac{\text{Occurrences of planned variant}}{\text{Total possible contexts}}$$

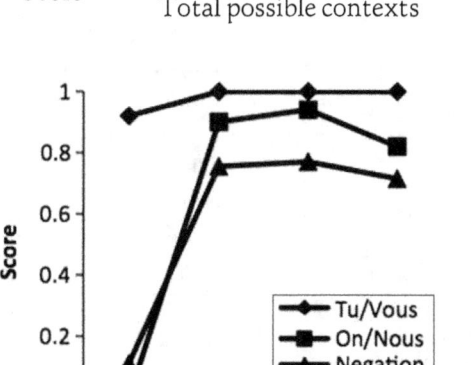

Figure 6.3 Control scores for informal scenarios

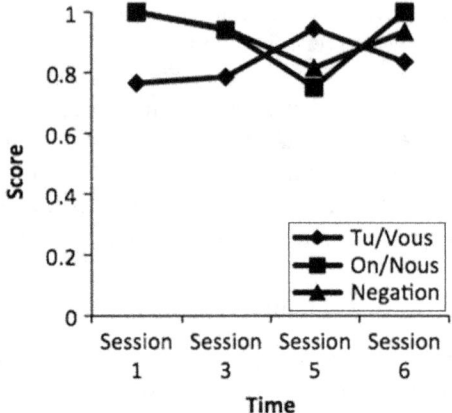

Figure 6.4 Control scores for formal scenarios

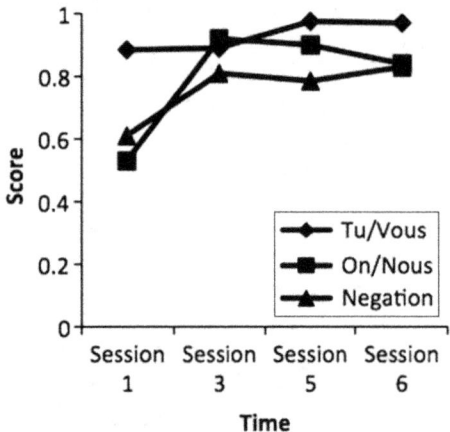

Figure 6.5 Combined control scores

Control scores therefore reflect learner-selected appropriate pragmalinguistic form use. Because of the dynamic nature of SIS administration, however, not all uses of an appropriate pragmalinguistic form were linked to a learner's independent control. As such, mediated pragmalinguistic performances (i.e. tokens of a variant produced with support from the tutor) were separated out from the tallies and assigned a half point in order to avoid skewing the scores. Thus, while such instances certainly count in the scores, they have less relative weight in comparison to uses of pragmalinguistic variants produced independently.

It should also be noted that scores for session 1 – that is, preenrichment – were calculated on the basis of conventionally appropriate language use since none of the learners indicated a preference for *on* versus *nous* 'we' or the presence versus absence of *ne* in verbal negation. Low scores for the informal scenario in session 1 reflect a lack of awareness of the informal forms, while high scores for the formal scenarios reflect the fact that the formal forms were the only ones in the learners' productive repertoires. Overall, the scores indicate a good level of control over performance across time. While there are certainly ups and downs, which are to be expected as learners were appropriating new forms into their productive repertoire with support from the tutor, control scores remained high in sessions 3, 5 and 6, following the start of the enrichment program. In session 6, control scores for negation and *on/nous* in informal scenarios (i.e. *ne* omission and *on* use) as well as scores for *tu/vous* (i.e. *vous* use) in formal scenarios wane to some degree, however, as support was withdrawn during the postenrichment SISs.

These difficulties – or inconsistencies in executing and controlling performance – were isolated to a few individuals. Pierre demonstrated considerable difficulty in remembering to omit *ne* during session 6 (three instances of infelicitous use of the *ne...pas* structure and only one token of *ne* omission), and Susan also used a *ne*-present structure once. Pierre also used *nous* 'we' twice when he had planned to use the more everyday variant *on*, and Leon and Mary each produced one instance of an infelicitous *nous*. As for the drop in *vous* control scores, this is accounted for by Susan and Conrad each using the tag *et toi?* 'and you?' once, which equated to about 17% of the group's total *tu/vous* tokens in session 6's formal scenario, thus somewhat skewing the figures negatively. It should, however, be borne in mind that development does not proceed in a straightforward and linear manner. As such, the isolated inconsistencies that occurred when support was being withdrawn should not be interpreted as a loss of effect over time, but as evidence that certain learners were still struggling to unlearn the more fixed or habituated forms resulting from their previous learning, even though they had made progress at the orientation stage.

Conclusion

The focus of this chapter was on the role of dynamically administered SISs in creating opportunities for the development of learners' pragmatic performance abilities. In contrast to more traditional assessments of speaking abilities in general and of pragmatic performance in particular, human mediation – that is, support from the tutor – was made available to learners not simply as corrective feedback to scaffold the performance itself, but as development-oriented assistance aimed at mediating all three stages of the formation of mental actions (Galperin, 1989, 1992; Poehner, 2008 for DA; Negueruela, 2003 for concept-based instruction): orientation, execution and control.

Development of pragmatic performance abilities therefore consists of learners becoming better able to plan (orientation) their performance (execution), and to monitor and evaluate their performance online (control). Because SISs were dynamically administered, the control function was distributed between the learner and the tutor, with the goal being to support the learner in progressively taking on greater responsibility for control. As we saw in Mary's case, DA procedures enabled the tutor to simultaneously diagnose her emerging capacities through intervention and to promote her continued growth. Mary demonstrated increasing control over the *ne*-absent negative structure; however, this control momentarily broke down during the final SIS, when she was confronted with non-performance-related cognitive demands (i.e. remembering task details). This is an important dimension of Mary's overall developmental profile because it shows the extent to which she was able to control her performance. Another important aspect of SISs was learners' emerging awareness of their own performance difficulties. Although learners may not always be able to fully control their performance, their awareness of this fact constitutes evidence of development of the control function: they are able to recognize and repair difficulties with little or no support from a human mediator. The quantitative figures provided an overall snapshot of learners' performances across time, documenting evidence of the incorporation of new pragmalinguistic forms into their productive repertoires as well as solid gains in their ability to control their performances. It should also be noted that, in the present study, SISs were specifically designed as tasks targeting control over linguistic performance, based on choices made in advance (i.e. during the planning stage). Accordingly, the performance stage did not entail the online application of concepts during language use, as one reviewer rightly pointed out. There is certainly room for improvement here (see Chapter 7), but it remains important to recognize that practice and control in implementing choices during performance is an important – though perhaps 'mechanistic' – dimension of L2 development.

Altogether, the findings reported above offer evidence that dynamically administered SISs assist learners' in accelerating (cf. *speeded up* in Paradis, 2009) access to their conscious pragmatic knowledge during performance. This is a crucial dimension of the SCT framework for instructional pragmatics, which is predicated on Vygotskian educational praxis – that is, the unification of knowledge and practical ability. In concluding this book in the next chapter, we revisit the dialectical relationship between knowledge and practice in an attempt to construct a future for Vygotskian approaches to L2 instructional pragmatics.

Notes

(1) During the rehearsal stage of the scenario, Mary and the tutor discussed which sociolinguistic variants would be appropriate to use. Mary decided that omitting *ne*, using *on*, and addressing her interlocutor with *tu* were the most appropriate choices. As such, she indicated that she would try to use those variants during the performance of the scenario.
(2) Recall that *on* always occurs with a singular third-person verb form, even when it is used for first-person plural reference (see Chapter 2).
(3) *Cooperative* interaction here refers to the fact that the tutor and Mary were *co*-operating, i.e. collectively working together to develop control over the variant (see Poehner & van Compernolle, 2011, on different frames of interaction in DA).

7 The Future of Vygotskian Approaches to Instructional Pragmatics

Introduction

To recall the opening lines of Chapter 1, my purpose in writing this book was to construct a framework for engaging in second language (L2) instructional pragmatics from the perspective of Vygotskian cultural-historical psychology, or sociocultural theory of mind (SCT) as it is more commonly known in applied linguistics and L2 acquisition research (SLA) (Lantolf & Thorne, 2006). The framework is grounded in a commitment to educational praxis (Vygotsky, 1997), wherein theory and practice inform each other in a dialectical relationship. This holds at the level of the conceptualization of the framework as such as well as at the more specific level of pedagogical activity carried out with learners: the framework emerges out of the dialectical unity of theory (e.g. SCT, pragmatics) and practice (e.g. teaching experience), and the pedagogical tasks and their administration within the framework in turn aim to unite theoretical (conceptual) knowledge of pragmatics and practical (performance) abilities in learners as they develop their pragmatic abilities.

The basic tenet of the SCT framework for L2 instructional pragmatics described in this book is that L2 development, including pragmatic development, is fundamentally a conceptual process. Culturally constructed concepts mediate cognition. Therefore, learning an L2 entails the appropriation, or internalization/personalization, of new concepts and/or modifying existing conceptual knowledge in relation to the linguistic means available in the L2. The SCT framework places concepts – meanings – squarely at the center of pedagogy (Negueruela, 2008), with the ultimate goal of supporting learners in mapping meanings onto forms. This is a reversal of more traditional approaches to instructed SLA in general and instructional pragmatics in particular where the emphasis has been on mapping forms (and functions) onto meanings.

The study reported on throughout this book drew on Galperin's (1989, 1992) theory of the formation of mental actions and his proposal for systemic-theoretical instruction. Recall that, for Galperin, mental actions consist of three processes: orientation, execution and control. The orientation process is the plan to be carried out in the execution, or performance, and the control process is responsible for monitoring and evaluating the execution in relation to the orientation. Thus, the orientation is central in Galperin's theory: the cultural tools available to learners as bases for orientation determine the quality of their achievements (Stetsenko & Arievitch, 2010). Consequently, his approach to pedagogy – systemic-theoretical instruction – emphasizes the development of coherent, systematic orientating bases for action through the internalization of scientific concepts (see Chapter 1). The SCT framework for L2 instructional pragmatics therefore compels us to search for appropriate pragmatic and sociolinguistic concepts (meanings) as the basis for instruction rather than the forms or functions that have traditionally guided research and practice in this domain. To be sure, forms (e.g. structures) and functions (e.g. speech acts) are important – they are the means by which concepts are instantiated in concrete communicative activity. In the SCT framework, they also serve the pedagogical function of illustrating how the concepts that learners are appropriating play out in actual language use.

As explained in Chapter 2, the SCT framework conceptualizes pragmatics as mediated action. Language use accomplishes social actions (functions), which are mediated by the particular pragmalinguistic resources (forms) available to speakers. The choice of one pragmalinguistic resource over another is in turn mediated by a speaker's sociopragmatic knowledge (meaning potential). In order to teach this basic principle to L2 learners, I have argued that Silverstein's (2003) concepts of orders of indexicality can be used as a leading concept to guide learners through a quasi-investigation (Davydov, 2004) of the pragmatics of the language they are learning. Silverstein's tripartite model of indexical meaning (i.e. the social meanings that language forms point to) encompassing conventions (first order), local social meaning (second order), and supra-local, ideological meaning (third order) offers a powerful way of understanding language in general and pragmatics in particular as a fluid indexical field (Eckert, 2008) in which social meaning is not fixed but highly malleable. I also proposed three subconcepts – self-presentation, social distance and power – aimed at guiding learners to an understanding of how indexicality works and of the pragmalinguistic practices that point to the indexical meanings available in the languaculture (Agar, 1994). The SCT framework is also meant to embrace the uniqueness of individuals, recognizing learners as people with diverse histories and potentials for internalizing/personalizing the concepts in ways that are personally relevant and significant to their own lives (see Chapter 3).

The pedagogical program illustrated in this book consisted of three specific types of tasks intended to lead to the internalization of the concepts, including learners' abilities to use the concepts to guide their use of French pragmalinguistic resources. Monologic and dialogic verbalized reflections (Chapter 4) served to render internal cognitive activity visible through externalization in language, so that existing pragmatic knowledge could be contemplated and revised in light of new ways of thinking that were mediated by the concepts. Appropriateness judgment tasks (Chapter 5) provided opportunities for learners to begin to put their emerging concept-based pragmatic knowledge into practice by using the concepts to select appropriate pragmalinguistic forms in a variety of hypothetical social-interactive contexts. The dynamic administration of these tasks – in which the tutor intervened to support learners – fostered new understandings of the concepts and their relevance to language choices. Strategic interaction scenarios (Chapter 6) then pushed learners to put their knowledge to use – that is, to plan (orientation) and perform (execution) scenarios using the pragmalinguistic forms they judged to be appropriate. Importantly, because scenarios were dynamically administered, control over performance was distributed between the learner and the tutor when performance began to falter. This not only supported the performance itself (i.e. use of forms), but also assisted learners in becoming more aware of their performance, thereby leading to greater control. Although the three tasks have been presented in separate chapters, it is important to bear in mind that they were not carried out in isolation. Rather, each task was an integral part of a larger program grounded in a dialectical, or praxis-based, perspective on the relationship between knowledge and ability for use. This relationship is depicted in Figure 7.1.

Pragmatic development is represented as a triangle. At the base of the triangle are conceptual knowledge and the ability to apply concepts to solve problems. These represent the foundation of pragmatic development, which ascends from the abstract (conceptual) to the concrete (Davydov, 2004) at the apex of the triangle: practical (material) activity. The two-way arrows connecting each point are meant to suggest bidirectionality, or mutual/dialectical influence. In the SCT framework, conceptual knowledge first develops through learners' interactions with the concept-based

The Future of Vygotskian Approaches to Instructional Pragmatics 187

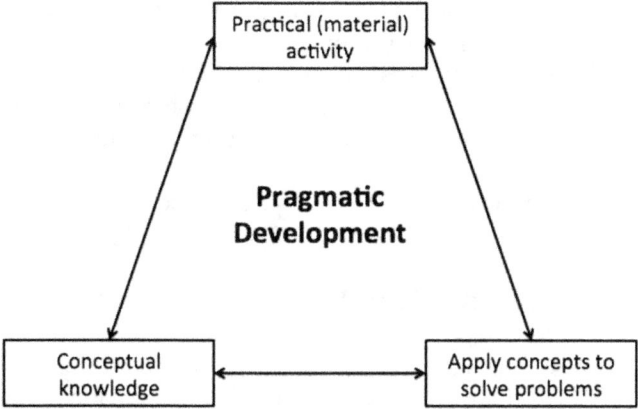

Figure 7.1 Dialectics in the SCT framework for instructional pragmatics

materials via verbalized reflections. This knowledge is then applied during appropriateness judgment tasks, where it may also be transformed. Conceptual knowledge is also applied, and potentially modified, in the orientation stage of strategic interaction scenarios. Practical (material) activity – the execution of scenarios – is therefore linked to conceptual knowledge and its application in solving problems, upon which it may in turn impact as the control function develops (i.e. the link between orientation and execution). The figure also implies that in the absence of one of the points there is no real pragmatic development. Vygotsky's (1997) conception of praxis-oriented education entails a dialectic relationship between knowledge and use: one without the other does not equate to development, but rather to rote learning and/or non-thoughtful performance gains.

One of the recurring themes running throughout the book is that human mediation, or development-oriented support, is a crucial dimension of the internalization process. The tutor supported learners in arriving at appropriate, yet personally significant, understandings of the concepts as such and in understanding how the concepts could be applied and modified in practice. The basic idea, to borrow from Kozulin (2003), is that human mediation creates a zone of proximal development (ZPD) wherein learners may be supported in internalizing psychological mediators – in the case of the SCT framework for instructional pragmatics, this means internalizing sociopragmatic concepts. Dialogic verbalized reflections and dynamically administered appropriateness judgment tasks and strategic interaction scenarios were not designed simply to evaluate the learners' progress, but to create the conditions under which learners' emerging competencies could be further nurtured, thereby leading to development.

In the remainder of this final chapter, we will turn our attention to the future of Vygotskian approaches to L2 instructional pragmatics. First, implications and future directions for research are sketched out. Second, I discuss how the SCT framework could be conceptualized for use in L2 classrooms. Third, the important domain of L2 teacher education is addressed.

Implications for Research

Implications and directions for future research that integrates the principles of the SCT framework for L2 instructional pragmatics are many. The discussion offered below is by no means exhaustive. Rather, I have selected a limited number of future directions that research in this area could take as a means of expanding and refining the SCT framework.

Addressing the limitations of the present study

The study reported in this book (see also van Compernolle, 2012) has exemplified one particular instantiation of the SCT framework for L2 instructional pragmatics. As with any empirical study, it is important to bear in mind its limitations when thinking of its contribution to the field and directions for future research.

One potential limitation of the study stems from its radically different orientation to teaching and developing L2 pragmatic capacities in comparison to previous L2 pragmatics research. The majority of data collected represent cooperative, intermental activity rather than individual competence. In addition, while in some ways similar to well-established data collection instruments (e.g. discourse completion tasks, role plays), the appropriateness judgment tasks and scenarios used during the course of the enrichment program were designed to integrate assessment and pedagogy as a unified activity through dynamic administration. Furthermore, this study was primarily concerned with the role of conceptual knowledge in the development of sociopragmatic capacity (i.e. mapping concepts onto forms), which entails a reversal of the traditional form-acquisition-to-meaning-association orientation within the field. As a result, directly comparing and contrasting the findings of this research with those reported in previous studies is at best tenuous because, despite having a common focus of interest, each originates from different, and ultimately incommensurable, theories of the relationship between *learning about* and *learning* language. However, this is not, in my estimation, a limitation or problem that needs resolution, but instead an important issue to recognize so that the questions, methods and findings of researchers working within one theory are not confused with, or reinterpreted within, the constructs and objectives of another (Dunn & Lantolf, 1998; Kinginger, 2001; Lantolf, 1996).

There are also limitations of the scope of the research design and methodology. This study included a small number of participants ($N = 8$) enrolled in only one particular intermediate-level US university French class. In addition, the qualitative treatment of developmental processes presented throughout the chapters captured only select moments in the developmental trajectories of certain individuals. Although the limited number of participants and careful selection of representative cases have allowed for a relatively in-depth look at sociopragmatic development from several angles, it will be necessary in the future to expand the breadth of the research design to include a greater number of participants as well as learners at different instructional levels and/or who are studying other languages. It should also be pointed out that this study was designed as a sort of test case for a concept-based approach to sociopragmatic instruction and, as such, was not intended to compare learners' achievements with a control group (i.e. no instruction) and/or a comparative group (i.e. an alternative pedagogical approach). Future comparative studies certainly have the potential to inform L2 sociopragmatics research, although such research focuses on product rather than process. As noted above, researchers should be careful not to confuse the constructs and goals of one theory of pedagogy and cognitive development with those of another. Instead, explorations of the particular qualities of development (i.e. what actually develops and how) may be more worthwhile than direct comparisons in which one approach is pitted against another and effectiveness of instructional intervention is measured on the basis of a single, standardized set of assessment instruments.

It is also noteworthy that this study involved one-on-one tutorials with an expert in French sociopragmatics and Vygotskian pedagogy rather than in a typical classroom. Although the materials and tasks designed for this study may not be wholly feasible in a typical classroom, they certainly lend themselves to being adapted for such use, and teachers would certainly be able to incorporate them into their courses. Nonetheless, it will be necessary to explore the extent to which teachers accept, reject and adapt concept-based approaches to pedagogy based on their previous learning and teaching histories and (folk) theories of language and learning. It may be that a reconceptualization of teacher education is needed that leads teachers to think about language and learning in new ways (Lantolf & Johnson, 2007).

Limitations of the scope of data collection are also apparent. Because this study focused heavily on putting concept-based pedagogy under a microscope, other potentially important sources of or influences on development were not emphasized. This is particularly clear when one considers that little information about learners' histories beyond the number of years of French study and current course enrollments as language learners was formally collected. Stories about past learning experiences evidencing a number of sources of language socialization did, however, emerge during the course of the study, often as anecdotes integrated into learners' explanations of performance and questions about the concepts. Likewise, this study did not formally attempt to collect data about the learners' concurrent educational experience in a formal classroom and how their participation in the enrichment program may have impacted upon it, nor did it include data (e.g. interviews) from the perspective of these students' regular classroom teachers. More formal approaches to collecting such information would certainly be beneficial to future studies.

Tasks and task administration

As noted above, the SCT framework for L2 instructional pragmatics centered around three principal types of tasks aimed at promoting the internalization of sociopragmatic concepts: verbalized reflections, appropriateness judgment tasks and strategic interaction scenarios. Dynamic assessment principles were implemented in the administration of these tasks as a means of co-constructing learners' ZPDs.

Two leading principles guided the design and administration of these tasks. First, because the SCT framework is grounded in a commitment to praxis, they aimed to develop both conceptual knowledge and practical ability for use. More specifically, they were designed to foster development in terms of the three processes involved in the formation of mental actions (Galperin, 1989, 1992): orientation, execution and control. Second, the tasks were designed and administered to promote verbalization, which is a central processes in internalization. Verbalization entails explanation of concepts as such (e.g. monologic and dialogic verbalized reflections) and explaining one's performance through concepts (e.g. appropriateness judgment tasks, scenarios). While the principles informing the design of these tasks is fundamental to the SCT framework, I do not wish to suggest that the specific tasks used in the study reported on in this book are the only possible options.

One particular area for improvement is in designing tasks that become increasingly difficult across time. In Chapter 5, for example, we saw how ambiguity and learner struggle were drivers of development within the context of appropriateness judgment tasks. The reason for this is that ambiguous social situations push learners not only to apply, but also to transcend (Poehner, 2007), their current understandings of the concepts in order to forge new linkages among the concepts, and how the demands of one may outweigh the demands of another. While ambiguity – meaning greater difficulty – was integrated into each appropriateness judgment task, this did not increase over time. A possible alternative approach would center around relatively straightforward task items where the selection of conventional pragmalinguistic forms is rather clear at the beginning of the enrichment program. The point here would be to orient learners to the relevance of the concepts for guiding language choices, as we saw again in Chapter 5 in Conrad's case. As the enrichment program continues, however, the situations would become increasingly ambiguous, pushing the learners to confront the potential conflicts between their existing knowledge and the demands of the task. It would therefore be possible to chart learners' developmental trajectories according to performance on near and far transfer tasks (Feuerstein *et al.*, 1988; Poehner, 2007) – that is, how far learners are able to take the concepts they are appropriating and use them in new and potentially unfamiliar contexts. Such would also naturally apply to strategic interaction scenarios.

A related idea for task improvement involves monologic verbalized reflections. As shown in Chapter 4, the think-aloud questions integrated into the concept-based materials were designed to lead learners to reflect on the meaning of the concepts by prompting them to think of examples of how the concepts apply to language use and/or social relationships. However, this proved to be too difficult a task for the learners when they were first reflecting on the concepts. It might be more beneficial to include specific examples at first, asking learners to explain how the concept that they are appropriating applies. Over the course of the enrichment program the explicit examples could be withdrawn, pushing the learners to rely on their own understandings of the concepts to develop relevant examples. In other words, more support would be provided in the materials themselves, which could be phased out over the course of enrichment.

There is also room for improving strategic interaction scenarios and their administration. As mentioned above, increasing the difficulty of scenarios over time by introducing greater levels of ambiguity could support learners in transcending their control over the concepts in practice to new and unfamiliar contexts. Another way of increasing the difficulty would be for the tutor/mediator to implicitly and/or explicitly initiate shifts in the level of discourse that diverge from the learner's orientation. For instance, for some of the conventionally more formal scenarios in the current study, several learners decided to use *vous* to create or maintain distance while at the same time opting for the more informal or everyday sociostylistic variants *on* 'we' and the absence of *ne* in negation. In future studies, the tutor could assess learners' sensitivity to the level of discourse of their interlocutor, and their ability to style shift, by using the more formal sociostylistic variants, *nous* 'we' and negation with *ne* (an implicit shift) or even by commenting on the learner's inappropriate informal style (an explicit shift). Alternatively, the tutor could implicitly or explicitly initiate a shift away from *vous* and toward *tu* as a means of pointing to increased social closeness in the scenario, or scenarios could be designed to include more than one interlocutor with differing social status vis-à-vis the learner and who enter the scenario at different times, meaning that the learner would be pushed to extend his or her conceptual knowledge to online language choices. The debriefing stage would be particularly important for gaining insights into learners' understandings of such shifts and dealing with changing social circumstances in the scenarios.

It is important to recognize that there exist alternative task types that may be used in order to foster the internalization of sociopragmatic concepts. Monologic verbalized reflections could, for example, be done and recorded at home (see Negueruela, 2003) rather than in the space where dialogic activity took place. This would give the tutor/mediator a chance to review the learners' verbalizations prior to engaging them in dialogic verbalized reflections. Appropriateness judgment tasks could also be modified depending on the illustrative pragmalinguistic forms/examples chosen for instruction. Multiple-choice and/or open-ended discourse completion tasks would likely be more appropriate than an either/or questionnaire format if speech act realizations (e.g. degrees of directness, internal and external modifiers) were used as illustrative examples of how self-presentation, social distance and power can be enacted through discourse. Strategic interaction scenarios could also be completed between two or more learners rather than between a tutor/mediator and a learner. (More about this will be said in the discussion of the extension to L2 classrooms.) Alternative production/performance tasks also exist. Because accelerated access to declarative knowledge is one of the goals of the SCT framework, it may be beneficial to include more restricted production tasks that push learners to produce specific phrases or speech acts that incorporate illustrative pragmalinguistic forms. This could be achieved through elicited imitation tasks where learners hear a recording of a particular speech act and are asked to repeat what they hear. Support could still be provided as a means of developing controlled performance: prompting verbalization after hearing the utterance would provide a context for supporting the orientation, and support provided during the execution of the orientation would aim to foster greater control in performance.

Computerized enrichment programs

A promising avenue for future instantiations of the SCT framework for L2 instructional pragmatics is the design of computerized enrichment programs. Web-based applications that require no software installations on the part of the user are particularly attractive since learners could access such programs from any device with an internet connection (e.g. desktop and laptop computers, tablets, smartphones). Although there would be a trade-off in terms of sensitivity to individual learner needs (i.e. ZPD), there is the potential for much greater educational impact than if one-on-one sessions with a human mediator were required because a much larger number of learners would be able to access the enrichment program simultaneously – and at their own convenience – via the internet.

The basic component of a computerized enrichment program would be a web-based concept tutorial program. A relatively simple – yet potentially powerful – format would adapt the 36-page course book designed for the study reported in this book for web-based/hypertext delivery. Learners would simply click through the pages of the course book in which the concepts are explained. At points where think-aloud/reflection questions are included, the web-based program could include a text box where the learner would reflect on the concept in writing and submit the response, which would be saved on a server for later analysis. Alternatively, it might be possible to incorporate a web-based audio recording program so that learners could verbally reflect on the concepts, which may reveal more spontaneous thinking-in-progress than would written reflections. Of course, audio recordings would require learners to be connected with a microphone-equipped device in a location where they could record their verbalized reflections without disruption, which would not necessarily be a concern if reflections were written. Written reflections would also make the analysis and evaluation of learners' thinking more efficient since there would be no need to transcribe speech, which is certainly an advantage for both researchers and teachers working with large numbers of learners.

Appropriateness judgment tasks could also be administered via a web-based platform. A simple survey-questionnaire format could be effective in eliciting learner responses: a situation could be presented, followed by a question eliciting the selection of a pragmalinguistic form (either multiple choice or open-ended, as appropriate), and then an open text box prompting the learner to explain the response (verbalization). Mediation could also be incorporated into the task following the procedures outlined in Poehner and Lantolf (2013) for computerized dynamic assessment. Mediating prompts would have to be prescripted and programed to respond to learners' choices.

In this case, multiple-choice tasks would be more feasible than open-ended tasks since open-ended tasks would require some form of artificial intelligence programming that could recognize and respond to a virtually infinite number of possible responses. Providing prescribed mediation would, however, require that there be a single correct response. As such, the task would shift focus away from what the learner would actually want to do in the situations (i.e. the meaning(s) he or she would want to make) and toward an assessment of the learner's knowledge of pragmatic conventions. A multiple-choice task with prescribed mediation would also allow for the calculation of scores that include both *independent performance* and *mediated performance*, which would be weighted to account for the level of support required to arrive at the conventionally appropriate response for each situation (i.e. fewer points awarded with each mediating prompt accessed by the learner). As Poehner and Lantolf argue, this allows teachers and researchers to arrive at rather detailed diagnoses of learner abilities and needs, as well as to calculate a *learning potential score* (Kozulin & Garb, 2002), which attempts to predict a learner's readiness to benefit from further instruction.

Other, more interactive web-based programs may also be feasible. Synthetic immersive environments (SIEs) incorporate aspects of online gaming to 'produce explicit, educationally related outcomes in simulated, relevant interactional contexts (Sykes, 2008). SIEs carry significant potential in that they allow creators to target specific skills and educational objectives, while creating a meaningful collaborative space in which learners themselves are at the center of their own learning' (Sykes *et al.*, 2008: 536). One recent SIE, *Croquelandia* (Sykes, 2008), has been designed for developing L2 Spanish pragmatic abilities. Learners are immersed in a three-dimensional interactive space in which they are guided through a series of goal-directed activities, or quests, in which they interact with non-player characters (i.e. computer avatars), native speakers and other learners. The SIE is a low-stakes, yet emotionally engaging, context in which learners are able to experiment with their pragmatic abilities. Learners are in turn provided with behavior-based corrective feedback. An adaptation of a *Croquelandia*-type SIE for the SCT framework would engage learners not only in selecting conventionally appropriate speech act realizations but, more importantly, in verbalizing their response processes by eliciting retrospective written or verbal/recorded protocols. In addition, rather than providing behavior-based *corrective* feedback, mediating prompts could be programed to guide learners toward conventionally appropriate pragmalinguistic choices in relation to the relevance of the sociopragmatic concepts learners are appropriating.

There may be a range of formats for implementing a computerized enrichment program that are appropriate for different purposes and learner needs. Some researchers and teachers may prefer only to develop a simple computerized concept-based tutorial, leaving other tasks (e.g. appropriateness judgments, performance tasks) for one-on-one, small group or even whole classroom formats. In other cases, a fully web-based module may be desirable. Decisions regarding the implementation of web-based materials and tasks will also certainly be determined by the availability of relevant technologies and by curricular constraints. More about this will be said in the section devoted to implications for the classroom.

The SCT framework as pre-study abroad enrichment

The study reported on in this book focused on a small group of students who volunteered to take part in a pragmatics enrichment program beyond their concurrent coursework – in essence, they participated for the sake of participating and potentially learning something new about French. An intriguing idea for future research is implementing the SCT framework for instructional pragmatics as a pre-study abroad enrichment program.

As Kinginger (2009) has reported in her critical survey of study abroad research, overseas sojourns can have a positive impact on all dimensions of L2 communicative competence, including sociolinguistic and pragmatic abilities. However, development is not guaranteed. Instead, the qualities of learners' experiences and the interpretive frames with which learners come into a study abroad experience shape the ways in which they notice, perceive and appropriate social rules and concepts for language use. In her own empirical work, Kinginger (2008) has shown that, although many learners make progress in decoding the social meaning of pragmatic features of language, they often lack a coherent, systematic way of understanding the languaculture (Agar, 1994) in which they are participating (or from which they are abstaining). Consequently, learners may appropriate somewhat piecemeal rules, based on empirical experience, that do not in fact reflect the larger, systematic indexical field of meaning potentials. In other words, in the absence of pedagogical arrangements targeting pragmatics, learners are left to their own devices to navigate and negotiate the complexities and ambiguities of the sociopragmatics and pragmalinguistics of the language they are studying.

Kinginger (2008: 111) identifies 'training [for study abroad participants] in ethnographic techniques of dispassionate observation' as a possible avenue to pursue. She continues:

> The goal of training in ethnography for language learners is a 'mix of learning to communicate appropriately and developing an analytic understanding of another group's system of meanings' (Roberts, Byram,

Barro, Jordan, & Street, 2001, p. 11). In such approaches, learners are trained in methods of observation, analysis, and writing, engaging them in observation of 'otherness' and representing what they observe not as a set of facts but as one interpretation mediated by their own cultural understandings. Learners come to understand the nature of language learning as socialization, to appreciate the extent to which language and culture are closely intertwined (as *languaculture*; Agar, 1994, p. 60), and to grasp the complexity of intercultural interaction. (Kinginger, 2008: 111)

Clearly, the SCT framework for instructional pragmatics articulates with the goals of training language learners in ethnography prior to their departure as a means of providing them with a systematic framework for observing 'otherness' and representing their observations as culturally mediated interpretations of communicative practices. In essence, it is about giving learners insights into the languaculture in which they will be studying.

Research in this domain would therefore entail designing a pre-study abroad concept-based enrichment program, which could be developed for face-to-face meetings (e.g. a small class) or using a web-based module, as described above. The goal would be twofold. On the one hand, the program would aim to provide learners with a coherent, systematic basis for understanding the ways in which sociopragmatic meanings are enacted in concrete communicative activity. On the other hand, learners would receive training in dispassionate observation techniques. Following learners' progress during their study abroad experience through such methods as journals and interviews (see Kinginger, 2008) would provide researchers with insights into the ways in which learners are able to interpret the pragmatic practices of members of the languaculture in which they are participating. Oral production tasks (e.g. strategic interaction scenarios) would also have the potential to illuminate aspects of learners' control over pragmatic features of language in concrete communicative activity. The study abroad context, therefore, certainly represents a potentially fruitful area for future iterations of the SCT framework for instructional pragmatics.

Implications for the Classroom

The study reported on throughout this book involved a small number of students ($N = 8$) who voluntarily participated in a concept-based pragmatics enrichment program outside of their normal coursework. Although it may not be feasible to implement all of the particulars of the study into L2 classrooms, the basic principles outlined in Chapters 1–6 can be adapted for classroom teaching. In what follows, I offer recommendations for implementing the SCT framework for instructional pragmatics into existing curricula by adapting the materials and tasks for the classroom and utilizing technology-enhanced approaches to language pedagogy.

Adapting materials and tasks for the classroom

Language program coordinators and teachers often, and understandably, struggle to cover the material typically presented in learner textbooks (e.g. vocabulary, grammar) in a given academic term, and so they may wonder how additional pedagogical units focused on pragmatic concepts can feasibly be incorporated into classroom pedagogy. In addition, it is certainly the case that teaching in a classroom environment, where there are often 15, 20 or more students, is a dramatically different context from the one-on-one enrichment sessions organized for the current study. While these issues certainly present challenges for integrating the SCT framework for instructional pragmatics into existing curricula, the materials and tasks can be adapted in order to meet the demands of curricular constraints as well as the whole-classroom setting in which a teacher's attention is necessarily divided across a group of students.

The basis of the SCT framework is that learners need to develop a conceptually framed orientation to pragmatic performances focused on social meaning. Consequently, systematic pragmatic concepts (e.g. orders of indexicality, self-presentation, social distance) serve as the basic units of pedagogy. These concepts are presented verbally (e.g. written concept cards) and materially (e.g. pedagogical diagrams). In the present study, learners engaged with the concepts through monologic (independent) and then dialogic (with the tutor) verbalized reflections. A number of adaptations for the classroom are possible. For example, students could simply be given the concept-based materials to be read and reflected on at home. For teachers interested in tracking their students' verbalized reflections, learners could be asked to audio record their verbalized reflections as homework (Negueruela, 2003). Alternatively, teachers could ask their students to write their verbalized reflections, which may be more feasible since it would not require any transcription of spoken language. Teachers could also initially present the concepts in class in a whole-group format and elicit group verbalized reflections through instructional conversation (van Compernolle & Williams, 2012a). In this way, teachers would be able to support individual learners as well as the group as a whole since all classroom participants would – ostensibly at least – be party to the interaction and forms of mediation being offered (Ohta, 2001; Poehner, 2009). Students could also work in pairs or small groups to foster collaborative peer dialogue in the classroom (Swain & Lapkin, 2002) before proceeding to a whole-group discussion. Teachers may of course wish to present each of the concepts at different points in time, depending on curricular constraints. For instance, if there is not enough time to present all of the concepts at once, a teacher might consider presenting the orders of indexicality one day, to be followed by self-presentation a week or two later, social distance after that, and so on.

Appropriateness judgment tasks could be adapted for the classroom as well. One option would be to assign an appropriateness judgment task as homework, and to ask students not only to mark their pragmalinguistic choices but also to use the concepts to explain their choices. In class, the teacher could then lead an instructional conversation centered on learners' choices and their justifications for those choices. In this way, the teacher could help students understand how the concepts are relevant to making pragmalinguistic choices, especially in cases where there may be different orientations to appropriateness among students. Teachers would be able to guide learners toward an understanding of pragmatics as choices, rather than as sets of rules where there is one correct answer. This would provide an opportunity for learners to engage with perspectives on appropriateness that may differ from their own. Another option would be to have students work individually or in pairs/small groups in class before turning to a whole-group discussion of responses. Whatever format the teacher decides is most suitable for his/her classroom, it will be important to focus learners' attention on the relevance of the concepts for making pragmalinguistic choices (see Chapter 5).

Adaptations of strategic interactions scenarios are also certainly possible in a classroom context. Teachers could design scenarios as in-class communicative tasks that push learners not only to use the L2 (and target pragmatic features) but also to reflect on the relationship between context, meaning and language form. Orientation stages could be accomplished individually (e.g. as homework) or collaboratively in class – for example, scenarios do not necessarily need to be based on one-on-one interactions but may incorporate multiparty (e.g. three to four students) interactional contexts. Scenarios could then be performed in front of the class, after which all classroom participants (i.e. the performers, the teacher and the audience) could participate in the debriefing stage. Teachers could also ask students to design their own scenarios as a means of fostering critical reflection on the context-meaning-form relationship (Negueruela, 2003). In addition, group dynamic assessment (Poehner, 2009) may be feasible in a classroom context, where the teacher – and possibly the student audience – could intervene during the performance of scenarios to support the performers in controlling the execution of their orientation.

Additional and/or alternative tasks may also be relevant for classroom pedagogy. Awareness-raising tasks in which learners analyze authentic language-in-use in order to explain the differences and similarities in terms of pragmalinguistic forms in relation to the context can be helpful (van Compernolle & Williams, 2012b, 2012c). Films are particularly good resources for finding authentic language examples (Etienne & Sax, 2006, 2009). Learners could, for example, be asked to work in small groups to compare two different spoken interactions (e.g. an informal conversation and a more formal interaction such as a new interview). They would first be asked to discuss social-contextual factors (e.g. perceived formality, relationship status of the interlocutors) and make predictions – based on the concepts they are appropriating – about the type of language they expect to be used in each context. Then they would identify relevant pragmalinguistic practices and explain their use through the concepts. In a whole-class instructional conversation, the teacher would then lead a discussion of the findings as a means of fostering critical reflection on the relevance and significance of the concepts in relation to the pragmalinguistic forms identified by students.

Technology-enhanced approaches

The recommendations for adapting materials and tasks for the classroom described above privilege face-to-face interactions between teachers and students, which may or may not always be feasible depending on curricular and/or institutional constraints. Consequently, technology-enhanced approaches to language learning and language teaching may offer a number of advantages for teachers and students.

Integrating technology-enhanced approaches will depend on a number of factors, most notably the availability of technological resources (e.g. access to computers and/or other networked devices) and teachers' familiarity and comfort with computer technology. For example, a web-based tutorial program and/or an SIE (see above) may be ideal for teachers who are not able for whatever reason(s) to dedicate course contact hours to introducing concept-based materials, since learners would be able to engage with the materials on their own time outside of class. However, this would require teachers to have the time and skills to create such programs, or at least access to a technology expert who could assist them, which is likely not the case in the majority of educational contexts. A more feasible approach entails a combination of in-class or at-home pen-and-paper concept-based instruction (i.e. using non-computerized concept explanations and diagrams) with other tasks that utilize readily available forms of computer-mediated communication (CMC). The recommendations offered below center on technology-enhanced awareness-raising and language performance tasks that would complement in-class or at-home concept-based instructional materials.

In introducing their edited volume, *Electronic Discourse in Language Learning and Language Teaching*, Abraham and Williams note that internet technologies and various forms of CMC offer language learners an expanded range of opportunities to observe and analyze communicative practices of speakers of the language they are studying beyond what may be introduced in the classroom. They continue: 'It is also important to point out that the social and linguistic practices of online communities (i.e. environments) are shaped by users for particular purposes with specific participants in different contexts (Lam, 2004; Thorne, 2003, 2008). As such, understanding how participants shape the discourse of these communities (e.g. chat, discussion forums, blogs, and so forth) is also of fundamental interest' (Abraham & Williams, 2009: 2). Several of the chapters included in the volume explicitly address ways of supporting learners' access to and participation in online communities, with specific reference to the sociolinguistics and pragmatics of discussion forums (Blattner & Williams, 2009; Farrell Whitworth, 2009), blogs (Douglass, 2009), synchronous text-based chat (van Compernolle & Pierozak, 2009) and podcasts (Guikema, 2009). Although the specific recommendations vary across the chapters, the common theme running throughout them is one of fostering motivated and thoughtful observation of online community members' communicative practices, with the teacher's role being one of guiding learners to a critical and culturally relevant understanding of such practices. These approaches articulate well with the principles and goals of the SCT framework for instructional pragmatics.

One particularly attractive option involves engaging learners in ethnographic observation projects (see above with regard to ethnography in the study abroad context). Teachers could identify specific online communities (e.g. chatrooms, blogs, forums), or have learners search on their own, to explore over the course of an academic term. Learners would be instructed to gather language samples (i.e. data), for example, from a discussion thread or chat transcript and to identify relevant pragmalinguistic practices in their data. They would then be asked to explain how the pragmatic concepts (e.g. orders of indexicality, self-presentation, social distance) relate to the observed communicative practices. This could be done as a homework assignment, which students could report on in class where the teacher and other students could provide feedback and/or support presenters in interpreting the indexical meanings (i.e. concepts) of their findings. Ideally, this would be done multiple times throughout an academic term, thus giving learners the opportunity to explore and compare several different online communities. As an alternative to assigning such tasks as individual work, learners could instead work with a partner or in a small group.

CMC technologies also offer many opportunities for language use both within and beyond traditional, structured educational environments. Web course management systems (e.g. Angel, Blackboard) and social networking technologies (e.g. Facebook, Google, Twitter) provide text-based communication environments and automatic archiving options that may be useful for teachers and students. Strategic interaction scenarios involving two or more students could be assigned outside of class in a synchronous chat environment. For example, for the scenario involving a job interview used in the present study, students could be assigned the role of either the interviewer or the interviewee. For the initial planning (orientation) stage, all of the interviewers and all of the interviewees could meet in class or online to discuss and rehearse their plan of action for that role. Then, for the performance (execution) stage, students would meet in pairs in a chatroom, each with one student performing one of the roles. Because text-based chat transcripts can be archived, students (and teachers) would then have access to the discourse produced following the performance. These transcripts could then be used for the debriefing stage: learners could be asked to critically reflect on and evaluate their performance in relation to their orientation as homework. Teachers could also review selected excerpts of the transcripts in class.

Telecollaborative interaction with *extra muros* partners (Belz & Thorne, 2006) is another possibility for teachers fortunate enough to have a working relationship with another teacher or program coordinator in a country where the language learners are studying is spoken. Such interactions in and of themselves can foster pragmatic development if and when native speaker interactants provide peer assistance on pragmatic conventions (Belz & Kinginger, 2002). However, telecollaboration can also be integrated as part of a larger pedagogical program in which transcripts of learners' interactions with their native speaker telecollaborative partners are analyzed and reflected upon in class in conjunction with explicit pragmatics instruction (Belz & Vyatkina, 2008). Telecollaboration also offers the unique advantage of being a 'real life' extension of the classroom where there exist real and immediate social consequences of learners' pragmatic actions that do not exist in more pedagogized tasks, such as strategic interaction scenarios. Of course, this depends on the degree to which learners perceive and participate in the telecollaborative context as language practice or an opportunity to build and maintain social relationships (Thorne, 2003). It should also be borne in mind that, while telecollaboration has the potential to foster the establishment of social relationships where pragmatic practices are highly consequential, there is a drawback in that learners may not have opportunities to vary their use of pragmatic features of discourse. As such, teachers fortunate enough to have access to telecollaborative partnerships may wish to have their students engage in strategic interaction scenarios as well, where scenarios can be designed to represent a wide range of communicative contexts and elicit sociosituational and pragmatic variation.

Implications for Teacher Education

One of the major challenges for the future of the SCT framework for instructional pragmatics entails addressing what Lantolf and Johnson (2007: 884) describe as language teachers' 'largely unarticulated, yet deeply ingrained, everyday concepts about language, language learning and language teaching that are based on their own L2 instructional histories and lived experiences'. As noted throughout this book, the SCT framework represents a radical departure from traditional conceptions of appropriateness and principles of language teaching. There are, therefore, important implications for L2 teacher education, most notably with regard to developing L2 teachers' knowledge base. As Johnson (2009) observes in her formulation of an SCT perspective on teacher education:

> in order to raise the professional stature of the L2 teaching profession, the knowledge-base of L2 teacher education has drawn heavily from the disciplinary knowledge in linguistics and SLA to define what it is that L2 teachers need to know about language and [L2] learning (Freeman & Johnson, 1998). Yet how knowledge about language is presented to teachers in their teacher education programs or how it is instantiated in their instructional materials is contingent on how language is defined and how SLA is understood. (Johnson, 2009: 41)

In the following paragraphs, I offer a brief outline of the principal areas of L2 teacher education for which the SCT framework for instructional pragmatics has important consequences: beliefs about language, correctness and appropriateness, the development of pedagogical content knowledge, and educating teachers as researchers.

Challenging beliefs about language

Johnson (2009) argues that the most pervasive conceptualization of language in L2 teacher education programs draws from the Saussurian–Bloomfieldian approach to semiology, which posits an abstract linguistic system that is separable from language use and the people who use it. Such a view of language has continued to pervade linguistic theory and, by extension, SLA and L2 teacher education because of the dominant place of Chomskian generative grammar since the 1960s (e.g. Chomsky, 1965).

Consequently, according to Johnson (2009), the prevailing view of language is one of a collection of discrete phonological, morphological, lexical and syntactic features that are governed by universal and immutable rules. Even in light of theories of communicative competence (Hymes, 1972) and approaches to communicative language teaching (Canale & Swain, 1980) that privilege language use and appropriateness over knowledge of discrete linguistic forms, the knowledge base of L2 teacher education has traditionally centered around an individualist-mentalist rule-governed linguistic system:

> The profession has long assumed that L2 teachers need to have a theoretical understanding of the syntactic, phonological, and morphological rules of a language, and that once they have consciously acquired that knowledge they should be able to help L2 learners acquire it, or, within the [communicative language teaching] movement, use it to engage in meaningful communication. (Johnson, 2009: 42)

Johnson goes on to argue that L2 teacher education research 'suggests that the traditional definition of language that has permeated the context of L2 teacher education programs may not provide teachers with a conceptualization of language that is amenable or useful to L2 instruction' (Johnson, 2009: 43). The alternative proposed by Johnson (2009) is a view of language as social practice, a perspective that articulates with the principles of the SCT framework for instructional pragmatics, and which has already been argued for in this book (see Chapter 2). Briefly put, a view of language as social practice positions culturally mediated conceptual meaning rather than linguistic form as the central feature of language and communicative activity, or what Agar (1994) refers to as *languaculture*. Thus, 'L2 teachers need to be able to open up the *languaculture* for conscious inspection' (Johnson, 2009: 46; see also Lantolf & Johnson, 2007).

Johnson's (2009) comments are particularly relevant for L2 instructional pragmatics. On the basis of the prevailing L2 teacher knowledge base, teachers often acquire rather doctrinal, prescriptivist views of language that tend to privilege a single correct usage over the possibility of sociosituational and pragmatic variation. Etienne and Sax (2009), for example, argue that teachers often resist incorporating less formal, or everyday, sociolinguistic features of discourse into the curriculum because they believe these forms to be derivative of, and therefore inferior to, standard, formal (textbook) language. While these beliefs are patently inaccurate, they are certainly understandable against a backdrop of L2 teacher education programs that promote and reinforce, rather than challenge, teachers' everyday concepts related to the nature of language as an abstract rule-governed linguistic system. From the perspective of the SCT framework for instructional pragmatics, what is needed in teacher education programs is an attempt to challenge these deeply ingrained beliefs about language and variation through investigations of the languacultural patterns of language use and meaning construction in the language teachers intend to teach.

As described in Chapter 2, the SCT framework draws heavily on a sociocultural orientation to language variation (van Compernolle, 2011a) in which four principles are proposed. First, language structure is emergent (Hopper, 1987, 1998), and therefore variation in language does not involve derivation from an underlying form, or the application of variable rules within the mind/brain of the individual, but rather the use of specific lexicogrammatical constructions available in the languaculture. Second, activity types (Levinson, 1992) mediate, and are mediated by, language in that participation in social activity and language form are mutually contingent. Third, language forms reflect, and transform, social-indexical meaning potentials (Silverstein, 2003). Fourth, language users do not simply inherit and use preexisting meanings but actively participate in the construction of new ones in concrete communicative activity. Such an understanding of the nature of language and meaning-making, with particular reference to sociolinguistic and pragmatic variation, could assist teachers in consciously reflecting on, and re-mediating, their beliefs about language and in developing 'the capacity to interpret and generate meanings that are appropriate within the relevant *languaculture*' (Johnson, 2009: 46). By extension, L2 teacher education programs ought to challenge teachers' beliefs about language appropriateness. Traditional approaches to instructional pragmatics privilege conformance to idealized social conventions. Yet appropriateness from the perspective of the SCT framework is a highly personal, culturally mediated interpretation of communicative practices (Chapter 2). Recall that pragmatics is conceptualized as mediated action: pragmalinguistic forms, the selection of which is mediated by one's sociopragmatic knowledge and intentions for the interaction, mediate social actions.

In an effort to develop teachers' awareness of language (languaculture) as social practice, teachers could themselves participate in a concept-based enrichment program as a means of internalizing the relevant pragmatic concepts that they will need to teach in the future. Teachers could also engage in ethnographic observation of online communities (see above) as a means of gaining empirical insights into specific languacultural practices that mediate, and are mediated by, activity types (e.g. informal conversation in a chatroom, political debates in comment threads hosted by online newspapers). The goal of such a program would be to push teachers to consider not only the formal characteristics of the language they intend to teach, but also to open up the underlying concepts that are relevant to language use consciousness. In other words, teachers would, ideally at least, internalize and personalize relevant pragmatic concepts as psychological tools to guide their own language use and teaching practices.

Developing pedagogical content knowledge

Historically, teacher education programs have separated disciplinary knowledge (i.e. linguistic and SLA theories) from the practical business of teaching (e.g. methods, approaches, techniques), with the assumption that knowledge of the structure, use and acquisition of languages should translate into effective classroom teaching. However, this is not necessarily the case (Freeman, 2004; Freeman & Johnson, 1998; Johnson, 2009): acquiring expertise in linguistics, SLA theory and teaching methods does not equate to teachers developing the relevant *pedagogical content knowledge* to make instructional content relevant and useful to their students.

From the perspective of the SCT framework for instructional pragmatics, disciplinary knowledge and pedagogical knowledge must be dialectically united (i.e. as pedagogical content knowledge), a view endorsed in Johnson's (2009) SCT perspective on L2 teacher education. In other words, it is not sufficient for teachers to gain expertise in Vygotskian SCT and pragmatic theory; rather, this knowledge must be linked to, and revised in, practical activity – that is, *teaching*. Johnson and Arshavshaya (2011) describe an innovative approach to developing L2 teachers' pedagogical content knowledge through a reconceptualization of the micro-teaching simulation and its relation to 'real' classroom teaching. In small groups, pre-service teachers collaborated to plan a short lesson, which they carried out in their teacher education course, and where they were given feedback aiming to mediate their future teaching practices. Later, the pre-service teachers taught a revised version of the lesson to an existing intact English as a Second Language class. The lesson was videorecorded for later review and reflection. In this way, the teachers were given opportunities not only to develop disciplinary knowledge, but also to develop knowledge of effective ways for making the content of their instruction relevant and accessible to their students.

Such an approach would certainly be beneficial to pre-service and in-service teachers in L2 teacher education programs that included units on instructional pragmatics. The focus of these units would not simply be on promoting the internalization of pragmatic concepts as such (i.e. disciplinary knowledge), but more importantly on effective teaching practices for presenting concepts to learners, supporting verbalized reflections, dynamically administering appropriateness judgment tasks and strategic interaction scenarios, and so forth. Put another way, teachers' pedagogical content knowledge would be forged in and through the very practice of teaching (e.g. micro-teaching simulations), access to appropriate meditating support from teacher educators and peers, and critical reflection on their teaching practices. In this way, teachers' developing theoretical knowledge would not only inform, but could be transformed by, their practical activity, which is the crux of the Vygotskian view of educational praxis (Vygotsky, 1997; see Chapter 1).

Educating teacher-researchers

In the field of SLA, and by extension L2 teacher education, there is a fundamental gap between an ordained class of *knowledge-producers* (i.e. SLA researchers), on the one hand, and *practitioners* (i.e. language teachers) who may apply – but not contribute to – knowledge, on the other (Block, 2000; Lantolf, 2008). L2 teacher education programs often reify this division through their focus on the application of SLA theory to classroom language teaching but leave little, if any, room for teachers to contribute to theory building (Lantolf & Johnson, 2007).

As argued in Chapter 1, however, Vygotskian developmental education (Davydov, 2004; Vygotsky, 1997) does not assume a unidirectional relationship between theory and practice wherein theory may inform practice, but where practical application has virtually no impact upon theory. Rather, because of the commitment to praxis, theory and practical activity are dialectically united – each informs each other in a potentially unending process. This perspective holds important implications for L2 teacher education because it positions teachers not as *pedagogical technicians* but as professionalized teacher-researchers who are competent to engage in critical praxis-oriented inquiry in their classrooms. As Johnson (2009: 121–123) forcefully argues, L2 teacher education programs should provide future teachers with training in the intellectual tools of inquiry so that they may critically engage with the broader field of L2 teaching and SLA research to become *transformative intellectuals* (Giroux, 1988) in their own right. This is not an argument in favor of requiring teachers to conduct formal research studies and to publish their findings in professional journals, as is the practice among (and expectation of) university SLA researchers, for example. But it is an argument in favor of teachers engaging in praxis-motivated inquiries into what Block (2000: 136) refers to as the 'multiple connotations of reality manifested through the multi-layered and textured social interaction which constitutes classroom language teaching and learning'. To achieve this goal, teacher education programs ought to equip teachers with the tools of inquiry required for research. This entails articulating and critically reflecting on their assumptions (i.e. theory) about the nature of language, language teaching and language learning, asking research questions and/or proposing hypotheses, developing appropriate methods for responding to questions and/or testing hypotheses, analyzing data, supporting claims about learning and development with evidence, and reflecting on the implications and limitations of their findings that may inform revisions of their assumptions and future practices in the classroom. There are certainly possibilities for collaborative partnerships between teachers and SLA researchers (e.g. Lantolf & Poehner, 2011), but teachers need not rely on such arrangements.

In fact, the SCT framework for instructional pragmatics already offers teachers a starting point for their own inquiries into the teaching of pragmatics in a classroom context. If pragmatic development is assumed to be largely a conceptual process, teachers may wish to investigate the extent to which their teaching practices do or do not support learners in internalizing pragmatic concepts. They may also wish to challenge the proposals for tasks and task administration that I have made throughout this book, and especially the recommended adaptations outlined earlier in this chapter. It may also be that teachers find the evidential basis I have relied on for making claims about pragmatic development to be unconvincing or misaligned with their own goals for, and experience in, classroom teaching. This is, for lack of a better phrase, a standing and open invitation for teachers to engage with the SCT framework for instructional pragmatics as teacher-researchers, as *transformative intellectuals*, and to challenge its assumptions, hypotheses, methods, evidence and claims.

Final Comments

This book represents an initial attempt at constructing a Vygotskian approach to L2 instructional pragmatics, and in this final chapter I have offered a brief sketch of the future of the framework in terms of research, classroom teaching and teacher education. By way of conclusion, I wish to reflect on two points that have been implied, yet not explicitly articulated in this book.

The first point speaks to an assertion I made in Chapter 1: the SCT framework does not represent a collection of tips or teaching techniques from which one can pick and choose at will. Rather, it is one particular instantiation of a coherently organized pedagogical program grounded in Vygotsky's cultural-historical psychological theory. To expand on this a bit, I would like to recount an interaction I had with a colleague only a few days prior to writing these final comments. While having tea at the university library's café, my colleague asked whether it was possible to be a 'partial Vygotskian' and borrow certain good ideas to be combined with others from different traditions, or if it was really necessary to buy into the theory *in toto*. My response – though certainly hesitant and likely garbled at first – was that, yes, it was possible to be a so-called 'partial Vygotskian', but in doing so, one will have likely abandoned the integrity of the theory in favor of a social-constructivist reinterpretation of Vygotsky's writings. To clarify, I explained that SCT is not a theory of assistance, a set of procedures for concept-based teaching or a set of techniques for the classroom; rather, it is a psychological theory that holds that culturally constructed artifacts mediate all higher, and specifically human, psychological processes. In essence, it is a theory of the dialectics of biology and culture, of mind and body, of individual and social. If this central tenet of the theory is abandoned, then what is left is a superficial perspective on social learning at best or, at worst, a de-theorized and unmotivated set of teaching techniques. As such, the future of the SCT framework for instructional pragmatics depends on a continued commitment to the integrity of the psychological theory from it derives and to which it contributes.

The second point I would like to make follows from the first. Although a commitment to the integrity of the theory is necessary, I do not claim to have presented the definitive or final articulation of an SCT-informed approach to instructional pragmatics. As should be clear from the contents of this final chapter, there are numerous directions for future instantiations of the framework in the domains of research, classroom pedagogy and teacher education programs. Far from being the final word on the topic, this book should be considered as the opening of a conversation about how Vygotsky's cultural-historical psychology and its contemporary interpretations can serve as the basis of pedagogical programs aiming to develop L2 learners' pragmatic capacities. In true Vygotskian spirit, this book should be regarded as a moment in praxis that can serve to inform future theoretical and practical innovations.

References

Abraham, L.B. and Williams, L. (2009) Introduction: Analyzing and exploring electronic discourse. In L.B. Abraham and L. Williams (eds) *Electronic Discourse in Language Learning and Language Teaching* (pp. 1–8). Amsterdam: John Benjamins.
Agar, M. (1994) *Culture Shock: Understanding the Culture of Conversation*. New York: Morrow.
Ager, D.E. (1990) *Sociolinguistics and Contemporary French*. New York: Cambridge University Press.
Ahearn, L. (2001) Language and agency. *Annual Review of Anthropology* 30, 109–137.
Alcón Soler, E. and Martínez-Flor, A. (2008) Pragmatics in foreign language contexts. In E. Alcón Soler and A. Martínez-Flor (eds) *Investigating Pragmatics in Foreign Language Learning, Teaching and Testing* (pp. 3–21). Bristol: Multilingual Matters.
Aljaafreh, A. and Lantolf, J.P. (1994) Negative feedback as regulation and second language learning in the zone of proximal development. *Modern Language Journal* 78, 465–483.
Antón, M. and DiCamilla, F.J. (1998) Socio-cognitive functions of L1 collaborative interaction in the L2 classroom. *Canadian Modern Language Review* 54, 314–353.
Austin, J.L. (1962) *How to Do Things with Words*. Oxford: Claredon Press.
Bachman, L.F. (1990) *Fundamental Considerations in Language Testing*. Oxford: Oxford University Press.
Becker, A.L. (1988) Language in particular: A lecture. In D. Tannen (ed.) *Linguistics in Context: Connecting Observation and Understanding* (pp. 17–35). Norwood: Ablex.
Beeching, K., Armstrong, N. and Gadet, F. (eds) (2009) *Sociolinguistic Variation in Contemporary French*. Amsterdam: John Benjamins.
Belz, J. and Kinginger, C. (2002) The cross-linguistic development of address form use in telecollaborative language learning: Two case studies. *Canadian Modern Language Review* 59, 189–214.
Belz, J.A. and Thorne, S.L. (eds) (2006) *Internet-mediated Intercultural Foreign Language Education*. Boston: Heinle & Heinle.
Belz, J.A. and Vyatkina, N. (2008) The pedagogical mediation of a developmental learner corpus for classroom-based language instruction. *Language Learning & Technology* 12, 33–52.
Biber, D. (2006) *University Language: A Corpus-based Study of Spoken and Written Registers*. Amsterdam: John Benjamins.
Blattner, G. and Williams, L. (2009) Linguistic and social dimensions of French-language discussion forums. In L.B. Abraham and L. Williams (eds) *Electronic Discourse in Language Learning and Language Teaching* (pp. 263–289). Amsterdam: John Benjamins.

Block, D. (2000) Revisiting the gap between SLA researchers and language teachers. *Links and Letters* 7, 129–143.
Block, D. (2007) The rise of identity in SLA research, post Firth and Wagner, 1997. *Modern Language Journal* 91 (S1), 863–876.
Blondeau, H. (2003) The old *nous* and the new *nous*. A comparison of 19th and 20th century spoken Quebec French. *Penn Working Papers in Linguistics* 9 (2), 1–15.
Bolden, G. (2006) Little words that matter: Discourse markers 'so' and 'oh' and the doing of other-attentiveness in social interaction. *Journal of Communication* 56, 661–688.
Brooks, L., Swain, M., Lapkin, S. and Knouzi, I. (2010) Mediating between scientific and spontaneous concepts through languaging. *Language Awareness* 19, 89–110.
Brown, P. and Levinson, S. (1987) *Politeness: Some Universals in Language Usage* (2nd edn). Cambridge: Cambridge University Press.
Bucholtz, M. and Hall, K. (2005) Identity and interaction: A sociocultural linguistic approach. *Discourse Studies* 7, 585–614.
Bybee, J.L. (2008) Usage-based grammar and second language acquisition. In P. Robinson and N.C. Ellis (eds) *Handbook of Cognitive Linguistic and Second Language Acquisition* (pp. 216–236). New York: Routledge.
Canale, M. (1983) From communicative competence to communicative language pedagogy. In J. Richards and R.W. Schmidt (eds) *Language and Communication* (pp. 2–27). London: Longman.
Canale, M. and Swain, M. (1980) Theoretical bases of communicative approaches to second language teaching and testing. *Applied Linguistics* 1, 1–47.
Celce-Murcia, M. (2007) Rethinking the role of communicative competence in language teaching. In E. Alcón Soler and M.P. Safont Jordà (eds) *Intercultural Language Use and Language Learning* (pp. 41–57). Berlin: Springer.
Celce-Murcia, M.A., Dörnyei, Z. and Thurrell, S. (1995) Communicative competence: A pedagogically motivated model with content specification. *Issues in Applied Linguistics* 6, 5–35.
Chaiklin, S. (2001) The category of 'personality' in cultural-historical psychology. In S. Chaiklin (ed.) *The Theory and Practice of Cultural-historical Psychology* (pp. 238–259). Aarhus: Aarhus University Press.
Chaiklin, S. (2002) A developmental teaching approach to schooling. In G. Wells and G. Claxton (eds) *Learning for Life in the 21st Century: Sociocultural Perspectives on the Future of Education* (pp. 167–180). London: Blackwell.
Chaiklin, S. (2003) The zone of proximal development in Vygotsky's analysis of learning and instruction. In A. Kozulin, B. Gindis, V. Ageyev and S. Miller (eds) *Vygotsky's Educational Theory in Cultural Context* (pp. 39–64). Cambridge: Cambridge University Press.
Chomsky, N. (1965) *Aspects of the Theory of Syntax*. Cambridge: MIT Press.
Cole, M. (1996) *Cultural Psychology: The Once and Future Discipline*. Cambridge: Bellknapp Press of Harvard University Press.
Cook, G. (1999) Communicative competence. In K. Johnson and H. Johnson (eds) *Encyclopedic Dictionary of Applied Linguistics* (pp. 62–68). Oxford: Blackwell.
Coveney, A. (1996) *Variability in Spoken French: A Sociolinguistic Study of Interrogation and Negation*. Exeter: Elm Bank Publications.
Coveney, A. (2000) Vestiges of *nous* and the 1st person plural verb in informal spoken French. *Language Sciences* 22, 447–481.
Coveney, A. (2010) *Vouvoiement* and *tutoiement*: Sociolinguistic reflections. *Journal of French Language Studies* 20, 127–150.

Crystal, D. (1997) *The Cambridge Encyclopedia of Language* (2nd edn). Cambridge: Cambridge University Press.
Davydov, V.V. (1995) The influence of L.S. Vygotsky on education theory, research, and practice (trans. S.T. Kerr). *Educational Researcher* 24 (3), 12–21.
Davydov, V.V. (2004) *Problems of Developmental Instruction: A Theoretical and Experimental Psychological Study* (trans. P. Moxay). Moscow: Akademyia Press.
de Saussure, F. (1913/1959) *Course in General Linguistics* (trans. W. Baskins). New York: Philosophical Library.
Dewaele, J-M. (2002) Using sociostylistic variants in advanced French interlanguage: The case of *nous/on*. *EUROSLA Yearbook* 2, 205–226.
Dewaele, J-M. (2004) Retention or omission of the *ne* in advanced French interlanguage: The variable effect of extralinguistic factors. *Journal of Sociolinguistics* 8, 433–450.
Dewaele, J-M. (2008) Appropriateness in foreign language acquisition and use: Some theoretical, methodological and ethical considerations. In R. Manchón and J. Cenoz (eds) *Doing SLA Research: Theoretical, Methodological, and Ethical Issues*. Special issue of the *International Review of Applied Linguistics* 46 (4), 235–255.
Dewaele, J-M. (2010) *Emotions in Multiple Languages*. Basingstoke: Palgrave Macmillan.
Dewaele, J-M. and Planchenault, G. (2006) 'Dites-moi tu?!' La perception de la difficulté du système des pronoms d'adresse en français ['Say tu to me?!' Perceptions of difficulty in the French system of address pronouns]. In M. Faraco (ed.) *La classe de langue: Théories, méthodes, pratiques* [The language classroom: Theories, methods, practice] (pp. 153–171). Aix-en-Provence: Publications de l'Université de Provence.
DeYoung, C.G. (2010) Personality neuroscience and the biology of traits. *Social and Personality Psychology Compass* 4, 1165–1180.
Di Pietro, R.J. (1982) The open-ended scenario: A new approach to conversation. *TESOL Quarterly* 16, 15–20.
Di Pietro, R.J. (1987) *Strategic Interaction: Learning Languages Through Scenarios*. Cambridge: Cambridge University Press.
Douglass, K. (2009) Second-person pronoun use in French-language blogs: Developing L2 sociopragmatic competence. In L.B. Abraham and L. Williams (eds) *Electronic Discourse in Language Learning and Language Teaching* (pp. 213–239). Amsterdam: John Benjamins.
Dunn, W. and Lantolf, J.P. (1998) Vygotsky's zone of proximal development and Krashen's i + 1: Incommensurable constructs; incommensurable theories. *Language Learning* 48, 411–442.
Eckert, P. (2008) Variation and the indexical field. *Journal of Sociolinguistics* 12, 453–476.
Engeström, Y. (1987) *Learning by Expanding: An Activity-theoretical Approach to Developmental Research*. Helsinki: Orienta-Konsultit Oy.
Etienne, C. and Sax, K. (2006) Teaching stylistic variation through film. *French Review* 79, 934–950.
Etienne, C. and Sax, K. (2009) Stylistic variation in French: Bridging the gap between research and textbooks. *Modern Language Journal* 93, 584–606.
Farrell Whitworth, K. (2009) The discussion forum as a locus for developing L2 pragmatic awareness. In L.B. Abraham and L. Williams (eds) *Electronic Discourse in Language Learning and Language Teaching* (pp. 291–317). Amsterdam: John Benjamins.
Ferreira, M. (2005) A Concept-based approach to writing instruction: From the abstract concept to the concrete performance. Unpublished doctoral dissertation, Pennsylvania State University.
Feuerstein, R., Rand, Y. and Rynders, J.E. (1988) *Don't Accept Me as I Am. Helping Retarded Performers Excel*. New York: Plenum.

Fonseca-Greber, B. and Waugh, L. (2003) On the radical difference between the subject personal pronouns in written and spoken European French. In P. Leistyna and C.F. Meyer (eds) *Corpus Analysis: Language Structure and Language Use* (pp. 225–240). Amsterdam: Rodopi.

Frawley, W. (1997) *Vygotsky and Cognitive Science. Language and the Unification of the Social and Computational Mind*. Cambridge: Harvard University Press.

Freeman, D. (2004) Language, sociocultural theory, and L2 teacher education: Examining the technology of subject matter and the architecture of instruction. In M.R. Hawkins (ed.) *Language Learning and Teacher Education: A Sociocultural Approach* (pp. 167–197). Clevedon: Multilingual Matters.

Freeman, D. and Johnson, K.E. (1998) Reconceptualizing the knowledge-base of L2 teacher education. *TESOL Quarterly* 32, 397–417.

Galperin, P.I. (1989) Organization of mental activity and the effectiveness of learning. *Soviet Psychology* 27 (3), 45–65.

Galperin, P.I. (1992) Stage-by-stage formation as a method of psychological investigation. *Journal of Russian and East European Psychology* July/August 30 (4), 60–80.

Gánem-Gutiérrez, G.A. and Roehr, K. (2011) Use of L2, metalanguage, and discourse markers: L2 learners' regulation during individual task performance. *International Journal of Applied Linguistics* 21, 297–318.

Gardner-Chloros, P. (2007) T/V choices: An act of identity? In W. Ayres-Bennett and M.C. Jones (eds) *The French Language and Questions of Identity* (pp. 106–115). Oxford: Legenda.

Gass, S. and Mackey, A. (2006) Input, interaction and output: An overview. *AILA Review* 19, 3–17.

Giroux, H. (1988) *Teachers as Intellectuals: Toward a Critical Pedagogy of Learning*. Brandy: Bergin & Garvey.

Goldenberg, C. (1991) *Instructional conversations and their classroom applications*. Paper No. EPR02. NCRCDSLL Educational Practice Reports. Center for Research on Education, Diversity & Excellence.

Goodwin, C. (2007) Participation, stance and affect in the organization of activities. *Discourse and Society* 18, 53–73.

Guikema, J.P. (2004) Learners as agents of development: An activity theory and folk linguistic analysis of foreign language literacy. Unpublished PhD thesis, Pennsylvania State University.

Guikema, J.P. (2009) Discourse analysis of podcasts in French: Implications for foreign language listening development. In L.B. Abraham and L. Williams (eds) *Electronic Discourse in Language Learning and Language Teaching* (pp. 169–189). Amsterdam: John Benjamins.

Gumperz, J. and Hymes, D. (1972) *Directions in Sociolinguistics: The Ethnography of Communication*. New York: Holt, Rinehart & Winston.

Haenen, J. (1996) *Piotr Gal'perin: Psychologist in Vygotsky's footsteps*. New York: Nova Science Publishers.

Hall, J.K. (2001) *Methods for Teaching Foreign Languages: Creating a Community of Learners in the Classroom*. Upper Saddle River: Prentice Hall.

Halliday, M.A.K. (1973) *Explorations in the Functions of Language*. London: Edward Arnold.

Halliday, M.A.K. (1978) *Language as Social Semiotic. The Social Interpretation of Language and Meaning*. London: Edward Arnold.

Harley, B., Cummins J., Swain, M. and Allen, P. (1990) The nature of language proficiency. In B. Harley, P. Allen, J. Cummins and M. Swain (eds) *The Development of Second Language Proficiency* (pp. 7–25). Cambridge: Cambridge University Press.

Haywood, H.C. and Lidz, C.S. (2007) *Dynamic Assessment in Practice. Clinical and Educational Applications.* Cambridge: Cambridge University Press.

Hellermann, J. (2007) The development of practices for action in classroom dyadic interaction: Focus on task openings. *Modern Language Journal* 91, 83–96.

Holzman, L. (2009) *Vygotsky at Work and Play.* London: Routledge.

Hopper, P. (1987) Emergent grammar [Electronic version]. *Berkeley Linguistics Society* 13, 139–157. See http://elanguage.net/journals/bls/article/view/2492. Accessed 15 October 2012.

Hopper, P.J. (1998) Emergent grammar. In M. Tomasello (ed.) *The New Psychology of Language: Cognitive and Functional Approaches to Language Structure* (pp. 155–176). Mahwah: Lawrence Erlbaum.

Horwitz, E.K., Horwitz, M.B. and Cope, J. (1986) Foreign language classroom anxiety. *Modern Language Journal* 70, 125–132.

Hulstijn, J.H. (2007) Psycholinguistic perspectives on language acquisition. In J. Cummings and C. Davidson (eds) *The International Handbook on English Language Teaching* (pp. 701–713). Norwell: Springer.

Hymes, D. (1964) Formal discussion of a conference paper. In U. Bellugi and R. Brown (eds) *The Acquisition of Language.* Monographs of the Society for Research in Child Development. Malden: Blackwell.

Hymes, D. (1972) Models of the interaction of language and social life. In J.J. Gumperz and D. Hymes (eds) *Directions in Sociolinguistics: The Ethnography of Communication* (pp. 35–71). New York: Holt, Rinehart, & Winston.

Ilyenkov, E.V. (1982) *The Dialectics of the Abstract and the Concrete in Marx's Capital.* Moscow: Progress.

Imai, Y. (2010) Emotions in SLA: New insights from collaborative learning for an EFL classroom. *Modern Language Journal* 94, 278–292.

Ishihara, N. (2010) Instructional pragmatics: Bridging teaching, research, and teacher education. *Language and Linguistics Compass* 4, 938–953.

Johnson, K.E. (2009) *Second Language Teacher Education: A Sociocultural Perspective.* New York: Routledge.

Johnson, K.E. and Arshavskaya. E. (2011) Reconceptualizing the micro-teaching simulation in an MA TESL course. In K.E. Johnson and P.R. Golombek (eds) *Research on Second Language Teacher Education: A Sociocultural Perspective on Professional Development* (pp. 168–186). New York: Routledge.

John-Steiner, V.P. (2007) Vygotsky on thinking and speaking. In H. Daniels, M. Cole and J.V. Wertsch (eds) *The Cambridge Companion to Vygotsky* (pp. 136–152). Cambridge: Cambridge University Press.

Johnstone, B. (2011) Making Pittsburghese: Communication technology, expertise, and the discursive construction of a regional dialect. *Language & Communication* 31, 3–15.

Johnstone, B. and Kiesling, S.F. (2008) Indexicality and experience: Exploring the meaning of /aw/-monophthongization in Pittsburg. *Journal of Sociolinguistics* 12, 5–33.

Karpov, Y.V. (2003) Vygotsky's doctrine of scientific concepts: Its role for contemporary education. In A. Kozulin, B. Gindis, V.S. Ageyev and S. Miller (eds) *Vygotsky's Educational Theory in Cultural Context* (pp. 39–64). Cambridge: Cambridge University Press.

Kasper, G. (1997) *Can Pragmatic Competence be Taught?* Honolulu: Second Language Teaching & Curriculum Center, University of Hawai'i. See http://www.nflrc.hawaii.edu/NetWorks/NW06/.

Kasper, G. (2001) Four perspectives on L2 pragmatic development. *Applied Linguistics* 22, 502–530.

Kasper, G. (2004) Speech acts in (inter)action: Repeated questions. *Intercultural Pragmatics* 1, 105–114.

Kasper, G. and Roever, C. (2005) Pragmatics in second language learning. In E. Hinkel (ed.) *Handbook of Research in Second Language Learning and Teaching* (pp. 317–334). Mahwah: Lawrence Erlbaum.

Kasper, G. and Rose, K. (2002) *Pragmatic Development in a Second Language. Language Learning* 52 (Suppl. 1). Oxford: Blackwell.

Kinginger, C. (2001) i + 1 ≠ ZPD. *Foreign Language Annals* 34, 417–425.

Kinginger, C. (2004) Alice doesn't live here anymore: Foreign language learning and identity. In A. Pavlenko and A. Blackledge (eds) *Negotiation of Identities in Multilingual Contexts* (pp. 219–242). Clevedon: Multilingual Matters.

Kinginger, C. (2008) Language learning in study abroad: Case studies of Americans in France. *Modern Language Journal* 92 (Suppl. 1).

Kinginger, C. (2009) *Language Learning and Study Abroad: A Critical Reading of Research.* Basingstoke: Palgrave Macmillan.

Knouzi, I., Swain, M., Lapkin, S. and Brooks, L. (2010) Self-scaffolding mediated by languaging: Microgenetic analysis of high and low performers. *International Journal of Applied Linguistics* 20, 23–49.

Kozulin, A. (1995) The learning process: Vygotsky's theory in the mirror of its interpretations. *School Psychology International* 16, 117–129.

Kozulin, A. (2003) Psychological tools and mediated learning. In A. Kozulin, B. Gindis, V.S. Ageyev and S.M. Miller (eds) *Vygotsky's Educational Theory in Cultural Contexts* (pp. 15–38). Cambridge: Cambridge University Press.

Kozulin, A. and Garb, E. (2002) Dynamic assessment of EFL text comprehension of at-risk students. *School Psychology International* 23, 112–127.

Labov, W. (1972) *Sociolinguistic Patterns.* Philadelphia: University of Pennsylvania Press.

Lam, W.S.E. (2004) Second language socialization in a bilingual chat room: Global and local considerations. *Language Learning & Technology* 8, 44–65.

Lantolf, J.P. (1996) SLA theory building: 'Letting all the flowers bloom!' *Language Learning* 46, 713–749.

Lantolf, J.P. (2003) Intrapersonal communication and internalization in the second language classroom. In A. Kozulin, B. Gindis, V.S. Ageyev and S.M. Miller (eds) *Vygotsky's Educational Theory in Cultural Context* (pp. 349–370). Cambridge: Cambridge University Press.

Lantolf, J.P. (2006) Sociocultural theory and L2. *Studies in Second Language Acquisition* 28, 67–109.

Lantolf, J.P. (2007) Conceptual knowledge and instructed second language learning. In S. Fotos and H. Nassaji (eds) *Form-focused Instruction and Teacher Education: Studies in Honour of Rod Ellis* (pp. 35–54). Oxford: Oxford University Press.

Lantolf, J.P. (2008) Praxis and classroom L2 development. *Estudios de lingüística inglesia aplicada* 8, 13–44.

Lantolf, J.P. (2010) Sociocultural theory and the pedagogical imperative. In R.B. Kaplan (ed.) *The Oxford Handbook of Applied Linguistics* (2nd edn) (pp. 163–177). New York: Oxford University Press.

Lantolf, J.P. and Genung, P. (2002) 'I'd rather switch than fight': An activity theoretic study of power, success and failure in a foreign language classroom. In C. Kramsch (ed.) *Language Acquisition and Language Socialization: Ecological Perspectives* (pp. 175–196). London: Continuum.

Lantolf, J.P. and Johnson, K.E. (2007) Extending Firth and Wagner's (1997) Ontological perspective to L2 classroom praxis and teacher education. *Modern Language Journal* 91 (Suppl. 1), 877–892.

Lantolf, J.P. and Pavlenko, A. (2001) (S)econd (L)anguage (A)ctivity theory: Understanding learners as people. In M. Breen (ed.) *Learner Contributions to Language Learning: New Directions in Research* (pp. 141–158). London: Pearson.

Lantolf, J.P. and Poehner, M.E. (2004) Dynamic assessment: Bringing the past into the future. *Journal of Applied Linguistics* 1, 49–74.

Lantolf, J.P. and Poehner, M.E. (2011) Dynamic assessment in the classroom: Vygotskian praxis for second language development. *Language Teaching Research* 15, 11–33.

Lantolf, J.P. and Thorne, S.L. (2006) *Sociocultural Theory and the Genesis of Second Language Development*. Oxford: Oxford University Press.

Lapkin, S., Swain, M. and Knouzi, I. (2008) French as a second language: University students learn the grammatical concept of voice: Study design, materials development and pilot data. In J.P. Lantolf and M.E. Poehner (eds) *Sociocultural Theory and the Teaching of Second Languages* (pp. 228–255). London: Equinox.

Lave, J. and Wenger, E. (1991) *Situated Learning: Legitimate Peripheral Participation*. New York: Cambridge University Press.

Leech, G. (1983) *The Principles of Pragmatics*. London: Longman.

Leontiev, A.A. (1981) *Psychology and the Language Learning Process*. London: Pergamon.

Leung, C. (2005) Convivial communication: Recontextualizing communicative competence. *International Journal of Applied Linguistics* 15, 119–144.

Levinson, S. (1992) Activity types and language. In P. Drew and J. Heritage (eds) *Talk at Work: Interaction in Institutional Settings* (pp. 66–100). Cambridge: Cambridge University Press.

Lyster, R. (1994) The effect of functional-analytic teaching on aspects of French immersion students' sociolinguistic competence. *Applied Linguistics* 15, 263–287.

Lyster, R. and Rebuffot, J. (2002) Acquisition des pronoms d'allocution en classe de français immersif. *Acquisition et Interaction en Langue Étrangère* 17 [np]. See http://aile.revues.org/document842.html (accessed December 2008).

MacIntyre, P.D. (2002) Motivation, anxiety and emotion in second language acquisition. In P. Robinson (ed.) *Individual Differences in Second Language Acquisition* (pp. 45–68). Amsterdam: John Benjamins.

Mahn, H. and John-Steiner, V. (2002) The gift of confidence: A Vygotskian view of emotions. In G. Wells and G. Claxton (eds) *Learning for Life in the 21st Century: Sociocultural Perspectives on the Future of Education* (pp. 45–58). London: Blackwell.

Martínez-Flor, A. and Usó-Juan, E. (2006) A comprehensive pedagogical framework to develop pragmatics in the foreign language classroom: The 6Rs approach. *Applied Language Learning* 16 (2), 39–64.

Martínez-Flor, A. and Usó-Juan, E. (eds) (2010) *Speech Act Performance: Theoretical, Empirical and Methodological Issues*. Amsterdam: John Benjamins.

McCafferty, S. G. (1998) Nonverbal expression and L2 private speech. *Applied Linguistics* 19, 73–96.

McCafferty, S.G. (2004) Space for cognition: Gesture and second language learning. *International Journal of Applied Linguistics* 14, 148–165.

McCourt, C.A. (2009) Pragmatic variation among learners of French in real-time chat communication. In R. Oxford and J. Oxford (eds) *Second Language Teaching and*

Learning in the Net Generation (pp. 143–154). Honolulu: National Foreign Language Resource Center, University of Hawai'i.
McNeill, D. (2005) Gesture and Thought. Chicago: University of Chicago Press.
Morford, J. (1997) Social indexicality in French pronominal address. *Journal of Linguistic Anthropology* 7, 3–37.
Mougeon, R., Nadasdi, T. and Rehner, K. (2010) *The Sociolinguistic Competence of Immersion Students*. Bristol: Multilingual Matters.
Mühlhäusler, P. and Harré, R. (1990) *Pronouns and People: The Linguistic Construction of Social and Personal Identity*. Oxford: Basil Blackwell.
Nassaji, H. and Swain, M. (2000) Vygotskian perspective on corrective feedback in L2: The effect of random versus negotiated help on the learning of English articles. *Language Awareness* 9, 34–51.
Negueruela, E. (2003) A sociocultural approach to teaching and researching second language: Systemic-theoretical instruction and second language development. Unpublished PhD thesis, Pennsylvania State University.
Negueruela, E. (2008) Revolutionary pedagogies: Learning that leads (to) second language development. In J.P. Lantolf and M.E. Poehner (eds) *Sociocultural Theory and the Teaching of Second Languages* (pp. 189–227). London: Equinox.
Negueruela, E. and Lantolf, J.P. (2006) Concept-based pedagogy and the acquisition of L2 Spanish. In R. Salaberry and B.A. Lafford (eds) *The Art of Teaching Spanish: Second Language Acquisition from Research to Practice* (pp. 79–102). Washington, DC: Georgetown University Press.
New London Group (1996) A pedagogy of multiliteracies: Designing social futures. *Harvard Educational Review* 66, 60–92.
Niedzielski, N. and Preston, D. (eds) (2000) *Folk Linguistics*. Berlin: Mouton de Gruyter.
Norton, B. (1995) Social identity, investment, and language learning. *TESOL Quarterly* 29, 9–31.
Norton, B. (2000) *Identity and Language Learning: Social Processes and Educational Practice*. London: Longman.
Ohta, A.S. (2001) *Second Language Acquisition Processes in the Classroom: Learning Japanese*. Mahwah: Lawrence Erlbaum.
Paradis, M. (2004) *A Neurolinguistic Theory of Bilingualism*. Amsterdam: John Benjamins.
Paradis, M. (2009) *Declarative and Procedural Determinants of Second Languages*. Amsterdam: John Benjamins.
Pavlenko, A. (2005) *Emotions and Multilingualism*. New York: Cambridge University Press.
Pavlenko, A. (ed.) (2006) *Bilingual Minds: Emotional Experience, Expression and Representation*. Clevedon: Multilingual Matters.
Pavlenko, A. and Lantolf, J.P. (2000) Second language learning as participation and the (re)construction of selves. In J.P. Lantolf (ed.) *Sociocultural Theory and Second Language Learning* (pp. 156–177). Oxford: Oxford University Press.
Peeters, B. (2006) Nous on vous tu (e): La guerre (pacifique) des pronoms personnels. *Zeitschrift für romanische Philologie* 122, 201–220.
Perkins, D.N. (1993) Person-plus: A distributed view of thinking and learning. In G. Salamon (ed.) *Distributed Cognitions. Psychological and Educational Considerations* (pp. 88–110). Cambridge: Cambridge University Press.
Poehner, M.E. (2007) Beyond the test: L2 dynamic assessment and the transcendence of mediated learning. *Modern Language Journal* 91, 323–340.
Poehner, M.E. (2008) *Dynamic Assessment: A Vygotskian Approach to Understanding and Promoting Second Language Development*. Berlin: Springer Publishing.

Poehner, M.E. (2009) Group dynamic assessment: Mediation for the L2 classroom. *TESOL Quarterly* 43 (3), 471–491.
Poehner, M.E. and Lantolf, J.P. (2010) Vygotsky's teaching-assessment dialectic and L2 education: The case for dynamic assessment. *Mind, Culture, and Activity* 17, 312–330.
Poehner, M.E. and Lantolf, J.P. (2013) Bringing the ZPD into the equation: Capturing L2 development during computerized dynamic assessment (C-DA). In R.A. van Compernolle and L. Williams (eds) *Sociocultural Theory and Second Language Pedagogy* [Special issue]. *Language Teaching Research* 17, 323–342.
Poehner, M.E. and van Compernolle, R.A. (2011) Frames of interaction in dynamic assessment: Developmental diagnoses of second language learning. In M.E. Poehner and P. Rae-Dickens (eds) *Addressing Issues of Access and Fairness in Education Through Dynamic Assessment* [Special issue]. *Assessment in Education: Principles, Policy and Practice* 18 (2), 183–198.
Poehner, M.E. and van Compernolle, R.A. (forthcoming) L2 development around tests: Response processes and dynamic assessment. *International Review of Applied Linguistics in Language Teaching*.
Regan, V., Howard, M. and Lemée, I. (2009) *The Acquisition of Sociolinguistic Competence in a Study Abroad Context*. Bristol: Multilingual Matters.
Rose, K.R. (1999) Teachers and students learning about requests in Hong Kong. In E. Hinkel (ed.) *Culture in Second Language Teaching and Learning* (pp. 167–180). Cambridge: Cambridge University Press.
Rose, K.R. (2005) On the effects of instruction in second language pragmatics. *System* 33, 385–399.
Rose, K. and Kasper, G. (ed.) (2001) *Pragmatics in Language Teaching*. Cambridge: Cambridge University Press.
Sacks, H., Schegloff, E. and Jefferson, G. (1974) A simplest systematic for the organization of turn-taking for conversation. *Language* 50, 696–735.
Savignon, S.J. (1972) *Communicative Competence: An Experiment in Foreign-language Teaching*. Philadelphia: Center for Curriculum Development.
Savignon, S.J. (1983) *Communicative Competence: Theory and Classroom Practice*. Reading: Addison-Wesley
Savignon, S.J. (1997) *Communicative Competence: Theory and Classroom Practice* (2nd edn). New York: McGraw Hill
Sax, K. (2003) The acquisition of stylistic variation by American learners of French. Doctoral dissertation, Indiana University.
Searle, J. (1969) *Speech Acts: An Essay in the Philosophy of Language*. Cambridge: Cambridge University Press.
Serrano-Lopez, M. and Poehner, M.E. (2008) Materializing linguistic concepts through 3-D clay modeling: A tool-and-result approach to mediating L2 Spanish development. In J.P. Lantolf and M.E. Poehner (eds) *Sociocultural Theory and the Teaching of Second Languages* (pp. 321–346). London: Equinox.
Sfard, A. (1998) On two metaphors. *Educational Researcher* 27, 4–13.
Silverstein, M. (2003) Indexical order and the dialectics of sociolinguistic life. *Language and Communication* 23, 193–229.
Stetsenko, A. and Arievitch, I.M. (2010) Cultural-historical activity theory: Foundational worldview, major principles, and the relevance of sociocultural context. In S.R. Kirschner and J. Martin (eds) *The Sociocultural Turn in Psychology: The Contextual Emergence of Mind and Self* (pp. 231–252). New York: Columbia University Press.

Swain, M. (2006) Languaging, agency and collaboration in advanced language proficiency. In H. Byrnes (ed.) *Advanced Language Learning: The Contribution of Halliday and Vygotsky* (pp. 95–108). London: Continuum.

Swain, M. (2013) The inseparability of cognition and emotion in second language learning. *Language Teaching* 46 (2), 195–207.

Swain, M. and Lapkin, S. (1990) Aspects of the sociolinguistic performance of early and later French immersion students. In R.C. Scarcella, E.S. Andersen and S.D. Krashen (eds) *Developing Communicative Competence in a Second Language* (pp. 41–54). Rowley: Newbury House.

Swain, S. and Lapkin, S. (2002) Talking it through: Two French immersion learners' response to reformulation. *International Journal of Educational Research* 37, 285–304.

Swain, M., Lapkin, S., Knouzi, I., Suzuki, W. and Brooks, L. (2009) Languaging: University students learn the grammatical concept of voice in French. *Modern Language Journal* 93, 5–29.

Sykes, J.M. (2008) A dynamic approach to social interaction: SCMC, synthetic immersive environments & Spanish pragmatics. Unpublished PhD thesis, University of Minnesota.

Sykes, J., Oskoz, A. and S.L. Thorne (2008) Web 2.0, synthetic immersive environments, and mobile resources for language education. *CALICO Journal* 25, 528–546.

Taguchi, N. (2011) Teaching pragmatics: Trends and issues. *Annual Review of Applied Linguistics* 31, 289–310.

Takahashi, S. (2010) The effect of pragmatic instruction on speech act performance. In A. Martínez-Flor and E. Usó-Juan (eds) *Speech Act Performance: Theoretical, Empirical and Methodological Issues* (pp. 127–142). Amsterdam: John Benjamins.

Tarone, E. (1988) *Variation in Interlanguage*. London: Edward Arnold.

Tharp, R. and Gallimore, R. (1988) *Rousing Minds to Life: Teaching, Learning and Schooling in Social Context*. Cambridge: Cambridge University Press.

Thomas, J. (1983) Cross-cultural pragmatic failure. *Applied Linguistics* 4, 91–112.

Thorne, S.L. (2003) Artifacts and cultures-of-use in intercultural communication. *Language Learning & Technology* 7, 38–67.

Thorne, S.L. (2008) Transcultural communication in pen Internet environments and massively multiplayer online games. In S. Magnan (ed.) *Mediating Discourse Online* (pp. 305–327). Amsterdam: John Benjamins.

Thorne, S.L. and Lantolf, J.P. (2007) A linguistics of communicative activity. In S. Makoni and A. Pennycook (eds) *Disinventing and Reconstituting Languages* (pp. 170–195). Clevedon: Multilingual Matters.

Tomasello, M. (2003) *Constructing a Language: A Usage-based Theory of Language Acquisition*. Cambridge: Harvard University Press.

Trudgill, P. (1999) New-dialect formation and dedialectalization: Embryonic and vestigial variants. *Journal of English Linguistics* 27, 319–327.

Valsiner, J. (2001) Process structure of semiotic mediation in human development. *Human Development* 44, 84–97.

Valsiner, J. and Van der Veer, R. (2000) *The Social Mind: Development of the Idea*. Cambridge: Cambridge University Press.

van Compernolle, R.A. (2008a) Morphosyntactic and phonological constraints on negative particle variation in French-language chat discourse. *Language Variation and Change* 20, 317–339.

van Compernolle, R.A. (2008b) *Nous* versus *on*: Pronouns with first-person plural reference in synchronous French chat. *Canadian Journal of Applied Linguistics* 11, 85–110.

van Compernolle, R.A. (2008c) Second-person pronoun use and address strategies in on-line personal advertisements from Quebec. *Journal of Pragmatics* 40, 2062–2076.
van Compernolle, R.A. (2010a) Towards a sociolinguistically responsive pedagogy: Teaching second-person address forms in French. *Canadian Modern Language Review* 66, 445–463.
van Compernolle, R.A. (2010b) The (slightly more) productive use of *ne* in Montreal French chat. *Language Sciences* 32, 447–463.
van Compernolle, R.A. (2011a) Developing a sociocultural orientation to variation in language. *Language and Communication* 31, 86–94.
van Compernolle, R.A. (2011b) Developing second language sociopragmatic knowledge through concept-based instruction: A microgenetic case study. *Journal of Pragmatics* 43 (13), 3267–3283.
van Compernolle, R.A. (2012) Developing sociopragmatic capacity in a second language through concept-based instruction. Unpublished PhD thesis, Pennsylvania State University.
van Compernolle, R.A. (2013) From verbal protocols to cooperative dialogue in the assessment of second language pragmatic competence. *Intercultural Pragmatics* 10, 71–100.
van Compernolle, R.A. (forthcoming) Interactional competence and the dynamic assessment of L2 pragmatic abilities. In S. Ross and G. Kasper (eds) *Assessing Second Language Pragmatics*. Basingstoke: Palgrave Macmillan.
van Compernolle, R.A. and Kinginger, C. (2013) Promoting metapragmatic development through assessment in the ZPD. In R.A. van Compernolle and L. Williams (eds) *Sociocultural Theory and Second Language Pedagogy* [Special issue]. *Language Teaching Research* 17, 282–302.
van Compernolle, R.A. and Pierozak, I. (2009) Teaching language variation in French through authentic chat discourse. In L. Abraham and L. Williams (eds) *Electronic Discourse in Language Learning and Language Teaching* (pp. 111–126). Amsterdam: John Benjamins.
van Compernolle, R.A. and Williams, L. (2009a) Variable omission of *ne* in real-time French chat: A corpus-driven comparison of educational and non-educational contexts. *Canadian Modern Language Review* 65, 413–440.
van Compernolle, R.A. and Williams, L. (2009b) Learner versus non-learner patterns of stylistic variation in synchronous computer-mediated French: *Yes/no questions* and *nous* versus *on*. *Studies in Second Language Acquisition* 31, 471–500.
van Compernolle, R.A. and Williams, L. (2011a) Metalinguistic explanations and self-reports as triangulation data for interpreting L2 sociolinguistic performance. *International Journal of Applied Linguistics* 21, 26–50.
van Compernolle, R.A. and Williams, L. (2011b) Thinking with your hands: Speech-gesture activity during an L2 awareness-raising task. *Language Awareness* 20 (3), 203–219.
van Compernolle, R.A. and Williams, L. (2012a) Promoting sociolinguistic competence in the classroom zone of proximal development. *Language Teaching Research* 16, 39–60.
van Compernolle, R.A. and Williams, L. (2012b) Reconceptualizing sociolinguistic competence as mediated action: Identity, meaning-making, agency. *Modern Language Journal* 96, 234–250.
van Compernolle, R.A. and Williams, L. (2012c) Teaching, learning, and developing L2 French sociolinguistic competence: A sociocultural perspective. *Applied Linguistics* 33, 184–205.
van Compernolle, R.A., Williams, L. and McCourt, C. (2011) A corpus-driven study of second-person pronoun variation in L2 French synchronous computer-mediated communication. *Intercultural Pragmatics* 8, 67–91.

van Lier, L. (1988) *The Classroom and the Language Learner*. London: Longman.
van Lier, L. (1996) *Interaction in the Language Curriculum: Awareness, Autonomy, and Authenticity*. Harlow: Longman.
van Lier, L. (2004) *The Ecology and Semiotics of Language Learning: A Sociocultural Perspective*. Boston: Kluwer Academic.
van Lier, L. (2008) Agency in the classroom. In J.P. Lantolf and M.E. Poehner (eds) *Sociocultural Theory and the Teaching of Second Languages* (pp. 163–186). London: Equinox.
Vygotsky, L.S. (1978) *Mind in Society: The Development of Higher Mental Processes*. Cambridge: Harvard University Press.
Vygotsky, L.S. (1986) *Thought and Language*. Cambridge, MA: MIT Press.
Vygotsky, L.S. (1987) *The Collected Works of L.S. Vygotsky. Volume 1. Problems of General Psychology. Including the Volume Thinking and Speech* (ed. R.W. Rieber and A.S. Carton). New York: Plenum.
Vygotsky, L.S. (1997) *Educational Psychology*. Boca Raton: St. Lucie Press.
Vygotsky, L.S. (2000) *Thought and Language* (revised) (ed. A. Kozulin). Cambridge: MIT Press.
Vygotsky. L.S. (2004) The historical meaning of the crisis in psychology: A methodological investigation. In R.W. Rieber and D.K. Robinson (eds) *The Essential Vygotsky* (pp. 227–344). New York: Kluwer/Plenum.
Wartofsky, M. (1973) *Models: Representation and the Scientific Understanding*. Dordrecht: Reidel.
Wells, G. (1999) *Dialogic Inquiry: Toward a Sociocultural Practice and Theory of Education*. Cambridge: Cambridge University Press.
Wertsch, J. (1985) *Vygotsky and the Social Formation of Mind*. Cambridge: Harvard University Press.
Wertsch, J. (1998) *Mind as Action*. Oxford: Oxford University Press.
Wertsch, J. (2007) Mediation. In H. Daniels, M. Cole and J. Wertsch (eds) *The Cambridge Companion to Vygotsky* (pp. 178–192). Cambridge: Cambridge University Press.
Widdowson, H.G. (1989) Knowledge of language and ability for use. *Applied Linguistics* 10, 128–137.
Widdowson, H.G. (2003) *Defining Issues in English Language Teaching*. Oxford: Oxford University Press.
Widdowson, H.G. (2007) Un-applied linguistics and communicative language teaching: A reaction to Keith Johnson's review of *Notional Syllabuses*. *International Journal of Applied Linguistics* 17, 214–220.
Wiley, N. (1994) *The Semiotic Self*. Chicago: University of Chicago Press.
Williams, L. and van Compernolle, R.A. (2007) Second-person pronoun use in on-line French-language chat environments. *French Review* 80 (4), 804–820.
Williams, L. and van Compernolle, R.A. (2009) Second-person pronoun use in French language discussion fora. *Journal of French Language Studies* 19 (3), 363–380.
Woodfield, H. (2010) What lies beneath?: Verbal report in interlanguage requests in English. *Multilingua* 29, 1–27.
Yáñez-Prieto, M.-C. (2008) On literature and the secret art of (im)possible worlds: Teaching literature-through-language. Unpublished PhD thesis, Pennsylvania State University.
Zinchenko, V.P. (2002) From classical to organic psychology. *Journal of Russian and East European Psychology* 39, 32–77.
Zinchenko, V.P. (2007) Thought and word: The approaches of L.S. Vygotsky and G.G. Shpet. In H. Daniels, M. Cole and J. Wertsch (eds) *The Cambridge Companion to Vygotsky* (pp. 212–245). Cambridge: Cambridge University Press.

For Product Safety Concerns and Information please contact our EU Authorised Representative:

Easy Access System Europe

Mustamäe tee 50

10621 Tallinn

Estonia

gpsr.requests@easproject.com